THE SUPERNATURAL SIDE OF MAINE

C. J. Stevens

John Wade, Publisher

Published by John Wade, Publisher
P. O. Box 303
Phillips, Maine 04966

Acknowledgments for permission to use previously published or un-published material will be found on pages 263-266.

The Supernatural Side of Maine
1. Paranormal and supernatural encounters
2. Psychic and occult adventures in Maine
3. 19th and 20th century—history, profiles, and controversy

Library of Congress Control Number:
2002110314

ISBN # 1-882425-17-0 (paper)
ISBN # 1-882425-16-2 (cloth)

Manufactured in the United States of America

FIRST EDITION

Books by C. J. Stevens

Poetry
Beginnings and Other Poems
Circling at the Chain's Length
Hang-Ups
Selected Poems
Shepherd Without Sheep
Collected Poems

Biography
Lawrence at Tregerthen (D. H. Lawrence in Cornwall)
The Cornish Nightmare (D. H. Lawrence)
Storyteller: A Life of Erskine Caldwell

History and Adventure
The Next Bend in the River (Gold Mining in Maine)
Maine Mining Adventures
The Buried Treasures of Maine
The Supernatural Side of Maine

Translations
Poems from Holland and Belgium

Animal Behavior
One Day With a Goat Herd

Fiction
The Folks From Greeley's Mill
Confessions

I dedicate this book to my wife, Stella Stevens, who shaped its beginnings and graced every page with her presence.

Contents

PREFACE

This book had its beginnings early in my life, and it is written with the hope that readers will look upon these pages as an adventure while exploring the mysterious frontier leading to a supernatural side of Maine. What follows is not meant to be broad in orientation or scope—such a presentation would render my intentions meaningless and perform a disservice to the book's contributors. I do, however, include accounts of extraordinary happenings from elsewhere; they seem to possess informational magic, and I don't look upon them as details held captive in regional settings.

An awareness of the supernatural became part of the huge jumble of impressions from childhood as I studied faces and listened to stories. What the grown-ups told me was taken for granted, and I rarely questioned anything—there were just too many marvels nudging my awkwardness and gullibility.

When a dog in the neighborhood began howling and continued for several nights, my grandmother nodded knowingly and said: "It's Ambrose Seekins—he's been poorly." Down on our Maine farm, a baying dog was probably the most frequent announcement of an impending death, though crows flocking in barnyards or cornfields were harbingers, and another sign was the nervous behavior of cows in the tie-up after milking. Approaching storms were read as portents, and it was worrisome if a chair fell over backwards when a person stood up.

I do recall a fixation when it came to doors—my family never trusted them much. It was thought to be unlucky to enter the house through the back door, and I remember that my grandfather's coffin was cumbersomely carried through the front portal after an aunt or some elderly mourner reminded one of the pallbearers that there had been "enough sickness and dying in the family for the time being"—my grandmother had passed away six months earlier after a long illness.

It puzzles me now that I let so many wondrous tidbits slip past me when the elders paraded their superstitions or allowed slivers of the paranormal to prickle their conversations with solemnity and innuendo. I cite witches as an example. "They always ride brooms and worship the Devil"—that was the unsolicited commentary from an uncle after the extracurricular activities of a "busybody" in the neighborhood had been cataloged.

Years later, in researching this book and realizing that the supernatural is only a step away from the world we sometimes arrogantly describe as "real," I learned that people ran through the fields astride a broom in rural Europe to coax the grain to grow, and it was not uncommon for a peasant to jump over one to instruct his crop to rise to the highest leap—these straws-on-a-stick antics soon led to stories of cackling hags flying their cleaning instruments across the spooky face of a moon.

When I told an acquaintance that I was writing a book about supernatural happenings in Maine, the man asked me: "Will your stuff include witches?"

"Probably."

"Flying saucers, haunted houses, and telling fortunes are fun things to read about, but I wouldn't fool around much with witchcraft."

"Why not?" I asked.

"Because you could get yourself into a pack of trouble," he warned. "Say something those people don't like and you could be jinxed."

I'm sure he meant well, and I had heard such things from grandparents, parents, uncles and aunts. It's a cultural thing, I was thinking, powerful superstition—that fear of the hex, curse, spell—often roaming the troubled faces of grown-ups.

I never shall forget the look on my mother's face the day she broke her mirror. "Seven years of bad luck," she proclaimed as the two of us stood in the kitchen and she stared at the glittering remains of a broken world that only moments before had been a reflection of herself. There was little I could do to comfort her—such a proclamation was beyond the competence of my seven years—and what she prophesied for herself came true in a painful divorce and an unhappy second marriage. She had no luck in life, my mother, before or after the flimsy antique frame came apart in her hands and the glass shattered in shards of gloom.

The breaking of that mirror came shortly before I found myself forecasting a nearly fatal event in our lives. My parents couldn't understand why a seven year old would race his shiny new cart down a sloping driveway and at the bottom intentionally upend the little wagon in the ditch. It was a game I invented and called "Accident." The more I scratched and dented the metal sides and twisted the steering handle, the greater my satisfaction. We didn't realize that this destructive and solitary pursuit of mine was a sort of rehearsal—I was sensing an occurrence before its time.

Sunday was the day set aside to see more of Maine, and I enjoyed those automobile trips in the backseat of my father's sedan—Popham Beach, Rangeley, Mount Katahdin, Moosehead Lake. Then came the Sunday my parents decided to visit Bar Harbor.

"I don't want to go," I told them.

"Why on earth not?" asked my mother.

"Because we're going to get into a bad accident and people will get hurt."

"That's nonsense, Sonny," said my father.

"Please!" I begged them, my voice choking into a whimper.

I was being unreasonable, they scolded, and my kicking and screaming on the living room carpet didn't change their minds. I began the trip sulking, but my mood brightened as the August scenery rolled dizzily past the car windows.

The head-on collision occurred on the way home from Bar Harbor. My father and mother were badly bruised and shaken, my injuries were a broken hip and a fractured skull, and two elderly passengers in the other automobile were hospitalized for weeks.

How did the author of this book know there was going to be an auto accident? He "just knew."

It took me time to realize that the unexplained freshens the imagination and gives one a vacation from the ordinary, though I do recall that some stories jolted me: the face appearing in the upstairs window of a deserted house, lanterns flickering in cemeteries, and the creak of footsteps in an attic three nights in succession—just when a hallway clock grumbles its midnight. Then there is a memory of amazed silence at our supper table after grandfather told us how a fortune-teller's crystal ball at the county fair and the sloshed tea leaves in grandmother's cup contradicted the steadfast almanac and accurately predicted a windfall from a cash crop of corn.

Such mysteries hovered in the background throughout my childhood and teenage years; they were just out of reach—maybe "lingered" is the better word to describe their durability since I only half believed such things existed. In a way, I considered them to be remnants from the glow of storytelling, and they remained closeted. A shrug of the shoulder or condescending smile usually dismissed such goings-on.

On another level, more secretive and mystifying, were the unexpected flares from the residual influences of just being alive—I'm thinking of the intuitive information one gets from tastes and smells. An unpleasant sensation in the mouth may occur when something doesn't seem right, and a certain odor can carry a person instantly back in time.

When I smell bleach, I see a *Maytag* washing machine in a kitchen and clothes being run through the two rollers of an old-fashioned wringer. I also hear the creaking and snapping sounds of shirts and underwear on a clothesline above a crusty March snow. This is a scene from the early 1940s—that time when my parents were in the process of separating and I felt torn emotionally. Could it be possible that this unhappiness explains why I am extremely allergic to bleach?

Cousin Ethemer Stevens of Norridgewock, Maine gave me my start as a dowser. He showed me how to hold the crotched stick he had cut from a branch, and just before I passed over a vein of water he stood behind me and held both my wrists with a firm grip. "This is what got me on the right track," Ethemer said with a chuckle. "You could call it the laying on of hands!" I felt a tingle, a twitch or throb along the Y-shaped wood, and the stick slowly began twisting in my hands over the water vein. How a dowser can pass on such magic to an incompetent fascinates me, and this is not unusual. Dowsing does seem to be something "handed down" when there is a need to search further for the earth's nectar. "You now have the touch," Ethemer told me, "and it should improve with practice."

It wasn't until the late 1970s, when my wife, Stella, and I got interested in gold prospecting, that I allowed my slight dowsing talent a further range. In addition to the gold pan, sluice, and recreational dredge, we began using a dowser—one of those shiny, expensive instruments with an antenna and a stainless steel chamber for loading specimens. Without realizing it, I was becoming more involved with the supernatural as we dowsed the wilderness rivers and watershed streams of northwestern Maine in search of an elusive mother lode of gold.

In 1967, when we were living in Monmouth, Maine, a stationary object, larger and brighter than the North Star, was visible for several minutes in a sunset sky before disappearing with unbelievable speed. Because of this sighting, one of Stella's inevitable questions when we met strangers or small talk got mired in banalities, was "Have you ever seen a flying saucer?" I half expected people to exhibits signs of uneasiness. Instead, the query usually generated a social incandescence that swiftly illuminated other phenomena, such as reincarnation, out-of-body and near-death experiences.

I didn't get to see the light over Monmouth, but there was a UFO incident in my past a decade earlier. In 1955, I worked at the front desk of the Windsor Park Hotel in Washington, DC, where Colonial Airlines rented several rooms for their crews on stops between flights. Over a period of weeks, I got to know the pilots and stewardesses by their names. They were a friendly group, and when they registered, usually around 11 p.m., they always appreciated the midnight snacks I had the porter bring to their rooms.

Never have I seen four people more troubled, almost helpless in their motions as they entered the lobby that February night and approached the desk for their keys. The four crew members were in uniform, and with them was a dour-faced man in civilian dress, a stranger, but someone obviously in charge of a situation that had been out of control. Gone was all conviviality; not one of them smiled, and they didn't react when I asked if they would like refreshments sent up. "We are not accepting any telephone calls," the scowling executive instructed. "If there should be inquiries, Colonial Airlines is not available. Is that understood?" I nodded as he briskly turned away and herded his crew of zombies into the elevator.

I didn't have long to wait before the telephone switchboard blazed and a caller was on the line. He identified himself immediately.

"This is Donald Keyhoe speaking," he said, "and I would like to get in touch with the Colonial Airline pilot who is registered at your hotel."

I wanted to be helpful and would have given much to eavesdrop on such a conversation; Keyhoe's reputation as a UFO expert was internationally established, and his hurried call pretty much explained the demeanor of the troubled crew. Some terrifying encounter must have occurred—there was little doubt in my mind.

Of course I had to say no to Mr. Keyhoe—respecting the privacy of guests is an unwritten mandate in hotels. The incident was never mentioned by the crew as they checked in and out of the hotel between flights, but I sometimes wonder if they were ever quite the same people after that night in the sky.

In 1983, Stella began immersing herself in studies of the supernatural and paranormal, and she often highlighted her reading excursion in conversations with me. Maybe, by this time, I was responding more tolerantly, though some of the concepts and bizarre incidents she shared seemed lopsided and far-fetched—that imp from my conservative background was still capable of dispatching ridicule when there were extreme deviations from the ordinary.

I don't know who gave me the idea to write this book. Certainly my wife was an influence, and the project overcame both of us with its momentum—all we had to do was hang on for dear life as the pages galloped out of sight. This adventure has been the trip of a lifetime, and I owe so much to the book's many contributors. I feel privileged to have been a participant in that rule-breaking game of making a new truth out of an old knowledge.

THE SUPERNATURAL SIDE OF MAINE

THE ALLAGASH ABDUCTIONS

In late August of 1976, four men went on an eleven-day fishing trip along the wilderness waterway of the Allagash in Maine. The journey began with a hike up Mount Katahdin, and the following day the four went to Shin Pond where they rented canoes and were flown to remote Telos Lake, the embarkation point of their incredible adventure.

Chuck Rak, an avid outdoorsman who had camped in the region the previous year, asked friends he had met in college to accompany him. It was decided that Rak would act as a guide for Charlie Foltz, and twin brothers Jack and Jim Weiner.

A northerly wind slowed their progress the first full day of canoeing, and it was just after dusk when they reached Mud Brook Campsite at the entrance of Chamberlain Lake. The night sky was crammed with stars as the men gathered firewood and set up camp.

Suddenly a light blazed on the horizon. Jim Weiner, who had studied ceramics, described the illumination as suffused with the same intensity that one would see when viewing the inside of a pottery kiln at more than 2,000 degrees Fahrenheit—it seemed three to five times brighter than the most visible star and appeared to be only a few miles away. Weiner got out his binoculars and immediately realized that this was no ordinary light. "It hovered perfectly still for a few seconds," he recalled, "and then extinguished from the outside edge of the light to the center. I did not really think much about it, except that I had never observed a light implode like that before."

Heavy rains kept the foursome in camp on Wednesday morning, and it was mid-afternoon before they paddled towards Allagash Lake for some trout fishing. Currents slowed their progress, and they finally had to bivouac at an intersection of a river and Chamberlain Lake. The cloud covering scattered at dusk, and the tired canoeists watched a theatrical display of northern lights as they sat around a campfire and replanned their fishing trip.

Thursday broke warm and sunny with diminishing winds. The four soon reached the portage between Chamberlain and Eagle Lakes. It was afternoon when they arrived at Smith Brook Campsite, the most remote spot on Eagle. They quickly unloaded the canoes, stored their belongings, and paddled to the mouth of Smith Brook spurred by hopes of hooking a string of trout. Only an inedible chub was lifted from the depths and thrown back.

The last of the fresh meat was consumed that night, and since they had planned to replenish their food supply with fish, they decided to try some night angling. A huge pile of logs was collected and kindled—this would serve as a beacon for them to find their way back. The four men crowded into one canoe: Foltz in front as bowman, the Weiner twins in the middle, and Rak at the back as helmsman.

Chuck Rak was the first to sense that they were not alone as the canoe sliced the dark waters of the lake a quarter mile offshore. He turned and saw a sphere of light hovering soundlessly about 200 feet above the southeastern timberline. "That's a hell of a case of swamp gas!" he said, alerting the others. They all stared as a strange fluid spread over the face of the object in a change of colors from red to green to yellowish white. When they became more aware of the intense glow, a gyroscopic motion was detected, a sort of energy surging up and down. As the light boiled in its saucepan of night sky, the four wondered what would happen.

For nearly five minutes it hovered. This was no moon, star, or helicopter, the men decided. Weather balloons and marsh gas were ruled out; the thing seemed to lack solidity; there was an edgeless whirl of motion—the same kind of light that they had seen at the campsite by Chamberlain Lake.

It was Charlie Foltz's idea to signal the glowing energy mass with his flashlight. Three short, three long, and three short flashes were sent upward. The result was instantaneous: the shiny presence halted its swirl and slowly approached their canoe. The men agreed to sit still and see if the light reflected or churned the waters of the lake. It was now at an altitude of only 50 feet and edging closer.

Bolts of fear stiffened the three in front before they panicked—only Chuck Rak remained calm. Then pandemonium as the light kept bearing down in an obvious attempt to encompass them. "We decided to get off the water and onto solid ground," recalled Foltz under hypnosis. The men started paddling towards shore, all except an entranced Rak who kept staring at the object. An eerie beam of light now was prowling the surface of the lake as it advanced on them.

Memories can be tricksters: each of the four had a slightly different version of what happened next. Chuck Rak remembered remaining in the canoe after the others were onshore—he couldn't stop staring at the phenomenon. Slowly, the beam of light shifted away from them, and when it did Rak saw the sphere change from a full-moon outline to a thin crescent. It had the same imploding characteristics that the men had observed at the Mud Brook Campground two nights before.

Charlie Foltz recalled the frantic paddling towards shore and standing with the others as they watched the object depart. He flashed his light skyward once more but there was no response. As the spinning ball met two small clouds head-on, a beam of intense light cut through the bundled mist and the object was lost among the stars.

Jack Weiner's memory was somewhat more graphic; he remembered paddling and looking over his shoulder at the light with fear. "Holy shit!" he thought. "This is it! We'll never get away." Then he was at the shore and getting out of the canoe; there was no more need to save himself. But the thing still spun, nearly a stone's throw away, about 30 feet above the calm waters of the lake. For nearly five minutes it silently hovered, and Jack recalled feeling out of himself. A giant had grabbed and lifted him—he was sick to his stomach.

Jim Weiner was left with the same terrifying document posted in his memory when he spoke of the chase on the lake. He, too, was suspended in time while the light hovered and then disappeared.

Then all were weary. Even in their partly anesthetized state the men were dumbfounded: the huge campfire they had built was now a bed of coals; logs that should have burned for several hours had been consumed in an estimated twenty minutes. Too exhausted from the ordeal to start another fire, they fell asleep and woke the next morning still bone tired and confused.

"We broke camp and continued on our way to the next campsite," remembered Jack Weiner, "where we signalled a forest ranger. When he arrived at camp, we told him the whole story, but he didn't believe a word of it."

For the remainder of the trip, they moved in a state of bewilderment, each believing and half-believing that the incident had happened. One gnawing puzzle to them all was the lapse of memory while a huge bonfire became coals.

At a 1988 symposium on UFOs in Waltham, Massachusetts, planetarium operator Raymond E. Fowler, later author of *The Allagash Abductions*, 1993, was approached by Jim Weiner. Fowler was highly qualified and the ufologist to consult; he had been researching UFO and abduction incidents for more than 35 years, beginning with the astonishing Barney and Betty Hill case in 1961. Jim had been diagnosed as having temporolimbic epilepsy, a condition that caused extreme chest pains and numbness along one side of his body. Weiner had revealed to his doctor that he was experiencing nighttime aberrations which included waking to find strange beings by his bedside. He claimed that while he was in a state of temporary paralysis and unable to defend himself, these creatures had performed some medical procedure on him in the area of his genitals. Could this have anything to do with the UFO encounter in Maine? "Does it occur frequently?" Fowler asked. "Ever since we came back from the Allagash," Jim replied.

Tony Constantino, a qualified hypnotherapist who was skilled in regression techniques, was chosen to conduct a series of interviews, and Fowler asked David Webb, solar physicist and UFO investigator, to help as a consultant. The first session with Jim Weiner substantiated the opening minutes of the encounter, and much more.

Then, in an even deeper level of hypnosis, Weiner crossed into the territory where suppressed memories surface to the conscious mind. The reaction was noticeable agitation: "I can feel my heart pounding," the twin gasped. "I'm afraid of that light." Chuck Rak couldn't be seen because he was in the tube—this was a tunnel of light, claimed Weiner, with moving walls, and one was caught like particles of dust in a beam. When asked what happened on the other end of the tube, the response was painful. "Jack! They hurt Jack." Strange things, suited beings, were conducting medical experiments on his brother while Rak and Foltz were sitting naked on a bench. Jim was standing only a few feet away from the two; his back was against a wall and he was unable to move.

It was in the second hypnosis session that Jim Weiner gave a more detailed description of the aliens. They were like bugs, had bug eyes that didn't blink, blackish-brown pools on a noseless face with only a trace of a mouth and holes for ears. There were three or four of them dressed in bluish-gray suits made of shiny material—small things they were, perhaps five feet in height. Jim watched as the creatures probed Jack's eyes with a gleaming instrument that had a blinking light—it didn't seem to hurt him. His brother's scrotum, penis, and the inside of thighs were scrutinized. Then it was Jim Weiner's turn on the table, and he was examined with the same methodical care; one could tell by their gestures—their communication was telepathic—they were interested in the fact that two of the earthlings looked alike and the other two didn't.

Hypnotherapist Constantino had all he could do to calm Jim when the captors led Weiner down a dark hallway to another illuminated room. "I'm not going in there!" he shouted. "No! No fucking way! Just leave me alone!" The bugs now had him on a metal or thick plastic table and there was a "pokey thing" in one of the creature's three- or four-fingered hands. An erection was demanded as they lowered a silvery container which was five or six inches in length with an inch and a half insertion collar. Weiner was given a wordless command to ejaculate. Humiliated and afraid, he thought of naked women, of having sex with his girl-friend, anything as long as they stopped probing him with pointed in-struments and he could escape those fingers that felt like crawling caterpillars. Finally, it was over, he was led back to the others, they let him put on his clothes, and he was back in the canoe.

Television found the Allagash adventure irresistible; the incident had pictorial charisma from the moment the four men lowered their canoes into the water until they stared in wonder at the untimely coals of a huge bonfire. Ted Turner's TBS showed a documentary filmed by a Maine-based company, and *Unsolved Mysteries* featured a segment of it in one of their nationwide weekly programs.

WCSH television in Portland, Maine interviewed Chuck Rak when the station carried the Allagash waterway episode in a documentary called *Maine Mysteries*—this was in 1998, five years after the book publication of Raymond E. Fowler's *The Allagash Abductions*. WCSH wanted to question the other participants so they could tell their versions, but a lawyer for the three declined. Foltz and the Weiner twins were "trying to get film rights to their tale."

Channel 6 told its viewing audience: "Chuck Rak once believed this happened to him (the abduction), but he no longer does." The event did not traumatize him, he claimed, it was just imagery from a vivid dream. "This disagreement, along with twenty-two years of stuff," the report continued, "has caused a split between Chuck and the other guys. In a phone conversation, Jack Weiner angrily called his one-time friend a 'debunker.' But even if you take the abduction part out, all four men agree they saw a UFO back on that night in 1976, and it is a pretty good story."

"Maine would be a good place for aliens to conduct experiments," said a UFO enthusiast who requested anonymity. "If they abducted one or two, nobody would ever know the difference because there aren't that many folks up here to see them do it. Visitors from other planets or dimensions could have whole complexes somewhere in the woods—up in Aroostook County—and no one would ever know it."

The abduction story that caught the attention of the country and be-came a forerunner for countless hobnobbing adventures with aliens was the Barney and Betty Hill encounter near Indian Head in the White Mountains of New Hampshire on the evening of September 19, 1961.

"We were driving along on a tarred road," Betty Hill stated in an interview under hypnosis, "and all of a sudden without any warning or rhyme or reason or anything, Barney stopped suddenly and made this sharp turn off the highway." Then she saw it. An enormous disk-shaped craft with two rows of windows had descended.

Hill crept within 50 feet of the ship and looked up to see six creatures peering through a row of windows. Terrified, he ran back to the car and sped away. Not far down the road, the vehicle began vibrating and a haze engulfed the couple. When the Hills returned home and checked their watches, they realized that several hours had been "lost" somewhere along the way.

After the incident, Barney and Betty Hill began having disturbing dreams—scary enough for them to seek help from Boston psychiatrist Benjamin Simon. Four months of hypnotic regression revealed a terrifying visit aboard the spacecraft where they were subjected to medical examinations conducted by five-foot-tall, hairless creatures with grayish skin, pear-shaped heads and large slanting eyes. Betty Hill spoke of a pregnancy test; skin scrapings, samples of earwax, hair and fingernail clippings were taken. Before leaving the ship she was shown a "Star Map" of their home base called "Zeta Reticuli."

This New Hampshire encounter captivated reporters and commentators while critics bayed at a bad moon. What the Hills had seen was nothing more than Jupiter, the pundits howled, and there were incongruities: for instance, the spacemen used colloquial English and asked banal questions: "What are vegetables? What is yellow?"

The Hill case was remembered and brought up repeatedly because of the role that hypnotism was given in confirming what the couple believed happened to them that evening—many skeptics and UFO researchers argued that an inexact science had been overplayed and too much credence placed on its effectiveness.

Are people really being abducted, taken aboard spaceships, and subjected to medical examinations? There is no conclusive evidence—such as photographs; there is only the testimony from involuntary participants, and this alone isn't enough to convince scoffers that these adventures are plausible.

If one traced the history of abduction before it became a popular entertainment centerpiece for television and before the public was aware that certain patterns occur in spaceship kidnapping, there may be only two possible explanations: that people are really being abducted or that we, as a species, share a curious mass hallucination.

Would an altered state of consciousness explain the phenomenon?

Scientists are reluctant to accept abduction reports even when impressed with the sincerity of those who make such claims. The human brain is capable of producing a wide panorama of mind states, though we are jarred when anything bizarre intrudes. We don't like our realities messed with; it is easier to say abductions can't happen.

One would doubt the tellers of such tales if these were isolated incidents. What nudges John Q. Public into believing that the events take place is the firm conviction of those reporting such encounters. The average abductee appears to be an honest and reliable witness; someone you might know from your neighborhood, and certainly not a person attempting to hoodwink one with a fanciful yarn.

Abduction scenes have few niceties, and when such things are staged, they inevitably become productions that would set Dracula's teeth on edge: frightened captives are fully conscious but shackled within a state of paralysis as implants are inserted behind eyes or crunched into skulls, scoops and pointed rods become vicious instruments, blood and urine are collected, and finally there is the humiliation of having semen or ova extracted—aliens have a fascination for reproductive organs and their functions. In the final act of this script, once the seeds of life have been seized and somehow altered, they are planted in the uterus during a return visit. After the fetus has gestated for some weeks in the mother, it is removed and placed in a tank to incubate. Both parents are sometimes brought back to see their offspring and are encouraged to hold and love the child.

Abductees come from many backgrounds, and most of them hesitate before sharing their ordeals with others, even with family members. Because of highly publicized accounts of corralling in desert settings, the Barney and Betty Hill abduction, and the Allagash incident, a majority of people conclude that aliens are more likely to grab a person in a barren or wooded area—it can happen, so say many ufologists, just as readily on the side street of a city or in a suburban bedroom.

A number of researchers believe that abductions often begin in childhood, sometimes as early as the age of three or four. Once an abductee is designated a prime specimen for ongoing genetic evaluation, there is no release—during an entire lifetime one can be picked up and examined. Many hypnotic regression experts are convinced that the memories of these visitations can easily be retrieved.

Stories of late-night callers are commonplace. Peculiar images invade a troubled sleep and upon waking one is aware of a figure by the bed—a creature familiar only in rare flashbacks or when its hazy presence is seen lingering by the portals of the subconscious. Another preliminary is the ball-of-light announcement: a glowing aura dissipates and the entity appears.

There are eighty or more people in Maine who claim that they have been abducted. "Many of them attend meetings in the Bangor area—in a missile silo that has been deactivated." ("I hope to God it was!" interjected the man whose wife was telling the story.) There were thirty-nine present on the night the couple in the above parentheses visited.

"We sat in a circle," said the wife, "and they gave their testimony. A middle-aged woman—maybe closer to sixty—said she hated the creatures that came for her. She was worn out from nursing strange babies all night long."

"I'm more accepting," declared the husband. "The people present were friendly, and they seemed in every other way logical and down-to-earth. There was a need to meet and talk. If they didn't, they would explode."

"I thought they were just bug-eyed," said the wife. "Some of the women of the gathering claimed that they were made pregnant and the babies were taken and never seen again."

"I wouldn't rule out the possibility entirely," the husband defended. "It's far-out—there is no question about that—but who knows?"

A 1991 Roper Organization poll on "unusual experiences" startled the general public. Analysis showed that one out of every fifty people in this country claims to have had an abduction experience at some time or another. Should this be true—and there are many who dismiss such testimony—there must be an increase in the number of defenders of the paranormal. What once was scoffed at and shelved as nonsense is fast becoming mainstream.

There are individuals who take strong issue with the negative views concerning aliens and abductions—people who once had little patience for such things. What happened to one convert has happened countless times to others. A friend of this man tells the story: "Joe Smith (not his real name) woke up one night and two little guys were standing by his bed. He reached out to feel them and claimed their arms were soft. When they were about to leave, they looked back at him and said they would come again. Then he realized that he wasn't afraid of them at all. The next morning his eight-year-old son came to him and asked: 'Dad, who were those two men next to your bed last night?' Even to this day, he believes these creatures were benign and had kind intentions. I have read too many things about aliens; they may be good or evil—perhaps they may be coming from different places."

"Here is a thought," said a UFO defender, "UFOs could be monitoring certain people with implants. I think we must allow for that possibility, no matter how incredible. For example, a man in Wilton, Maine told of an experience he had out in Indiana—a close encounter. He, his grandmother, and some other people saw this object; they were on a farm and this thing came in around the barn and circled them. His wife had a UFO encounter over in New Sharon, Maine and it scared the living daylights out of him because his daughter also had seen them. He got panicky because he was aware that this often runs in families."

270 abduction cases were analyzed by folklorist Dr. Thomas Bullard in 1987, and after he weeded out the likely hoaxes and self-delusions, the study confirmed what many ufologists have suspected all along: the sequence of events occurred over and over to people of entirely different nationalities, backgrounds, and occupations.

One of the difficulties an investigator has in getting a clear view of an abduction is the participant's inability to place the experience in a logical time frame. There is an unrolling of disoriented sequences and too much confusion prompted by fear—the film gets snarled in the projector, and what one sees on the screen is distortion.

Abductees are in agreement that aliens are detached as they go about the business of performing medical examinations. There seems to be an air of clinical responsibility as they probe, test, and take samples. They are disinterested doctors—all of them—and no effort is made to get better acquainted with their captives on a personal level.

Time implodes into a moment of terror as the abductee is unable to speak or move. Only the eyes can function in their frightened focus as nightmarish creatures engulf them in surroundings that are not of this planet. There is no need for language here; commands take over the mind without gesture or sound; no gentleness is exhibited, only the suggestion of remaining calm to avoid harm.

The mystery of the log fire had troubled the four men after they left Maine and resumed their lives. Jack Weiner, in his hypnosis session, also described the beam of light as hollow and there were rings on the water as it came after them. "It's going to get us!" he shouted to the others moments before they were engulfed. He, too, couldn't look out once inside the cylindrical belly with its walls which drifted like smoke in a room. Then there was a blazing light in front of him before he saw his brother and the two friends sitting naked on a bench. Something was coming toward him, Jack remembered. "Oh-h-h! Is it going to hurt me?"

Small mouth, no nose and ears, but big eyes that were long and round "like eggs." And behind the creature another followed. The aliens were thin and small, had turtle mouths, and when they approached their joints "didn't move right."

Jack's armpits, legs, the inside of thighs, the backs of calves and knees were scraped with a shiny metal gouge. The instrument inserted into his penis was less kind: "It's hurting me! It hurts!" Afterwards, he was assisted into another room for more examinations. Their faces were in his face, and they began explaining things to him; their eyes were shining, and he heard words in his head. "Don't be afraid," he was told. "We won't harm you. Just do what we say." Jack Weiner used his eyes to communicate—his mouth was frozen shut. "Where's Jim?" he asked. And one of the creatures up close said in his head: "Jim is all right. You're almost finished. Just a little while longer."

They led Jack to a bench, and Jim was brought into the room by two of the aliens. There was a long wait before he saw Chuck and finally Charlie. They were all naked, stiff with the inoculation of fear and caught in a spell that bewildered them. "We're almost done," they were told.

Apprehension continued as they were taken into another place and helped into their clothes. Before them was a machine of tubelike glass, "big as a Volkswagen," and they were directed to stand next to it. The apparatus moved, and Jack Weiner felt that he was coming apart, flying in different directions. Jack saw the others, and they were all screaming as the walls crowded them; he even saw himself coming towards himself—his eyes wide, mouth wide, tongue sticking out, and ears falling off. Then they were all back in the canoe and paddling away from the beam of light.

Charlie Foltz had no recollection of going to bed that night; under hypnosis, he stated that they talked for hours. As he remembered it, the tube of light was solid glass, a blue-glass tunnel that overtook them. Instead of being in the canoe, he was suddenly lying on his back with his eyes closed—Foltz was afraid to open them, but when he did there were his toes, and he realized his clothes had been removed. The place was "like a doctor's office" with Jim, Chuck, and Jack sitting naked on a bench "doing nothing, just looking." He could see the back of one of the aliens. This creature was facing his friends, and the thing's backside reminded him of "a kid." There was no hair on the head; it was about four feet eight in height; a girl's neck it had, long and thin; the eyes were almond-shaped, Asian, without lids, but a flash of something came across them occasionally instead of a blink; the nostrils and ears were smaller than his; its clothing was smooth, "close-fitting but loose," a grayish-white in color, reflective, and cut like an aerobic costume.

A tray or panel had been placed on Foltz's chest during the scraping procedure and the taking of blood and saliva samples. Urine and feces were also collected, even toe and fingernail clippings. He was helped up and led to a bench when they were through, and a nearby porthole or window in the wall gave him a glimpse of their canoe on the lake.

The machine of "tubelike glass" described by Jack was a panel of light in a wall to Charlie. The hollow insides that acted as their transport also moored the canoe. Foltz had difficulty recalling the beaming down—he had been instructed in his head to forget everything. With its eyes, the alien helping him into the canoe had commanded him: "Don't be afraid. Relax."

To Chuck Rak, the tube also was a tunnel, almost a barrier and solid. Beyond was a circular room, "sort of a yellowish-silver-blue." And once in this bright enclosure, he had no voluntary control over himself. Three or four figures were present as Rak was led to a table where his midsection was closely examined with a light that fluttered "like a butterfly" as it prowled downward. Something began oozing from his penis. The sperm sample was taken away in a black contraption that had joints—a gadget one might see in a dental office. Finally, he was lifted from the table and led to a bench. Jim and Charlie were there and Jack was on the other side of the room in a "kind of harness." The twin was being told to raise his arms, and three-fingered hands began probing his upper rib cage and an armpit.

Rak now counted four or five entities in the room. They had "embryonic chicken heads, craniums oblongated from front to back," duck-shaped with black eyes and only froglike membranes for lids. Chuck felt drugged, and the surroundings were hazy, but he noticed their bald heads, translucent skins and "turkey-gizzard" necks. He knew what the aliens wanted without language.

After it was over, the four were helped into their clothes and taken to what Rak described as a "portal"—some place in a wall where things happened. It was as if they were "penetrating a membrane of blue-gray tubes." Chuck saw nothing during the painful passage, but he did get a glimpse of the lake sixty feet or so below. There seemed to be a "floating" motion as he descended. Two of the creatures, waist-deep in the lake beside the canoe, seated a befuddled Rak.

Did all this really happen? Chuck Rak was asked later. He definitely had seen something in Maine, but the onboard experiences were jumbled, as if he had been led through a series of events—Rak was the only one of the four who showed little fear when recalling abduction incidents under hypnosis. For him, the adventure was a chance to learn, and the reactions of his three companions—their fears—were brought forth because of a "parochial Sunday-school upbringing." Raymond Fowler and Tony Constantino nicknamed Chuck their "Macho-Man." Very little bothered him, and he was quick to tell people that he could iron his way through most difficulties. Rak was analytic and introspective when reviewing the sequence of abduction events: he wondered if the troubled dreams that the Weiner twins had years after the Maine trip contaminated his response to questions. Maybe reading too many UFO books had twisted or softened him.

There are a number of physical problems for abductees after an incident: muscle pains, genital disorders, bruises, neurological scarring, and pregnancy anomalies. One of the body locations that aliens supposedly examine frequently is the tibia. It is along the leg that circular or scooplike traces, about one-eighth to three quarters of an inch in diameter and as much as a quarter-inch deep, are sometimes found. Many abductees claim that devices have been inserted, usually in the head as a tracking mechanism—X rays have been unable to reveal such extraterrestrial bugs, though some interesting skin irregularities have been found by doctors, such as unexplained burn marks, scars and bruises.

All four of the Allagash participants were left with some kind of scarring. A scoop mark suddenly appeared above an old operation scar on Jack Weiner's leg, and he also had skin deterioration on the bottom of one foot. Charlie Foltz discovered a pocket-like indentation on the inside of a leg, and Chuck Rak had a burn mark on his back, one that wasn't there before the Maine trip. In addition to Jim Weiner's neurological problems, there were typical scoop traces in the area of the tibia.

Charlie Foltz seemed unaffected by the Allagash waterway incident; he claimed to have no way of imparting how the adventure changed his life. Art had long been a fascination, and he thought of becoming a schoolteacher in his native Ohio. Instead, Foltz is a medical illustrator for scientists in the biotechnological fields and works as a volunteer at the Children's Hospital in Boston.

Chuck Rak is a caricature artist in shopping malls, does portrait commissions, and exhibits his oil and pastel paintings at an art center in Manchester, Vermont. He and Jack Weiner collaborated in producing a 32-page booklet of illustrations called *The Allagash Incident*. There are also original artworks based on the experience by Rak, and a limited-edition color computer print by Jack Weiner. The sale of such objects has raised doubts in the minds of some who wanted to believe that the Maine episode was authentic—"the story was cooked up to get money," declared a disbeliever.

Jack Weiner's career preference prior to the abduction was in the field of fine arts, but after the Allagash trip his interests shifted to science, mathematics, computers, and anything he can learn about "the ancient Mayans of Central America." He is not obsessed with trying to find out all that happened to him in Maine. "My life is still very typical," wrote Jack. "My time is spent doing all the normal things that people everywhere must be concerned with in order to survive from day to day."

Jim Weiner's nighttime encounters with aliens have become an accepted part of his conscious thought processes. Whenever he has a visitation, Weiner feels "a strong aura of malevolence emanating from the beings." Jim also criticizes the U.S. government and military: he thinks both are lying when they state that no such creatures exist. He is on the faculty of the Massachusetts College of Arts in their Computer Arts Learning Center and meets weekly as a member of a UFO abductee support group.

Each of the Allagash four took a polygraph test and passed. While it is clear that they believe that their memories are real, some skeptics feel that the stories do not stand up to scrutiny—like so many abductees, they may have been influenced by images from the entertainment world, such as scenes from the 1955 film *Invaders from Mars*.

"It is media driven; it is cyclical," declared William Cone, clinical psychologist who specializes in the study of hypnotic therapy and repressed memory. "You get some good cases on TV, people hear about them and think they may have had the same thing happen. It feeds upon itself."

"Usually, these are people who have had no interest in abduction," counters Dr. John Mack, Harvard psychiatrist who has done extensive work with abductees. "They have not read about it, are unfamiliar with the nature of such beings, and are astounded when they hear that there is material in the media about it."

"My investigators have a very clear-cut agenda of what they are looking for," Cone defended. "If you get somebody who is in UFO abduction research, this is a person who has already decided that such things are real, that thousands of people have had it happen to them; there is a symptom list, and if you come in the door with the symptoms, then you must have been abducted."

"It doesn't work that way," Mack replied. "People come because they have heard that I am open; I listen to things which other therapists or mental health professionals refuse to consider. Abductees are heavily doubtful—they don't want this to be true. It is not a club one wants to join."

After the hypnotic sessions were completed, Raymond Fowler brought the four together and they discovered that each of them recalled the same horrifying events. Jim Weiner was astonished. "Jack would say something, and Chuck would say the same thing."

Charlie Foltz concluded the drama with a look back: "If you were to tell somebody forty years ago that they would be able to see on television a meteorite crashing into a planet, that's a reality check, folks. And yet, forty years ago such a thing would be science fiction. The abduction happened. If you believe it, that's all right; if you don't believe it, I don't care. But it did."

HAUNTED LIGHTHOUSES

A 1996 poll revealed that a third of all adults in America believe in ghosts—an increase of twenty-two percent over a survey conducted six years earlier. "So, if you're not a believer," wrote John Richardson in the October 27, 1997 issue of the *Portland Press Herald*, "it may just be that your antennae are asleep or you're not in the right environment. Forget the Ouija board. Go visit a lighthouse."

There are several of these structures along the Maine coast that have long histories of hauntings, and what better sanctuary can be found? It's a kind of chapel for restless spirits; a meetinghouse that warns mariners of shoals and jagged obstacles; a place known to loosen tongues and widen the eyes of children when night pushes against windows. "You start listening to the wind howling through those old buildings and your imagination wanders," declared Tim Harrison of Wells, Maine, publisher of *Lighthouse Digest* magazine.

This tour begins with the lighthouse at Owls Head: it's a twenty-foot tower located on a rocky ledge a hundred feet above battering surf. The beacon was first lit on September 10, 1825, and not long after its construction the tower was manned by a frugal keeper whose obsession was conserving fuel. The Old Captain—a title given him by irritated employees over the years—still maintains a tight budget; the thermostat often is turned down and doors are slammed shut against a draft. There are other occurrences blamed on the old salt: furniture is moved, coats are taken from hooks and thrown on the floor, brass fixtures are found slippery with polish, and crockery can be heard chattering in the pantry. The spirit is sometimes forgetful and leaves the case around the lens ajar—as if he wanted to light the beacon but got distracted. The keeper's house stands about two hundred feet down a slanting boardwalk from the tower, and there have been reports of footprints on the walk after a snowfall or when the morning mist is heavy; these are prints of a man's boots—size 10½—and always found leading from the living quarters to the light. Once, a curious keeper followed the tracks and was in time to see a shadow, just when the steel door on the tower was closing.

The apparition of an attractive woman in her early twenties frequently paces the beach near the lighthouse in Southport, Maine. Her death is a mystery and has generated gossip. She had been seen by several residents the night before her body washed ashore with heavy weights strapped around the waist. They remembered greeting her but she had remained silent, "as if she wasn't there." For nearly eighty years her spirit has wandered this stretch of sand before disappearing in the mist. Did she commit suicide or was the girl murdered by rumrunners during Prohibition? The body was buried in the local cemetery, and to this day her identity is unknown.

Another apparition resides at the Ram Island Light in Boothbay Harbor. Several years before its construction in 1883, an old mariner was shipwrecked and died of exposure on the island. Since his demise, lights have been seen on the beach to warn passing ships, but when investigators looked for these beacons in daylight not one could be found. Many seamen have heard whistles but there are no sounding devices in the area. When local fishermen's tongues are loosened by grog, tales that are compellingly similar emerge: a ghost has been seen scurrying back and forth as if in a frantic effort to save lives.

Not all ocean outposts shelter restless presences. Guardians of the Cape Neddick Light near York Beach, better known as the Nubble Light, have only praise for their resident ghost. This is a happy and contented spirit. Strangers coming to the island and sensing the benevolent presence feel exhilarated as they bask in an atmosphere of cheerfulness. Here is an entity that enjoys its surroundings. There are no tricks played with windows and doors—all cups and saucers behave in the kitchen. In this tranquil stretch of coastline, harsh winds and heavy seas never cause keepers to be despondent, and many who serve here ask for an extension of their duties.

The Seguin Island Light near Popham Beach became one of Maine's most important lighthouse stations because of its location two miles south of the Kennebec River and an increase of schooner traffic. Known as the oldest (1795), windiest, loneliest, and foggiest outpost on the coast, the tower rises a hundred and eighty-six feet above sea level. Seguin is a difficult place to visit—the entrance to the living quarters is by a trolley ramp. A dolly is hauled up the track by a donkey engine, and it is a long climb from the boathouse to the main quarters.

One legend has it that a keeper and his wife brought a piano to the island. The wife practiced diligently but could play only one composition—composer unknown. She tinkled the keys over and over until her incessant hammering hastened the husband to madness. In a rage, he took a hatchet to the piano, his wife, and himself. This murder-suicide didn't assure silence: sometimes on quiet nights, sailors on passing ships can hear the same monotonous tune being played.

The man who wielded his axe has been sighted going up the narrow stairway to the tower, and a visitor on the island saw the ghost standing behind one of the keepers during a checkers game. Cold spots have been felt, and jackets have been found thrown on the floor. It is believed that there is a third ghost on the island: a little girl died there, and two workers saw her running up and down the stairs—she appeared to be a happy spirit: the child was laughing and she waved to the men.

An encounter with that irascible keeper occurred in 1985 when the lighthouse was being prepared for automation. All items on the premises had been packed for shipping to the mainland, and while the work crew slept on portable cots, the man in charge of the detail was awakened from a deep sleep. An apparition in oilskin stood before him. "Don't take the furniture!" the ghost lamented. "Please leave my house alone!" The crew foreman jumped up and made a hurried retreat to another room.

The following morning when furniture and sundry items were loaded on the dolly and orders were given to start the donkey engine, the chain holding the dolly broke and the load went full speed down the track, hit the water and sank. All the furniture and packing cases were lost. The crew foreman insisted that the late keeper caused this freak accident. That night, their last before leaving the place, the ghost made another appearance. In a whining voice the apparition complained: "I can't feed my family! Why did you do this to me?"

In a June 20, 2000 feature of the Brunswick, Maine *Times Record*, the current caretakers at Seguin, Rick and Jennifer Naugler, told reporter Jonathan White that there was continuous activity involving historical wall photographs in the island's lighthouse museum. "Every time I open up the museum," said Mrs. Naugler, "no matter the time of day, the pictures are all crooked again, even if I've straightened them 20 minutes before. They'll stay straight as long as I'm in there. When I leave, they move around."

The tools in her husband's workshop are also restless, and there are unexplained night noises. "I think that's just because you're out here, isolated," said Rick Naugler, "and you have a more active imagination. Things fall down in closets; this is a 144-year-old house. Even the gulls occasionally sound humanlike."

DOWSING ADVENTURES

A Maine farmer didn't have to travel far to find a dowser when a well ran dry in the nineteen thirties. There were plenty of old-timers around who could locate water for the farm family and livestock. In recent years, dowsing is less prevalent, and the most skeptical are those who never have placed themselves behind a rod or pendulum. No survey has been taken, but it is generally thought that more than sixty percent of Maine dowsers are over the age of fifty, and only one or two in a hundred successfully dowse for metals or minerals.

Generations of farmers went without scientific guidance to help find hidden veins of water crisscrossing the boulder-strewn landscape of Maine. Landowners had to hack their way through rock to make wells that never went dry. The water source for many of the old farmhouses is either on or nudging a vein—a fact that could not be accidental. Out of necessity, these wells had to be located by dowsers.

One popular explanation of how dowsing works is that a force emanates from unseen objects. This energy transmits itself to the instruments used by dowsers, and consequently to the humans holding sticks or pendulums. Such forces have been described as emissions, electromagnetic waves, and vibrations, though such theories fail to explain map dowsing. The ability to get a pendulum to respond over a sheet of paper with lines suggesting a particular territory argues for a psychic interpretation of dowsing. Could it be that a diviner's stimulation is not external but springs in some mysterious way from consciousness itself?

The principal use of dowsing is to find water, but the psychic premise that all objects, animate and inanimate, project some sort of aura or energy field isn't easily dismissed. There are thousands of stick and pendulum holders who believe that their methods can be used to locate buried treasures, oil, archeological relics, lost possessions, and missing people.

English dowser T. C. Lethbridge discovered that his pendulum would swing predictably for both material things and abstract concepts, such as love, hate, death, and even time. Author Colin Wilson, who did a study on Lethbridge's dowsing experiments, concluded that events imprint themselves on a particular place and a competent dowser can pick up vibrations from objects and events years afterwards.

Lethbridge, called the "Einstein of pendulum dowsing," conducted experiments on standing stones—the best known example being Stonehenge. He found that the pendulum reacted vehemently at these places and concluded that stones somehow amplify an energy from the earth, much in the same way as ley lines—a network of lines connecting old churches, hilltops, and mounds often found in the English countryside.

In 1960, Swiss dowser Edgar Devaux was asked to help find a missing housewife. He held his pendulum over a photograph of the woman and immediately announced that she was dead. Then, dowsing a map of the area, he traced a line along the bank of a river and made his cross a few feet offshore. Divers went down at the spot indicated and found her body. Such pinpointing cannot be explained in terms of magnetic fields; some impression of the tragedy must have been recorded to make possible such an exact reading. Perhaps humans possess the power of projecting their emotions under the stimulus of sudden danger or the prospect of death—a transmission that can be read by both psychic and dowser.

Many animals are not only affected by waterlines, but can instinctively find and use them. A remarkable water diviner is the burro. People living in sandy desert places of Mexico depend on these donkeys to show them where water can be found. The burros will dig until only their noses and ears are visible above the sand, and they are invariably successful in their search.

The earth acts as a weak magnet for birds and animals that use magnetic forces to find their way back to their nests and lairs. The homing pigeon has a small tissue between its eyes which contains the mineral magnetite, and when a magnet is strapped to the bird's back, the pigeon is unable to find its way home.

An experiment conducted in the late 1970s on two dowsers had similar results. They were taken by automobiles to unknown destinations, and each was asked to dowse in the direction of home. One dowser had a brass bar strapped to his head and the other rod carrier a bar magnet. The man with the brass fixture was remarkably accurate, but the person wearing the bar magnet was completely disoriented. Since the earth is surrounded by a magnetic field, certain frequencies may affect us. It has been ascertained that a greater number of traffic and industrial accidents occur when the earth measures a higher level of geomagnetic energy. Probably, in subtle ways, we are influenced by these forces.

Some dowsers are able to select radio broadcasts on different frequencies. This selection process is the same as when a practitioner looks for underground minerals and orders the pendulum or rod to ignore water—or when different articles are placed under a carpet and it is necessary to concentrate on the one that is being sought.

Physicist Z.V. Harvalik conducted a field experiment based on the theory that since a magnetometer is sensitive enough to pick up brain waves, why shouldn't a competent dowser also detect them? The physicist stood with his back to a screen, and wearing earplugs he asked people to walk towards him from the other side of the screen. Harvalik's divining rod revealed their presence when they were within ten feet of him. Then the doctor asked his subjects to think "exciting" thoughts as they approached the screen—"concentrate on sex," he suggested. When they did this, Harvalik was able to dowse them twenty feet away, not ten. (Maybe this explains why one feels uneasy when a person is staring at the back of one's head or why women often detect the gaze of a sexually interested male even when he is walking behind them.)

Experiments conducted on a group of dowsers in the 1960s revealed that their abilities improved after they drank several glasses of water, and people who showed no skills with a rod or pendulum became quite professional after consuming half a tumbler of whiskey. One of the observers concluded: "The alcohol seems to relax them to the point where they tune in."

"I could be up to my neck in water," said Frank Perham, a miner and expert on Maine minerals, "and the dowsing stick wouldn't twitch." But Perham has dynamited a lot of wells for people over the years, and he has seen his share of successful dowsers. One was an Austrian who stopped at their mineral store in West Paris and had a conversation with Frank and his father, Stanley Perham. The man had never been to Maine before, had no knowledge of the countryside, but he claimed that he could map dowse. Stan Perham gave the stranger a piece of nondescript feldspar that had been found in Leeds, Maine. "He took the rock," recalled Frank, "handled it a bit, and said: 'I have a feeling that this came from within a fifty mile radius of here.' " The Perhams wondered if this man was a clever charlatan. The visitor gripped the stone and moved a pendulum above a geological survey map. There were three possible sites in the Leeds area where the feldspar sample could have been found. "It is this one," said the Austrian dowser. "It came from right here." The man had pinpointed the exact spot.

Richard Longley of Caribou, Maine, described by his neighbors as being "an honest and decent man in every way," astonished everyone when he claimed that he had located five deposits of gold in Aroostook County by dowsing—most onlookers grin and shake their heads when they see someone on a river or in a quarry with a bent coat hanger or stick.

Longley's interest in dowsing for gold and silver began in 1895 when he was a logging boss in New Brunswick. A divining rod in a shop aroused his curiosity, and when he was told it would cost him more than he could afford, Longley decided to make his own. This consisted of two bands of steel one foot long, joined to form a V, and where the bands came together, a piece of leather was tied to serve as a strap for the cover of a small bottle. All Longley had to do was place a sample of whatever mineral or metal he wanted into the container for a reading.

A newspaper reporter, Phil Pendell, accompanied the Caribou dowser to a location where Longley claimed to have found gold. This 1939 mining site was on the bank of Madawaska Stream. With the help of several friends, a 40-foot trench, some 13 feet deep and 4 feet wide, had been dug with pick and shovel. "Still holding the rod," wrote Pendell, "he paced eastward away from the stream, and the end of the device continued to point eastward."

This adventure is anticlimactical. Longley's dream of finding a lode had the same conclusion as Maine dowser Henry Gross's hope of un-earthing tourmaline at Mount Mica: the outcome was left in limbo. Samples of ore had been sent to an assayer, but the results were never made public, and when Longley died his estate was described by family members as being "only modest."

(There are people who believe that the Jefferson Cattle Pound built by Silas Noyes in 1828 for $28 in Jefferson, Maine was not merely a pen for stray cows. "It was a temple," one sensitive told this author and his wife. "A friend and I tuned into it."

The stone slab crowning the entrance is reminiscent of a Stonehenge lintel, and one wonders why it was necessary to construct walls at least six to eight feet in height. A conservative estimate of the circle's diam-eter would be about forty feet, a sufficient area for performing tribal rites.

"I've taken different people there," said the sensitive, "and we've had meditation—this goes back to the oral tradition: that's when people gather

in a circle and the storyteller begins to tell the history of the place and
what more can be added to it."

As I listened, a picture of Celtic wanderers in Maine decorated my imagination.

"But the best thing of all is if you lie down in the very center, placing
yourself in a northeast-southwest direction, get into a meditative state,
and give permission to be taken out of your body, you go whoosh—and
you're gone!"

Perhaps the slight parting of my lips and a slackness along the jawline
were enough to register a hint of doubt—though I do take pride in my
showings of impartiality.

"You can take this with a grain of salt," I was told. "I cannot make you
believe my experiences, but I can share them—so you go whoosh. And
you're gone! There was this spacecraft and a door opening and a hand
reaching out and a voice in my head saying: 'Welcome aboard. We have
been waiting for you.' And then I came back."

The Jefferson Cattle Pound is an unusual construction, and my first
impression, when my wife and I visited the site the following week, was
the proud workmanship that went into the building of this enclosure—
one fieldstone locked tightly into the grip of two others, stone on stone,
with graceful circling lines. I didn't see it as an ancient temple; to me it
wasn't a Celtic sacred place. As I stood leaning against the interior wall
and gazing at the lintel over the entrance, my thoughts were recreating
its history.

"Silas," I could hear one of the selectmen saying to Noyes as several
men sat at a long table with pipe smoke cushioning candlelight, "we
want a pen big enough to accommodate all those damned cows drifting
about town."

$28 seems a paltry sum for all the work that obviously went into the
pound's construction. The stones probably were placed on a drag pulled
by oxen, transported to the site, sorted according to size and shapes, and
fitted into place—a formidable undertaking.

The world was very different in 1828, I thought as I studied the wall.
People who came to Maine in those days were pioneers busy clearing a
wilderness for crops and pastureland. Not all the stone walls on farms
were completed—there still were thousands of standing trees and an
endless tangle of roots cradling jagged boulders. I could hear in my mind
one of the town father's parting words: "You build that wall high, Silas.
The Town of Jefferson, Maine must set a good example!"

I drifted to the center of the pound and found remnants of charcoal;

someone had built a small fire in the exact spot where supernatural powers were supposedly pinpointed. Could it be ashes from some ritual, or kids toasting marshmallows over a bonfire? I looked up and saw Stella holding a small dowser in her hand. "Why don't you try this?" she suggested.

I wound the short piece of thread around a finger and lowered the small fisherman's sinker which served as the pendulum. When the lead weight stopped swaying, I paused several moments before asking my first question—a simple query that could be answered with a *yes* or *no*.

"Was this enclosure once a temple?"

The pendulum remained stationary, indicating a negative response.

"Was this a cattle pound?" I asked.

The lead sinker trembled and immediately began swaying in a clockwise motion with increased speed.

I had been given a resounding *yes*.

A number of dowsing questions followed, and the pendulum reacted predictably: yes, it was a cattle pound, built in 1828 by Silas Noyes, and for $28; no, it wasn't a jumping-off place for boarding spaceships and achieving paranormal highs—I must admit I found the responses disappointing; the dowser could have given me at least one swing in favor of those Celts.

When I told Stella what my readings were, she reminded me that I had already decided what the place was about before I picked up the lead sinker and thread. Probably the vehement *yeses* were mine, and not true reactions from the dowser. Then she remembered a conversation she had with Maine prospector and dowser Leigh Walton about the dangers of wishes and preconceived ideas and how they easily can influence an outcome. He solved the problem by having a friend with similar interests hold the pendulum while Leigh would pose the question in his mind—silently and strongly—and the companion holding the pendulum would give Walton the results.

My experience at the Jefferson Cattle Pound reminded me how easy it is to get sidetracked when you allow your feelings or hunches to interfere. Without an open mind and confidence in what you are doing, dowsing is an uncertain business. I'm not sensitive enough to be talented in this field; my negativism often gives me false readings.

As mentioned in my first Maine mining book, *The Next Bend in the River*, my wife and I went dowsing with prospector Harvey Packard one day in the Hartford, Maine area. Harvey, who has talent as a dowser, was trying to locate tourmaline in a ledge in the woods. It was a place remembered from his childhood. The mosquitoes were thicker than I had ever seen them, and we were being badly bitten. I was getting a different reading than Stella and Harvey, and since mine was more definite, they decided to follow my dowsing direction. What I located wasn't a pocket of tourmaline as they stumbled behind me over a fence and into a prickly blackberry patch. It was a beeline through the woods to our vehicle. My desire to get away from the mosquitoes was stronger than my urge to locate tourmaline.)

Maine game warden Henry Gross of Biddeford, the dowsing guru of the nineteen fifties, had few failures in finding water supplies, and he often amazed bystanders by correctly reading the number of people in a building. But when he used the pendulum to determine the sex of sixteen unborn babies at a Portland, Maine hospital, he predicted only six correctly. Novelist Kenneth Roberts gave Henry national recognition with the book *Henry Gross and his Dowsing Rod*, followed by two other studies, *The Seventh Sense*, and *Water Unlimited*. Kenneth Roberts and the dowser formed a company, and there were numerous dowsing adventures that the novelist recorded. But Henry had playfulness and visions of broadening his range of activities, while Roberts felt Gross should limit himself to locating water. An experiment with tourmaline chips proved disappointing. When the tip of the dowsing rod touched a green tourmaline, it thereafter gave a reading only on another green, never on a pink or watermelon stone. This test was conducted at Mount Mica, one of Maine's more productive mineral sites. Since the place was covered with tourmaline chips, both the dowser and his divining stick were confused. "We had no way of knowing," wrote Roberts, "whether Henry's rod was influenced by a single chip or by a vast deposit of crystals."

Once Henry placed coins in several pillboxes and mixed them with the same number of empty boxes. Both Gross and Roberts were surprised when this parlor experiment failed. More often than not, the pendulum misbehaved and the two men were unable to determine why the readings were so erratic. And yet Henry sometimes did have commanding control when dowsing: Gross discovered that he could stop a pendulum in anyone's hand—"not only by audibly ordering it to stop," recalled Roberts, "but by silently willing it to stop."

Henry Gross was a dowser who will be remembered—because of Roberts's international reputation as a writer. A dowser is frequently looked upon with disdain in our society—as a sort of misguided soothsayer flourishing a wooden wand. Roberts did indeed face a skeptical public when writing his three books on the subject. He noted in his personal copy of *The Seventh Sense* that the book's subtitle should read "Or How to Lose Friends & Alienate People." Some of the cries lodged against dowsing were "hokum," "hoax," "witchery," and "pseudo science."

Henry Gross and his Dowsing Rod was crammed with evidence of Henry's abilities, but both geologists and water scientists of the day persisted in saying that the proof didn't exist. "In every possible way they tried to discredit the book and destroy it," recalled Roberts. "The words of my detractors were so bitter, so false, so ill considered, that I was sure as soon as I saw them that they were inspired by fear of something: the fear, to be specific, of losing their prestige in the field of locating water supplies."

For a time Henry Gross experimented on food and drinks. When the tip of his dowsing rod was rubbed with rye whiskey, it would work only on the rye and not on scotch, blended whiskey, bourbon, or other liquors. When rubbed with brandy, the rod would work only on brandy, Cointreau and champagne. Even a fresh can of anchovies was used to illustrate Henry's culinary dowsing skills: the rod refused to respond when a can of spoiled anchovies was introduced.

When Henry's stick touched a half-dollar, and the coin was thrown into the grass, the dowser usually was successful in locating it. Both Gross and Roberts thought for a time that if a person held a half-dollar behind his back and switched the money from one hand to the other and then held both closed hands before him, Henry's rod would point to the clenched fist holding the coin. "We soon found that this wasn't so," wrote Roberts. "The rod worked as readily on a hand that had just held a half-dollar as it did on the hand containing the half-dollar. There was, at that time, no way of distinguishing between the two."

Gross astonished his game warden supervisor Verne Black of Kezar Falls, Maine during the summer of 1948. Black, the owner of a camp at Colcord Pond, contacted Henry when an outboard motor fell from a boat into deep water. On arrival, Gross cut a fresh stick and began asking the rod a series of questions: "How far is it from here to the motor?" He asked. "Is it 60 feet?" The rod dipped a *yes*. "Is it over 100 feet?" There was no motion to this question, indicating a *no*. Using this method, Henry was able to pinpoint the motor's location in the pond, and another interrogation revealed a depth of 16 feet. Gross stood in a boat with dowser poised while being rowed to the site. When his stick told them they were above the lost object, a grappling hook was sunk; it struck bottom at 16 feet, fumbled for the motor, and found it.

When Gross was told that Bermuda had gone for three hundred and forty years without groundwater—only rainwater caught from roofs—he got a map of the island and began some long-distance dowsing. The rod told him that Bermuda had three domes of good drinking water and one contaminated dome. Since this island is eight hundred miles from Maine, Henry's map dowsing was greeted with laughter by critics who gave little credence to such "witchcraft." After all, this Maine game warden, summer camp counselor, and fly-casting rustic had never been to Bermuda, knew nothing about the island, and had no way of sensing anything about its geological formation. But when Roberts, a frequent visitor to Bermuda, convinced local officials to verify this map dowsing, they found that Henry had pinpointed these domes of water with amazing accuracy.

Henry preferred a freshly cut piece of new-growth maple, but a branch cut from any kind of tree responded in his hands—he could even dowse with a long blade of grass. (After Gross's death, the Maine State Library acquired his papers and some memorabilia. Among these was a nylon dowsing rod which a librarian generously allowed this author to use for a number a days. I took it home and conducted several tests. The rod behaved well, but no differently than a freshly cut stick of willow. There was one problem which clouded my dowsing commands: I was unable to shake the awareness that this nylon rod once belonged to the legendary Henry Gross.)

GUARDIAN ANGELS

A poll published by *Time* magazine showed that 69 percent of American adults believe in angels, and 46 percent of this over two-thirds majority feel that they have a personal guardian angel. 506 teenagers—most of them believing in several paranormal phenomena—gave pollsters these responses: 74% thought angels existed, 22% added ghosts to their lists, ESP 50%, witchcraft 29%, and the Loch Ness monster 16%.

The Western concept of the angel evolved from the mythologies of Babylonia and Persia, with Egyptian and Greek cultural influences. The Hebrews adopted this idea which in turn was absorbed by the Christians. The Bible presents angels as representatives of God, existing in a celestial realm. They have the ability of assuming different forms and passing as mortals, sometimes appearing as beings of brilliant light, lightning, and fire. The Angel Lucifer's sins of exaggerated pride and self-confidence caused him to be cast out of heaven, and one third of the heavenly host followed him—these fallen angels became devils, and among them are the demonized gods of pagan cultures.

Today's angels can be male or female of any race, but often they are male, youthful, invariably well-dressed, polite, and skillful in handling a crisis. They go about their tasks saying little, and vanish when the problem has been solved. It is the sudden appearance and mysterious disappearance that people find confusing, and they are left wondering whether they have been helped by a flesh-and-blood human or an angel.

Over the years, the word *angel* has broadened its base—its usage is no longer limited to religious or metaphysical topics. "Oh what a little angel!" the lady in the shopping mall tells a delighted mother as they both hover over the baby carriage. "You are my angel!" the groom whispers to his bride as they share moments of endearment, and the stranded motorist expresses appreciation by saying to the stranger who stopped to help her: "You sure are an angel in disguise!"

Angel-related organizations and businesses are flourishing now that people are more willing to reveal their encounters with celestial guardians. What once was considered a taboo subject has storytelling impact for a receptive audience. The AngelWatch Network in New Jersey monitors angelic appearances and publishes a newsletter for its 1,800 subscribers. At last count, there were more than 100 specialty stores and catalog houses across the country, each devoted exclusively to angel paraphernalia: books, calendars, dolls, pins, diaries, watches, rings, plates, even thank-you notes. Neiman Marcus and Saks Fifth Avenue carry an "Angel" perfume from French clothing designer Thierry Mugler, who believes "everyone has a guardian angel, or can at least smell like one." Not to be outdone, Crystal Connection, an environmentally concerned store in Austin, Texas, has available icons of river and plant angels to instill reverence for the planet.

Those who claim to have had encounters with angels describe experiences on various levels of perception and circumstance. A stranger appears on the scene—"out of nowhere"—just when help is needed, and afterwards the hero or heroine suddenly disappears, never to be seen again. A more subtle manifestation is by apparition—awake or in a dream: one is warned of danger, solutions are offered to resolve dilemmas, or comfort is given. Another kind of angelic visitation can be sound; a person hears a voice or noise and is distracted—this, too, may be to alert an individual to fortuitous opportunity or impending peril. A common occurrence reported is intervention: an unusual set of circumstances nudges one into a different direction or course of action. It is an invisible rescue, and the person who is undergoing this experience realizes that something incredible is happening. Synchronicity is another form of intervention—we are told that angels play games; they communicate by arranging coincidences to get attention. (Though this writer doesn't believe that a guardian was trying to communicate, the following synchronicity of numbers was startling. I went to the local hardware store one morning to purchase a tool for a home repair job and the price, including tax, was $9.20. I also needed a few items at the grocery shop and was amused when the cashier said, "That comes to $9.20." There were several letters and a parcel to be mailed at the post office, and the clerk rattled me when she, too, announced: "$9.20." What a coincidence! I was thinking as I drove home. Then I glanced at the clock on the dashboard. It was 9:20 a.m.)

People often claim to have had contact with angels through out-of-body experiences. One Bethel, Maine woman recalls being disciplined by her mother and sent to her room. The girl was four or five years old and having a tantrum. "I was jumping on my bed and crying real hard when I seemed to float right out of my body." She looked back and saw herself on the bed and then felt someone comforting her. "The arm I was holding hands with went up to the elbow, and a very bright light took the place of a person. The hand was warm and cold at the same time—it's hard to describe. Then I felt a jolt and was pulled back into my body." The anger was over and the child sat quietly on her bed for a long time. "This memory is so vivid, and I'm convinced it was my guardian angel. I don't know why she visited me that day, but the encounter has given me inspiration all my life."

In 1972, 15-year-old Monique Levesque took a photograph of a dramatic cloud formation over Sabattas Catholic Church in Lewiston, Maine. When the negative was developed, she was astonished to see a full-length image of an angel in the sky at the right side of the print—a female figure with hands extended and dressed in a white robe. "I had a miracle happen to me," explained Levesque, "and I like to think that people who have doubts or lack of faith will also be blessed when they see the picture."

Cindy Jones (not her real name), a young woman from a small Central Maine town who wishes to remain anonymous, had this angelic contact: It all began late one evening when two teenagers followed her in their car while she was walking along a deserted road about a mile from her home. "They started yelling four-letter words," said Cindy, "and recited all the dirty things they were going to do to me." Frightened, and re-gretting her love of walking at night under the stars, she hurried on her way with the hope that they would stop threatening her and drive off.

"They pulled their car up ahead of me," recalled Cindy, "and jumped out to block my path." As she turned to flee, a tall muscular stranger stood before her. "His eyes were gentle and suddenly I felt calm. I knew he wouldn't let anything bad happen to me."

The man approached the two teenagers and told them that he was the young lady's protector. They were to get back into their vehicle and leave immediately. The young men laughed, and as Cindy remembered it: "The next thing that happened was strange. Both boys tumbled to the ground as if pushed or hit. All of us looked at the stranger who acted as if nothing happened at all. The boys rushed to their car and left."

Cindy thanked the man and he offered to escort her home. Along the way, her protector suggested she get a big dog to take on her evening walks. "He never told me his name," she recalled, "but I'm positive he was an angel. How else could the invisible 'push' be explained? And the very next morning a big stray dog was sitting on my porch, waiting to be loved and taken for walks."

Dorothy Jordan of Warren, Maine was alone in her car and travelling about 55 mph when she heard a distinct voice say, "Slow down!" She slowed to 35 mph and heard the voice say again: "Slow down!" A car was coming toward her in the other lane as she approached a sharp bend in the road. "As I came around the curve," said Dorothy, "I suddenly saw two small children playing in the street directly ahead of me." Since she was only going 15 mph, there was time to stop. Dorothy Jordan is convinced that what she heard was the voice of an angel.

An anonymous Maine contributor to the Internet wrote of a childhood incident that gave him a lifelong belief in angels: "I had a brother 18 months younger than myself—I was three or four at the time. We left our home one day and went to a nearby spring and my brother fell in. I went screaming to the house for my mother to help, and by the time we returned he was crawling out of the drain. I consider this a miracle. Without a guardian angel, my brother surely would have drowned."

Skeptics view angelic encounters as faulty interpretation. They feel that many religious people are likely to accept coincidence as divine intervention, and the mysterious stranger who appears on the scene in time of need as a messenger from God, when in fact, the passing hero is just a benevolent human.

"There are no angels!" a husband told his wife when she insisted on taking her good-luck figurine on a motor trip—the kind of ornament that can be dangled from a dashboard or rearview mirror.

(The two were visiting us at our summer home in Maine, and I further fueled differences when I showed them Monique Levesque's photograph of an angel visible in the sky over the Lewiston church.)

"Could be a case of double exposure," said the skeptic after glancing at the print. "Such things don't exist."

"Well, *I* believe in them," the wife replied. "There are endless possibilities in this life and beyond."

"That's a lot of nonsense if you ask me," the husband countered.

"I don't know why everything must be black and white," she fired back. "That's leaving one closed to so many possibilities—for instance, out-of-body and near-death experiences, reincarnation..."

"When you die, you're dead, and you don't come back!" he replied with finality.

"Don't take my word for it," she said. "Just go read the Bible—it's loaded with angels."

Numerically, she had a point: angels are mentioned over 300 times in the Old and New Testaments. Most of these messengers are wingless beings who appear in the form of men. The only exceptions are the cherubim and the seraphim as described in Ezekiel and Revelations. Oddly enough, winged women and children who pose as angels are found frequently in pagan mythology—Cupid, who made lovers out of humans by shooting them with special arrows, preceded the airborne children popular during the Renaissance and in Victorian times.

Angelic visitations include a wide range of appearances. One person may only sense a presence while another sees shifting rays of light or a hovering halo. They sometimes come forth as humans, vague outlines, and even animals. Many contactees are convinced that angels are more likely to appear to those who are suffering emotionally or physically, though there are encounters of minuscule proportions, such as being helped in finding lost objects or winning a lottery. "I was touched by an angel," said the pedestrian who felt himself being pushed moments before a speeding vehicle rushed the crosswalk. There is that old wives' tale: "If you hear your name called and you look around to find yourself alone, your guardian angel just saved you from danger or temptation."

PHINEAS PARKHURST QUIMBY

Phineas Parkhurst Quimby was born in Lebanon, New Hampshire on February 16, 1802, and he was two years old when his family moved to Belfast, Maine. Quimby's formal education was limited, as he was apprenticed to a maker of clocks and watches at an early age. His eccentric spelling and scant knowledge of grammar would prove a lifelong difficulty, particularly when he began organizing the material for a book on his experiments in mesmerism and the healing arts. "Park," as he was called by friends—though he sometimes referred to himself playfully as "P.P.Q."—had a lively mind, was mechanically gifted, and proved to be a skillful daguerreotypist.

The first milestone in his peculiar life and career was passed when he developed tuberculosis and became disillusioned with treatments prescribed by physicians. A friend suggested that he take up horseback riding to restore his health, but Quimby, finding such exercise too rigorous, went on carriage rides instead. This course of action seemed to improve his condition and gave him a more optimistic attitude; it was a recovery which would influence his method of mental healing.

In 1838, Quimby learned of mesmerism and became expert in the practice. His fascination in the curing of diseases began when he hypnotized Lucius Burkmar, a teenager who was able to diagnose ailments and prescribe treatments. To his astonishment, P.P.Q. soon found that he also had the gift. The two traveled about Maine and New Brunswick giving exhibitions of their skills—Quimby displaying his mesmeric powers, and his companion concentrating on clairvoyance while in a state of deep hypnosis. Gradually, the watchmaker-mesmerist found that any medication Burkmar recommended would cure the patient. "This led me," Quimby wrote, "to realize that the cure is not in the medicine, but in the confidence of the doctor or medium." Most medical problems, he told clients, were brought about by unhealthy thoughts. If these were removed the body would cure itself. Quimby called this method "the Science of Health" or "Christian Science."

The Belfast man discovered, or was overcome with the revelation, that it wasn't necessary to cause a mesmeric trance in order to control the patient's mind—suggestion alone seemed to bring forth the desired results. The majority of people he treated remembered a burning sensation which seemed to be caused by emanations from his hands. When asked to identify this force, Quimby said he thought it was electricity passing from him to his patients.

Late in 1857, Quimby moved to Bangor and rented rooms at the Hatch House where he lived with his wife and children and held his practice for two years. Charles A. Norton, a medical student at the time, accompanied his mother when she visited the healer to have her facial neuralgia treated. There were thirty or more patients waiting to be seen. "Quimby asked but few questions," wrote Norton, "but in a loud voice demanded that each patient look him straight in the eye. An assistant followed him about the room holding a large dish of water. In most cases not a question was asked, in some however, Mr. Quimby would say: 'Where is your pain?' in others he would say: 'What ails you?' " The young medical student recalled that Quimby wetted both hands in a basin of water and gently pressed and stroked his mother's facial and neck muscles. "In a number of incidents," Norton concluded, "he would say, in a quick, sharp voice: 'Get up, walk away! You can walk, walk!' the patient almost always doing as bid. To one suffering with rheumatism he said: 'The pain is going, it is gone!' With a number he arranged for private treatments. All paid an assistant $1.00 as a fee as they passed out of the door."

A client in 1862 wrote: "He gives no medicine. The whole scope of his *Materia Medica* would comprehend water, and a pitcher to hold it. The application consists, if the case demands, in an imbibition of this fluid that would put the votaries of Lager to blush." Indeed, P.P.Q.'s confidence in water reached the point where he was advising distant clients to hold a tumbler of it in one hand and his letter in the other, a request which suggested that he wanted patients to think of the letter itself as magnetized, much as an amulet is blessed. It was imperative that those being treated should fasten their thoughts on the healer at the time of treatment and think of nothing else. One Quimby critic, when writing to a friend in 1843, jokingly offered, "Be assured, I have magnetized this letter with some of P.P.Q.'s personal sap-sugar." "Water," explained the mesmerist, was "a good conductor of vital energy, and when the hands are wet the current flows better from the treater to the patient."

Quimby depended on mental influences in his treatments, and one of his rules was that patients should never discuss their ailments. He had found that he could cure a number of patients simply by talking to them. In combination with rest, fresh air, diet, and those liberal doses of water inside and out, he could balance their minds by helping them to shed fears.

In the 1860s, the popular name for the "new science" was animal magnetism, although many felt more comfortable with the term mesmerism.

Most practitioners believed in the existence of a magnetic fluid by which one organism could influence another. J.P.F. Deleuze, author and later librarian at the French Museum of Natural History, offered the postulation: "A substance emanates from him who magnetizes, and is conveyed to the person magnetized." Since a fluid escaped, Deleuze felt there must be some will to give it direction. "Therefore we make use of our hands and eyes to magnetize."

One client cast further light on the doctor's approach to achieving a cure: "P.P. Quimby's perceptive powers were remarkable. He always told his patient at the first sitting what the latter thought was his disease; and, as he was able to do this, he never allowed the patient to tell him anything about the case. Quimby would also continue and tell the patient what the circumstances were which first caused the trouble, and then explain to him how he fell into his error, and then from this basis he would prove...that his state of suffering was purely a science, which proved itself. He taught his patients to understand and they were instructed in the truth as well as restored to health."

P.P.Q. moved his increasingly popular practice to Portland at the end of 1859, and the Quimby family settled into rooms at the International Hotel where he had his office—in the dining room of the establishment between meals. "He never told me how he healed," stated a patient who attended his treatment clinic as crockery was being taken away, "but employed rubbing in my case. He told me to look at him, and he looked me straight in the eyes for five or ten minutes, still holding my hands. After this process he dipped his hand in water and vigorously rubbed my head. Mr. Quimby told me that I must have explicit faith in him and believe that I had no pain at all. He told me stories while manipulating my scalp and neck muscles. He was of a happy disposition, jovial and honest and I had great respect for him."

Quimby's theories were both like and unlike the teachings and work of his imitators and followers—he undoubtedly possessed greater healing power and intuition than the therapists who adopted many of his techniques as their own; his reputation as a healer was achieved partly by his ability of going beyond nervous and functional diseases to cure organic disorders: a closet full of crutches and canes left by patients in the last years of his Portland practice was a verification of his remarkable methods.

An ailing Mary Patterson of Rumney, New Hampshire saw Quimby in 1862 and found herself "remarkably improved in health even before he administered treatment." So great was her faith in him that only a week later she was able to climb the one hundred and eighty-two steps that led to the dome of the City Hall, and every day she felt better. The patient, Mary Patterson, then wife of a dentist who eventually deserted her, was later known to the world as Mary Baker Eddy, founder of the Christian Science religion.

Mrs. Patterson had been ill "6 years with spinal inflammation, and its train of sufferings—gastric and bilious." Quimby's daughter, Augusta, saw the patient being lifted from a carriage and carried upstairs to a room in the International Hotel. Young George Quimby, who acted as his father's secretary, described the new client as being tall and "of consumptive appearance." She was eager to commence treatment with the "amazing doctor" and found him to be "a little man with shrewd piercing eyes, a genial manner," and radiating a confidence "that emanated from him like an electric current."

According to George Quimby, Mrs. Patterson talked at length with his father, and there were several visits in which the two held "silent sittings." She also attended group sessions where essays were read and discussed. It was in these meetings that Mrs. Patterson submitted some of her first attempts at expressing new ideas in her own way. She welcomed Quimby's criticism and had the opportunity of reading and copying extracts from the mesmerist's manuscript "Questions and Answers"—material later to be used as a base for her teachings.

Quimby described the clairvoyant faculty as the ability to detect the auras, or spiritual identities, of individuals. He would ask clients to think of him at a certain hour when long-range treatments were scheduled— one suggestion that would assuredly bring success was for the patients to massage their heads. When such directions were followed, Quimby's bodily presence would appear before them. Was this visible miracle the result of his power of suggestion? No, he inevitably replied. It only could be related to his theory of Christ. "I cannot tell how much I can condense my identity to the sick," he wrote one sufferer, "but I know I can touch them so they can feel the sensation. When you read this I will show you myself and also the number of persons in the room where I am writing this. Let me know the impression you may have of the number. This is the Christ that Jesus spoke of."

Mrs. Patterson found the healer's approach irresistible. "The trouble is in the mind," wrote Quimby, "for the body is only the house for the mind to dwell in. If your mind has been deceived by some invisible enemy into a belief, you have put it into the form of a disease, with or without your knowledge. By my theory or truth I come in contact with your enemy and restore you to health and happiness. This I do mentally and partly by talking till I correct the wrong impressions and establish the truth, and the truth is the cure....A sick man is like a criminal cast into prison for disobeying some law that man has set up. I plead his case, and if I get the verdict, the criminal is set at liberty. If I fail, I lose the case. His own judgment is his judge, his feelings are his evidence."

Quimby concluded early that it was necessary on occasion to relate his philosophy of "mind-cure" to the Bible in order to influence his devout, Bible-reading clients. Gradually, like many of the magnetizers of his day, Quimby became accustomed to speaking of his method of cure as that which was used by Jesus in healing the sick.

Although the healer gave passing mention to God as "First Cause," his religion is mostly subjective and empirical. The deity is absorbed into man as a principle to be *employed* by the individual—a technique to be learned in order to achieve healing. God, Christ, and Scientist are used as synonyms, and are identified as higher processes of the human mind. Quimby's son, George, proudly defended his father's methods in 1908 when confronted by critics. He believed that Mrs. Eddy had found a "prayer cure" through treatment entirely. "There was no asking assistance from God or any other divinity. He (Quimby) cured by his wisdom."

Mrs. Patterson spoke to the Spiritual Association in Portland's Mechanics Hall on January 10, 1864. Maine newspapers agreed that "the lady was not in the habit of public speaking" but spun an "exceedingly fine, silken thread" as her thoughts unraveled the borders of transcendentalism and perplexed many in her audience. "Having been cured of a disease by Dr. Quimby," one newspaper noted, "she endeavored to explain the cause of such diseases upon philosophical principles." Such assessments somewhat bewildered Quimby: he never gave his method of healing such considerations; his concern was more practical. The mesmerist's deity was a wisdom to be used to correct the mental mechanism which influenced the body; he felt more comfortable with the vision of living out his life as a watchmaker-inventor blessed with healing hands.

"He never spoke of God to me," one patient wrote, "or referred to any other power or person but himself. I distinctly recall that before he left our home that morning—I was too sick to visit his office—my father offered him a check for One thousand Dollars if he would impart to him or any member of our family his method of treating disease, to which the Doctor replied, 'I cannot. I don't understand it myself.' "

P.P. Quimby's concept that the mind governs the whole question of recovery was a revelation to a recovering Mary Patterson, and during the early months of 1864 there was growing in her mind a strong conviction that a real Science of Christianity existed—so much so that years later she looked upon this time with Quimby as crucial in her development: "I tried him, as a healer, and because he seemed to help me for a time, I praised him to the skies, wrote him letters,—they talk of my letters to Quimby as if they were something secret, they were not, I was enthusiastic, and couldn't say too much in praise of him; I actually loved him, I mean his high and noble character, and was literally unstinted in my praise of him, but when I found that Quimbyism was too short, and would not answer the cry of the human heart for succor, for real aid, I went, being driven hence by my extremity, to the Bible, and there I discovered Christian Science."

In a 1961 introduction to a selection of Quimby's unorganized but original writings on his system of spiritual mind treatment, *The Quimby Manuscripts*, it was noted by the book's editor, Ervin Seale, that "if it had not been for P.P. Quimby there would have been no Mrs. Eddy, and if it had not been for Mrs. Eddy we should never have known of Quimby."

Mrs. Patterson journeyed from Portland after a series of treatments and visited Mary Ann Jarvis, an ailing spinster of Warren, Maine. Miss Jarvis had been to Quimby earlier to seek help, and the most satisfying part of this March and April 1864 visit for the future founder of a religion was assisting her friend in getting well. Mary Baker Eddy's reliance on God was then weighted down by the mesmerist's theory of transference: that the healer must take over the patient's suffering to achieve a complete cure. "My dear friend does all in her power to make me enjoy my stay here," she wrote the Master, "but you know her body of belief 'is full of wounds and bruises' which in getting her out of I stumble." Patterson then asked Quimby to treat her for two symptoms "that Miss Jarvis has just got rid of and saddled on to me." At this time of her life, Eddy lacked assurance, and in the middle of a passage expressing her own views, she suddenly exclaimed: "Jesus taught as *man* does *not*; who then is wise but you! I am up and about today, i.e., by the help of the Lord (Quimby)." Shortly after this letter, Mrs. Patterson experienced a phenomenon familiar to many of the mesmerist's patients: his phantom form suddenly appeared in her room, complete in dress coat and hat. At that moment, he was directing his thoughts to her from Portland.

Quimby's manuscripts were not made available to the public until 1934. Very few of them were in the author's handwriting, most being copies made by his widow, son, and two secretaries. There also is the possibility that some of Mrs. Eddy's writings, emended by Quimby, may have been jumbled among the pages. An 1888 article in *Mental Science Magazine* by A. J. Swartz stated: "His (P.P. Quimby's) views were often written by those associated with him, and then submitted to him for approval or correction."

In the *History of Belfast*, 1877, Joseph Williamson wrote of Quimby: "Having become deeply interested in the act or science of mesmerism, then in its comparative infancy in this country, he devoted the last twenty years of his life to the development of its principles, especially with reference to the healing art." Homage to Quimby later appeared in the May 5, 1887 issue of the *Belfast Republican Journal*: "The good that he accomplished, the suffering that he averted, crippled forms that were restored under his kind magnetic hand, cannot be told in this simple tribute to his pleasant memory." There was no mention of the mesmerizer's "strange theories" that once aroused Belfast gossip and ridicule.

Judge Charles K. Miller of Camden, Maine stated in an affidavit that he had a severe case of rheumatic fever when he was thirteen and described Quimby's healing method: "He rubbed me and then they put me in a chair. He then looked me straight in the eye, and such eyes I never beheld before, told me to get up and walk. I told him I couldn't. He said you can. He took hold of me and pulled me on my feet and I walked two or three steps and fell, but he caught me and I was then put in bed again. The next day I went back home again and was able to ride on the seat with my parents (from Belfast to Camden). I was not treated mentally, but by rubbing and through mesmerism."

In May 1865, Quimby closed his Portland office and returned to his home in Belfast. He still saw an occasional patient but much of his time was spent in an unsuccessful attempt to get his chaotic notes into order for publication.

The *Portland Daily Press*, in their May 17 issue, lauded the mesmerist's efforts of two decades to find the origin and nature of disease. "By a method entirely novel," the article noted, "he has been slowly developing what he calls the science of health; that is, as he defines it, a science founded on principles that can be taught and practiced like that of mathematics, and not on opinion or experiments of any kind whatsoever."

The energetic little man who had transferred so much of his energy to clients was experiencing a growing weariness—a feeling of emptiness. He now sensed the frustration of having limited powers: so many of his patients were unable to help themselves. Not one of them—with the exception of Mrs. Eddy—seemed capable of extending his spiritual-physical crusade.

An internal tumor, which Quimby kept under control for several years, grew worse as his will to live weakened. The previous October, he had taken on the suffering of a patient and found himself unable to throw off the pain. Finally, he yielded to the entreaties of his family and received medical treatment, but it was too late. Phineas Parkhurst Quimby died on January 16, 1866.

THE SHAPLEIGH PLAINS GHOST

The Reverend Mr. Bryant was an itinerant Baptist preacher who lived in a small settlement near the Ossipee River, about twenty miles north of the Shapleigh Plains. It was 1801; a time when much of Maine was a wilderness where the backbreaking task of clearing land challenged the pioneer. Up and down the narrow pathways of his York County parish, Reverend Bryant traveled on horseback to deliver the gospel to parishioners.

His bible-thumping parables were preached with fervor: all must avoid sloth and greed, resist to the last breath the temptations of the flesh, keep a pure tongue and mind, and to the menfolks of his flock the stern reminder that rum was a devil's concoction. After these pronouncements and lengthy prayers came the selling of much-needed goods. The Reverend Mr. Bryant peddled an assortment of pots and pans, needles and thimbles, medicines and herbal remedies—any useful items that could be squeezed into his bulging satchel.

As he had done on several occasions when visiting the southern towns of his parish, Reverend Bryant spent the night at an inn which was the home of Mr. and Mrs. Joseph Hasty in the small settlement of Shapleigh. While the preacher was having breakfast the next morning, Hasty offered to accompany him on the first part of his trip back to his Ossipee River home. Some new paths had been cut through the dense forest of the Shapleigh Plains, his host informed him, and a person could lose his way easily, even become a victim of stray Indians or be mauled by bears. The thoughtful innkeeper saddled both horses and the two men rode off together.

Several days later, a dozen or more parishioners gathered at the home of Deacon Hill in one of the remote areas of the parish. Their preacher was expected to arrive early, but as the hours went by and it became late afternoon the group grew edgy. Where was the man? The idea of having to return to their homes in the dark disturbed them. Just as the disgruntled members were about to leave, a weary messenger on horseback galloped into Deacon Hill's dooryard. The rider had come all the way from the Ossipee River settlement; the Reverend's mother and sisters were frantic; they hadn't heard from him and were concerned for his safety.

The worshippers who had gathered at Deacon Hill's home joined in the search for their missing preacher but he wasn't to be found. Weeks went by, became months, then years, with never a sign of him. A disquieting development occurred when a riderless horse was seen trotting into the settlement at Shapleigh Corner—this was shortly after Bryant left Mr. Hasty's inn. Another troubling bit of news came from Mrs. Hasty herself when gossiping long with a neighbor: she had discovered a bundle and hat belonging to Mr. Bryant in one of her closets and remembered distinctly that the minister was wearing this hat when he left the inn. Mr. Hasty behaved strangely when curious settlers asked about the preacher's personal effects, and he later admonished his wife severely for having such a loose tongue.

The years passed, and stories began to be told of riders who were thrown from their mounts at a certain spot on the Shapleigh Plains, and some travelers felt a chill come over them as they approached a low-lying area of the trail, later known as Bryant's Hollow.

It was a timid young settler called Joe who had an unsettling encounter. He had been slow in transacting some tedious business and dusk had overtaken him as he trotted his horse along the misty path. Suddenly, the animal reared, almost throwing him. When Joe tried to urge the beast on, it froze with fear. "Come on, you nag!" he shouted nervously, getting down and tugging at the halter. "What is the matter with you!" It was then he saw a hatless figure, garbed in unbecoming gray, standing in the middle of the trail.

"In God's name," Joe cried out, "who are you? Why do you block my way?"

"I will not harm you," the gray one assured him. "Just hear what I am compelled to tell you and help me." The voice seemed to calm the horse, and it began grazing on tufts of grass by the wayside. "I once frequented this part of the world and did well in saving souls and discouraging evil ways. You are the first mortal who has spoken to me. This has unsealed my lips and it gives me the chance to tell you who I was and why I have frightened passersby on this forsaken trail."

Joe stared at the apparition as the voice continued.

"In life, I was known in these parts as a clergyman named Bryant. One day I was riding through the plains accompanied by Joseph Hasty, an innkeeper in whose house I had spent the preceding night. We were overtaken by a wretched settler named Warren—he was an evil and bold scoundrel, not one who ever attended my sermons. Warren took Hasty aside and began whispering, but I heard some of his urgings. He convinced Hasty that my purse was filled with sovereigns—which wasn't so. I had only my Bible that I shared freely with all sinners."

The phantom figure blocking the way turned and pointed at a sprawling oak by the path and to its trunk where the letter B had been deeply gouged. "That is the place," the voice softened with solemnity. "Beneath that tree they murdered me."

Joe stared at the letter for several long moments before daring to look into the eyes of the troubled spirit.

"If you will read the 69th Psalm," the gray-clad ghost continued, "you will know my feelings when I was in the hands of my destroyers. Follow me and I will show you where they buried me."

The young settler followed the misty presence as they made their way through a tangle of limbs and thick brush. Joe could hear only the sound of his own footsteps in the dry leaves. A few rods from the oak they stopped by a sheltered place.

"This is the lonely spot where they buried me," said the ghost. "Break off some branches so you may find it again. My journey is now fulfilled. I will be at peace in my eternal rest and will trouble this hollow no more."

Joe began blazing a trail of broken branches and when he looked back the ghostly figure was gone. The letter B was bright on the oak as he mounted his horse and galloped through a whiplash of brush and away from Bryant's Hollow. His mother was astonished when he asked her to read from the Bible. She opened her Good Book after staring at the son who had come home frightened and with scratched hands and face. He requested the 69th Psalm, and she was glad to oblige: the errant offspring, who early in life had strayed from the fold, now seemed more at peace as the words of the psalm worked a strange soothing spell.

Afterwards, Joe told his mother of the ghost he had faced on the path. This adventure excited her, and being amenable to gossip all her long life, she had things to tell him from the past. "After the disappearance of Mr. Bryant," said the mother, lowering her voice, "Joseph Hasty became a stranger to all who knew him. He even was afraid of his own shadow, and it got so bad that he refused to milk his cows after dark."

"What about that man Warren?" asked the son. "His guilt was as great as Hasty's."

"Yes," replied the mother, "he, too, was in an awful state of fear before his demise. I am told he sent for a loyal person of quality and under a promise of secrecy, made a full confession. This seemed to ease his spirit before he died."

Being by nature easygoing and a procrastinator, Joe let several weeks go by before setting out to find the spot that the ghost had marked for him. The B on the oak was still there, but too many settlers had heard the story of his encounter and the whole area had been so trampled that he was unable to find the grave.

Shortly after the Reverend's ghostly appearance on the trail, one of Mr. Bryant's elderly sisters began having a recurring dream that troubled her: a man she had never met kept promising that he would give her word of the missing brother. At her ancient mother's urging, the sister set out to find this stranger and was somehow guided to Joe's home. The moment the woman saw Joe, she cried out: "You are the one who appeared to me in my dreams! Tell me truthfully all you know of my dear departed brother." The sister felt at peace after hearing his story and thanked him warmly. "Now my mother who is old and ill will be freed from her miseries before she dies."

This story appeared in *A History of Shapleigh, Maine* by Rev. Amasa Loring, 1854, and was retold by Julia Anna Clark for the town's bicentennial, 1785-1985. Since Joe's encounter, no passerby has seen the apparition, though the mysterious circumstance of Mr. Bryant's passing still keeps this legend alive. Perhaps one day some bones will be unearthed on the plains by the giant paw of a backhoe. Supposedly based on fact, this folktale is mentioned whenever there is talk of supernatural happenings in that part of Maine.

EXTRASENSORY PERCEPTION

In 1882, when British and French experimentalists formed research centers to investigate psychic phenomena, both organizations encountered intense opposition from skeptics and scoffers around the world. Criticism and fun were poked at these scientific renegades for "dabbling in spooks." Paranormal happenings were interpreted as the works of the Devil, and to add to this confusion were the charlatans and magicians who purported to perform genuine feats of psychic power while hoodwinking audiences.

As late as the 1920s, most institutes of learning were emphatically negative to psychic research. A Cornell University psychologist reacted typically when he insisted that the journal of the *Society for Psychical Research* not be permitted in the campus library because it would "inflame the imagination and corrupt the minds of the students."

Even the most dedicated investigators admit that many premonitions prove to be faulty, and such admissions are quickly pounced on by critics. Skeptics, who point out that bull's-eyes are remembered longer than misses, believe that ESP research is merely an extension of quackery—the sideshow performances of mediums allegedly communicating with spirits of the dead.

One of the more significant experiments in ESP was conducted at Radcliffe College in 1942 by researcher Gertrude Schmeidler. She tested a group of students by asking them to guess cards. Before the experiment she asked which of them *believed* in the possibility of ESP. Those who did were classified as sheep and those who didn't were goats. Results showed the sheep scored significantly above the laws of chance. What seemed extraordinary to Dr. Schmeidler was that the goats somehow managed to score significantly below: they were unconsciously "cheating" to support their view that ESP was nonsense. They must have been ignoring their genuine hunches, Schmeidler concluded. In doing so, the goats revealed as much ESP as the sheep, but used it negatively.

Harvard parapsychologist Joseph B. Rhine was the one who coined the term "extrasensory perception." ESP allows a person to acquire information without the use of the five senses—this includes telepathy, precognition, clairvoyance, and psychometry. Such claims infuriate the traditional scientists; they show little tolerance for the paranormal; life after death, levitation, and out-of-body experiences threaten the whole fabric of their certitudes.

The three most commonly studied types of ESP are *telepathy*, thoughts transferred from one person to another without words—a kind of mind reading; *clairvoyance*, an awareness of distant events and objects, mental pictures and visions, such as murders taking place, or fires; and *precognition*, the knowledge of a future event, imparted either in a dream or in a waking state.

Telepathy seems to function best when strong emotions are involved. There seems to be a simultaneousness; telepaths share thoughts with clockwork accuracy—exactly at the time they occur. This is especially true when people sense that someone they know has died. This knowledge is transmitted at the very moment of death when there is no opportunity to see the person beforehand or to alter the circumstances.

Subjects who do well on ESP tests often possess the ability to manipulate objects without touching them. Such a skill (psychokinesis or PK) demonstrates that a human being can make contact with an outside world beyond the territory of the five senses. There is growing evidence that we do interact psychically with our environment and use these powers so subtly that they go unnoticed.

Most humans have some PK potential, but the effects are barely discernable in the frenzied fishbowl of existence. Researchers have found that many people—individuals who never thought of themselves as psychically gifted—could use psychokinesis to roll a die and make it land on a designated side more often than the laws of chance. Parapsychologists claim that during times of crises, particularly after the death of a loved one, a person is able to produce larger-scale PK results.

One may risk generalization by saying that women seem to be more apt in reading emotions and communicating, while men tend to be orderly in compartmentalizing task-oriented areas. Perhaps the connection between the left and right sides of the human brain accounts for these differences. It has been established that the two halves of the female brain are more closely connected than those of the male—a fact which may explain why women have a reputation for accurate intuition.

In their attempts to heal us, today's doctors are fully aware of the powerful connection between our minds and bodies. There is still much to explore before the extent of psychic influences on our general health and well-being can be determined. Through medical practitioners and scientists, the public is gradually accepting experiences beyond the perimeters of the five senses: for example, if a loved one dies unexpectedly in a vivid dream, it is less likely to be regarded as a coincidence when the telephone rings to confirm the tragedy. There is a barrier between us and the nonphysical realm—we can't touch, feel, hear, taste, or smell the experience enough to achieve *reality*.

A person may react physically to stress: the stomach is in knots after a difficult matter has been decided—this is probably where the expression "following your gut instinct" originated. The body frequently sends messages to the mind. As one's fingers touch an object, feelings of sadness or happiness may surface—the psychometry of detecting vibrations that accompany an object's past. A room can reflect the emotions of the occupants; the walls can indeed talk. Concerned husbands sometimes experience sympathy pains when their wives are in labor, and there is the headache that serves as a warning that one is overstressed and must slow down.

Though many scientists regard it to be a fraudulent activity, psychometry, the ability to hold objects and read their history, is one of the commonest of paranormal faculties. In 1843, Dr. Joseph Rodes Buchanan discovered that he could distinguish brass in the dark—all he had to do was touch the metal to get a "brassy" taste in his mouth. Buchanan conducted experiments with students in his medical class and was fascinated to find that many of them could identify various substances with their fingertips in a pitch-black room, even when the objects were bound in thick paper. Astonishment followed when he found that several of his more talented pupils could hold a sealed letter in their hands and describe in detail the person who had written it. A few were able to tell that person's mood while the letter was being composed.

Tests conducted by geology professor William Denton in Boston revealed that some "sensitives" could hold specimens of prehistoric bone fragments or minerals in their hands and pinpoint on a map where the objects originated—this was done without the use of a dowsing pendulum. Lava from Hawaii gave one psychometrist a picture of an ocean of fire flowing over a cliff; a pebble of glacial limestone produced a view of the substance deep under the sea and locked in ice. Denton was now convinced that the entire history of the earth was imprinted in objects and could be read by many humans if they took the time to develop that faculty. He estimated that one man in ten and one woman in four can develop the ability of reading the past in this manner.

Coincidences that may have ESP origins occur in literature and publications. In the month preceding the World War II invasion of Normandy by Allied forces, a crossword puzzle in London's *Daily Telegraph* gave most of the code words for the coming military action: Mulberry, Neptune, Utah and Overload—the last being the name for the entire operation. When worried authorities investigated, they found that the compiler of the puzzle was a schoolmaster named Dawe who had no knowledge of the coming operation, nor why he chose those words for his puzzle.

Another startling coincidence occurred in 1972 when writer James Rusk, under a pseudonym, published a pornographic novel called *Black Abductor*. The plot was identical to what transpired in the kidnapping of heiress Patty Hearst by the Symbionese Liberation Army two years later—even the name of the victim in the story was the same: Patricia. The FBI interrogated Rusk to determine whether he had any involvement. He was totally nonplussed, and investigators concluded that what Rusk had written was "pure coincidence."

There are among us those who believe that all methods of fortune-telling are based on synchronicity: in other words, the message from the fortune cookie is no coincidence, and tea leaves tell us what we need to know at the moment; such thinking suggests that the "voice" of the Ouija board is rising up from deep within us—as the proverbial stone thrown into a glassy pond creates a ripple effect that exceeds itself.

The most haunting example of synchronicity took place in 1898 when novelist Morgan Robertson produced a book about a ship called the *Titan*. It was "the safest vessel in the world," which hit an iceberg on her maiden voyage across the Atlantic. Fourteen years later, Morgan's novel came to life in the tragic maiden voyage of the *Titanic*. This was not the only bizarre coincidence: W. T. Stead, an author and editor, had written a tale about a ship that sank, and he concluded his story by saying: "This is exactly what might take place, and what will take place if liners are sent to sea short of boats." Like the vessel in Robertson's novel, the *Titanic* did not have enough lifeboats, and W. T. Stead was one of the passengers who drowned after this ship struck an iceberg and sank.

Rhine and his colleague Karl Zener came upon a simple way of measuring ESP. They designed a set of symbols now known as Zener cards. Each pack has twenty-five cards of five different symbols: a green star, black square, orange circle, red cross, and blue wavy lines. The cards are shuffled by the "sender" and turned over one by one. The "receiver" tries to identify each card and makes a note of the images seen.

Pure chance gives a maximum score of five correct guesses, and more than this indicates the presence of ESP. Rhine got surprising results when conducting tests on psychic Hubert E. Pearce. To eliminate future accusations of fraud from their critics, Pearce was placed in a separate building and carefully monitored. He averaged approximately 32 hits out of every 100 ESP cards—much better odds than chance would have yielded.

Irish-born Eileen Garrett, one of the giants among psychics, explained that she shifted her whole field of awareness when receiving paranormal information; it was a kind of *turning inward*, a form of self-hypnosis. Asked to explain further, Garrett replied: "It is a withdrawal from the conscious self into an area of the nonconscious self. And...within this other mind, life is being worked out on a different level." The sensation could only be described as "living in two worlds at once," and these "glimpses" were not something she achieved with conscious effort; they just happened. "You open a door for a moment, and are confronted with it. The door closes, as it opened, and the image is gone."

Harold Sherman, noted author of *How to Make ESP Work For You*, would startle Rotarians and members of other clubs at their luncheon meetings where he appeared as a guest speaker. "How many of you know enough about the mechanics of your car motor to be able to fix it?" he would ask. Nearly two-thirds of the businessmen present would proudly raise their hands. "That's fine, gentlemen," said Sherman. "Now let me ask you another question. You are each walking around with the most sensitized instrument in the world inside your head—your very own mind—upon which you have relied for everything that you have accomplished." Then pausing, he would ask: "This being true, how many of you can tell me how your mind operates?" According to Sherman, not one hand was raised "from coast to coast!"

Though our five senses reign, our powers are restricted. What sort of universe would we perceive if instead of five we had six, seven, or eight different ways of experiencing life? Perhaps we have such inherent capacities. People all over the world, from time immemorial, have been aware of a sixth sense, a perception called the third eye and second sight.

It has been proved scientifically that some sensitives can be enclosed in shielded booths lined with thick lead slabs—an insulation that makes the conveying of electromagnetic waves an impossibility—and despite this elaborate shielding, telepathic messages can be sent and received.

Two people in love, or a happily-married couple who have lived together for many years, are more likely to have thoughts flowing between them. The same communication occurs between mothers and their newborn babies. Psychologists discovered that if a sleeping infant is isolated in a soundproof room, the mother often knows when her baby starts crying.

The line between sensory and extrasensory perception may be finer than imagined. Animals have sense organs that respond to stimuli inaccessible to humans. Several species of birds hear sounds in ultralow frequencies indiscernible to our ears. "Birds are not living in the same sensory world that we live in," said Stephen T. Emlen, an avian researcher at Cornell University. "They are hearing, seeing, and sensing a world expanded from ours."

One of the miracles here in Maine is that tiny summer tourist, the ruby-throated hummingbird—it winters in Mexico. Schools of fish move and change direction simultaneously by using flawless underwater signals; they never bump into each other. Some bats are equipped not only with this species' directional abilities, but also with the capacity of distinguishing poisonous from nonpoisonous prey by sensors on their mouths. Many researchers believe that senses such as these may once have been part of our survival equipment, only to have been discarded (or perhaps submerged) in our evolutionary process.

Melissa (last name omitted) told *Paranormal Phenomena*, an internet newsletter, of an experience that took place in Byrant Pond, Maine in 1978 when she was eleven years old. The girl was spending the night with a school friend on the other side of town. At 8:00 p.m., when the two schoolmates were in bed and the lights still on, Melissa suddenly had a "vision" of her beloved golden retriever, Tippy, running into the road and being hit by a small red truck. "A woman with light brown wavy hair," Melissa informed the newsletter, "wearing a brown corduroy blazer got out of the driver's seat and bent down over Tippy. She was crying hard as she picked him up and carried him up the driveway to my front door." Melissa began weeping uncontrollably, and her friend's mother had difficulty quieting her.

When the child came home the next day, her parents met her at the door with tears in their eyes. At 8:00 p.m. the night before, the events she saw in her vision had occurred in exact detail. "As sad and gruesome as this may seem," concluded Melissa, "it proved to me that our minds are capable of far greater things in this universe than we have yet to discover. This experience will forever be an enigma to me."

In spontaneous cases of hunches or vivid dreams one may have foresight of the coming death of a relative, or of some disaster on the other side of the world. If these were acted upon, lives might be saved, though when the normal sensory means are bypassed, people are reluctant to act for fear of being laughed at or accused of meddling in events that do not concern them.

An emergency medical technician from Bath tells this October 1979 story: "There had been a terrible automobile crash late one night in a remote area of Woolwich. One man was badly hurt, and before we had a chance to load him into the ambulance, a woman, who was later identified as Joan, walked up to where I was standing. I asked her if she was involved in the accident. She said she was home asleep when the crash happened but sensed that something was wrong and felt compelled to hurry to the scene. Upon further questioning, I found that she didn't own a police scanner and her house was several miles away. The most amazing thing of all was that the patient we loaded into the ambulance was *her son Larry*! He suffered a major brain injury and was unable to remember events leading to the crash. His mother, who rode with us to the hospital, has been very active in head-injury charity causes all over Maine since that fateful night."

There may be innumerable worlds and planes of being just beyond the reach of our five senses. The fact that we don't have the ability to perceive them is no proof that they don't exist. The paranormal has produced such widespread interest that many scholars no longer question *whether* this field should be investigated but how the subject may be dealt with more scientifically.

RITES OF EXORCISM

Rites of exorcism have been performed since ancient times, and in some cultures, where spirits are believed to interfere daily, seeing an exorcist is no more extraordinary than consulting a doctor for a sore throat. Depending on the context of an eruption, the intercessor designated to execute these rituals may be a priest, rabbi, shaman, lama, witch doctor, medicine man, witch or psychic—in some instances, demon expulsion may be attempted in the treatment of a personality disorder in which the patient is convinced that he or she is being taken over by an alien entity.

In recent years, exorcism was brought forth front and center on the stage of marvels with the film *The Exorcist*. Before this celluloid event, many moviegoers looked upon the expulsion of evil spirits by members of the clergy as rituals of old-fashioned superstition or last resort attempts to comfort deranged individuals. The majority of people were unaware that paranormal researchers had frequently flirted with the notion that there were "discarnate entities." Robert Monroe described several encounters he had with "mischievous" presences while on his out-of-body excursions.

Both spiritual and physical violence can occur in a demonic exorcism. The victim may suffer excruciating pain and have extreme spasms and contortions with diarrhea, vomiting, spitting, swearing, and disgusting body noises. The possessed person may levitate, exhibit superhuman strength, or speak in strange tongues. Furniture, clothing, and scattered objects become animated, and there are waves of cold and hot air rolling about the room.

Some methods involve strapping people to chairs and then attempting to scream the demons out of them; others encourage victims to vomit and curse while writhing on the floor, and these calisthenics are sometimes followed with mental health counseling.

The Catholic Church believes in diabolic possession, and its priests practice what Vatican officials call "real exorcism." Their methods are more disciplined than those observed by some evangelical sects. A 27-page manual approved by Pope John Paul II in 1998 is part of the accoutrements, along with various prayers, crucifix, incense, and holy water to drive out evil spirits.

There are no formal rituals for persuading a ghost to leave a particular place, and often the intermediary merely sprinkles holy water, burns incense, and exhorts the presence to depart. Various magical rites allegedly can coax troublesome spirits from cemeteries, especially those of suicides or murderers. First, a magic circle must be cast over the grave to protect the exorcist. At midnight, the ghost is summoned, and in hollow tones the spirit answers all questions. When the exorcist promises to carry out its wishes, the troubled presence vanishes, never to haunt again.

In Catholic exorcism, there is a spiritual duel between exorcist and devil for the victim's soul. Whenever the demon snarls an invective, a priest must counter with a firm demand that the evil presence depart in the name of Christ or suffer everlasting pain and damnation. Exorcists must rely on stern language, prayer, starvation, electric shock, fumigation, and foul-tasting substances given to the possessed. Salt was believed to represent spiritual purity in medieval Europe, and still is used in rituals. Wine also is favored and symbolizes the blood of Christ.

Depending on how evil the spirit seems, exorcisms can range from cordial persuasions to elaborate rituals. The expulsion of demons, ghosts, and spirits is more a means of evoking a higher authority to force the offender to act contrary to its wishes than to expel forcibly. "I adjure thee, most evil spirit, by Almighty God" the Christian exorcism ritual begins, thus binding evil energies "by the triumph of Christ and through His power in and by His Church."

The Archbishop of Calcutta, Henry D'Souza, revealed that he ordered an exorcism performed on Mother Teresa shortly before her death in 1997. D'Souza stated that he thought she was being attacked by the Devil. Another headline appeared when the Italian media claimed that Pope John Paul II asked the Vatican's chief exorcist to coax evil spirits from a young woman displaying superhuman strength, but several attempts proved futile. A spokesman for the Catholic Church denied that exorcisms were conducted and said that the pontiff's only involvement had been to give the afflicted woman his blessing.

The Pentecostal Church recognizes what is known as "deliverance ministry," a practice in which the laying on of hands casts evil influences from possessed individuals. The healer, and sometimes an entire con-gregation, may confront the dark presence until the demon is forced to reveal its vices. Cries of joy and prayers of thanksgiving follow success-ful exorcisms as the afflicted are returned to Christ.

In Jewish folklore, some doomed soul or demon takes over a person's body and another personality manifests itself by speaking coarsely through the sufferer or causing inappropriate behavior—in Yiddish it is called a "dybbuk"—and must be exorcised by religious rite. (While we were living in Ireland, my wife got to know a person who was perhaps afflicted with this disorder. Mr. Kenny was a distinguished-looking gentleman, of friendly disposition, and he resided in the village hotel where my mother-in-law was staying. The three frequently sat in the lobby and had polite conversation while waiting for luncheon to be served. Sometimes, in the midst of casual observations on the weather or some topic of local interest, Mr. Kenny suddenly would grow silent, stretch his long legs from the chair, click his heels, and very spiritedly let loose three salvos of a four-letter word that vulgarizes the vagina. With this commentary accomplished, and unaware of a brief departure from decorum, Mr. Kenny would turn to my mother-in-law and with convivial aplomb ask: "And by the way, Mrs. Rayhart, what do you think they are featuring on the luncheon menu today?")

In 1991, ABC television aired an exorcism ritual performed on a young girl. Though the victim used foul language in a voice not her own, suffered fits and vomited, the program proved less dramatic for the television audience than anticipated. Skeptics called it a lackluster performance and remained unconvinced that such a ritual gave results. No permanent relief for the girl was realized, and she continued receiving psychiatric treatment.

In the rush to dissuade diabolical presences, exorcism has brought about a number of tragedies: In San Francisco, a teenager was pummeled to death during a 1995 exorcism—several rambunctious participants were unable to contain their enthusiasm while driving away his devil; a Wisconsin woman was awarded damages when she sued her psychiatrist for causing her to be suicidal—he diagnosed her as being possessed by 126 personalities, including the bride of Satan and a duck; and in 1998, a New York mother suffocated her 17-year-old daughter with a plastic bag while attempting to destroy a demon.

"Exorcism is more readily available today in the United States than perhaps ever before," wrote Fordham University sociologist Michael Cuneo in his book *American Exorcism*. Bizarre supernatural behavior featured in films had made people more aware of demons and their dark infestations. "By conservative estimates," claimed Cuneo, "there are at least five or six hundred evangelical exorcists." Not included in this count were the numerous devil-coaxing rites practiced by charismatic ministries.

"I think there is such a thing as demon influence, but I suspect it's rare," stated Pastor Steven Waterhouse, a Texas Evangelical Christian who has studied the differences between possession and mental influences. "People are too quick to diagnose demons. Human nature is plenty evil on its own."

A majority of those involved in exorcism point out that their rituals and prayers are safe methods that may bring comfort to many who are not actually being demonized. "If it's real to the person, you have to take it seriously," stated Eddie Gibbs, an Anglican priest and professor at Fuller Theological Seminary in Pasadena, California. "I do believe that there is an intelligence behind evil, but we mustn't be gullible."

THE EVIL AND THE JINXED

The automobile that Archduke Ferdinand and his wife were in when they were assassinated at Sarajevo—an event which precipitated World War I—was jinxed. Death or disaster awaited subsequent owners. An Austrian general, who took over the vehicle for a short time, later died insane; the next owner, a military subordinate to the general, broke his neck nine days after the purchase in a fall; the Governor of Jugoslavia lost an arm; a physician who bought the car was crushed to death when it overturned; a Swiss driver was thrown over a wall and died of injuries; a Serbian farmer was somehow killed while cranking the starter; and five people returning from a wedding died in a head-on collision when trying to pass it on a narrow road. Eventually, the vehicle was purchased by a museum in Vienna and placed on permanent display.

Even when dismantled, the racing car in which film star James Dean was killed in 1955 seemed to have the power to cause accidents. An owner of a garage purchased the vehicle, and as the wreck was being unloaded from a flatbed, the Porsche somehow slipped from its hoist and broke both legs of a mechanic. The engine was sold to a doctor, who was killed when the car in which it was placed went out of control during a race. In the same auto event that day, a racer equipped with the drive shaft from Dean's car rolled over and the driver was injured. Then the battered shell of the movie star's Porsche was displayed in a Sacramento highway-safety show, and during the exhibition the wreck fell off its mounting and broke a teenager's hip. Several weeks later, the truck carrying it to another display was involved in an accident—the driver was thrown out and killed by the hulk of Dean's car as it upended in a ditch. Another racing driver made the mistake of buying the tires from the Porsche; his penalty was a near-fatal collision when two of the tires exploded simultaneously and his car swerved into a wall. Later, in Oregon, a truck carrying the car slipped its hand brake and devastated the front of a store. In 1959, during a New Orleans exhibition, the battered vehicle astonished realists armed with rational explanations—this time the Porsche, secured on stationary supports, broke into eleven pieces. Finally, in 1960, the racer vanished forever while being shipped by train to Los Angeles.

A person buys a used car in mint condition at an unbelievably cheap price, and after driving it a few times the new owner discovers that the vehicle carries the unmistakable smell of death. Inquiries reveal that the previous owner died in the car and the body was not discovered until after it began to decompose. Just a story, skeptical readers may think, but this tale which probably originated in the 1930s has been told by people all across the United States. Details vary: the model of the car, year, where the death occurred and circumstances—the most common cause is suicide, followed by accident and murder. Efforts to rid the vehicle of the stench usually fails, and the owner either sells at a loss or has it hauled away for scrap metal. For some unknown reason, Buicks are the leading offenders, and others frequently noted are Chevrolets, Fords and sport cars, particularly convertibles.

Sailors take for granted that some ships are unlucky and refuse to sail on them. The British passenger *Great Eastern*, a 19,000-ton marvel and world's largest of its day, was notoriously ill-fated. It all began when a riveter and his young apprentice disappeared during the construction. Scheduled to be launched in June 1859, the vessel got stuck in the runway, and it took engineers three months to free it. When the *Great Eastern* finally reached water, the builder collapsed on deck with a fatal stroke. Early voyages were rarely without disasters: the funnel exploded when someone closed a safety valve and five stokers were killed, another sailor was crushed in the paddle wheel, the vessel was badly damaged in a storm, and the captain and a cabin boy were washed overboard. As the ship approached New York, another sailor was crushed by the paddle wheel and a passenger drowned in heavy seas. On a two-day cruise, the *Great Eastern* veered off course and drifted a hundred miles out to sea;

disgruntled customers left the ship upon reaching the first port and
returned home by train. The vessel's reputation was so scarred that the
owners had difficulty paying their crew of 400 as one disaster followed
another: broken paddle wheels, exploded funnels, and storm damage.
When the ship was hired to lay the transatlantic communication line, the
Great Eastern lost the cable halfway across and had to abandon the
project. Finally, fifteen years after its launch, the ship was left to rust in
an English port. In 1889, when it was broken up for scrap, the skeletons
of the missing riveter and his apprentice were found wedged in the double
hull.

Three years after the ill-fated *Great Eastern* was launched, the ship
Hinemoa began its history of disasters. The crew blamed the material
used as ballast for causing the vessel's instability in swelling seas—this
was gravel from a London graveyard. There was a different captain for
each of the first five voyages: one captain died in his cabin, one went
insane, another drank himself to death, one went to prison, and the fifth
committed suicide. The *Hinemoa* capsized on its sixth voyage, and two
sailors were washed overboard on the seventh. In 1908 the ship was
damaged beyond repair after floundering in an Atlantic storm.

Few vessels have been more jinxed than the German battle cruiser
Scharnhorst. Bad luck began before launching. When only half com-
pleted, it rolled over in dry dock and sixty men were crushed to death.
The next display of ghoulish trickery proved embarrassing to a number
of naval personnel: on the night before its October 1936 launch, with
Hitler and Goering waiting to take part in the lavish festivities, the
Scharnhorst broke loose from its moorings, slid down the ramp and
destroyed several barges in the harbor. The ship's first engagement in
World War II, the naval bombardment of Danzig, was another disaster:
a gun exploded, killing nine sailors, and the air-supply system broke
down, suffocating twelve more. When the cruiser attacked Oslo a year
later, its hull was struck by so many shells that the *Scharnhorst* had to be
towed away. Entering the River Elbe at night, it rammed the passenger
liner *SS Bremen*, causing extensive damage to both ships. After repairs,
the cruiser returned to sea and was spotted by a disabled British patrol
boat. The German vessel might have slipped away under cover of darkness, but an approaching British warship fired a broadside blindly—
more as an intimidating show of belligerence than in the hope of damaging
the ship—and being the vessel it was, the *Scharnhorst* took a direct hit
and sank. Among the few survivors, two crew members reached shore
on a raft, but died when an oil heater exploded.

Lockheed Constellation *Ahem-4* seemed to be jinxed from the moment a mechanic was cut to pieces by one of the plane's propellers in July 1945. Several people aboard this aircraft suffered heart attacks during flights, and deaths from unknown causes rose in disturbing numbers for passengers who had flown on this particular aircraft. One disaster after another continued until the plane crashed near Chicago in 1949, killing everyone on board.

Psychic Geraldine Cummins observed that if two letters are kept together for a time, the words written by the dominant personality is more likely to imprint itself on the other, much in the same way that a magnetic tape can print through and cause an echoing effect. This may be the basis of the ancient custom of blessing an object, or placing a curse on it. Tibetans extend this concept with their belief that objects can be "animated" by the thoughts of living beings and misbehave.

In the late 1950s, Marlborough Packard inherited a piece of furniture that had been in his family since the mid-1800s. It was a table about three and a half feet high with a marble top and mirror attached. Packard stored the furnishing in his garage, and when he married and moved into a two-family house on Long Island, New York the table was placed in the hallway of his residence. The Packards soon heard thumping sounds in different parts of their house. One night they were awakened by loud hammering, and when the couple tried to locate the source of the mysterious noise they became confused. The thumping began to playfully shift directions as they chased the rumpus into an attic where they lost its noisy trail.

The next morning, Packard brought up the subject with his neighbors who lived on the other side of the house.

"You folks must have been having quite a time for yourselves last night," he said with forced jocularity.

The neighbors looked surprised as they shook their heads and exchanged glances.

"I don't know what you mean," said the man. "We were out of town last night and just got back."

Several months later, Packard found different employment and moved to another part of the state. All their furniture, including the table, was shipped to the new house, and within the first week the thumping sounds were back. This home was made of cinder blocks, but the noise coming from the walls had the same persistent and irritating resonance.

The couple moved again, this time to Waterboro, Maine, in a home they occupied for five years, but the thumping continued and seemed to be more frantic.

"I've checked everywhere in the house," said a frustrated Packard, "from the basement to attic, and I still can't locate what is causing that noise—it really is beginning to get ridiculous!"

Finally, the Packards built a new house in Waterboro, but it made no difference. "An hour after we unpacked that thumping started up again," said the exasperated homeowner. "We just couldn't believe it."

It took time and a lengthy process of elimination before the couple realized that the houses they had occupied over the years had not been haunted; it was the table. Marlborough had noticed an illegible signature in pencil scrawled under the furnishing. It was probably the name of the person who had made the piece, he reasoned. But there was something unusual about this writing: the signature kept appearing and disappearing.

"I could usually find it," the owner recalled, "but when other people looked, sometimes it just wasn't there."

The thumping stopped when Packard brought the table to an antique dealer to be sold on consignment, and after a year the man decided to buy the piece for his own home.

Packard met the dealer one day and asked after the table that had given him so much trouble.

"Oh the table is fine," the new owner assured him. "But there have been the weirdest sounds going on in my house lately—like footsteps or thumping, and I can't figure it out."

Another piece of furniture, this one a chair, seemed to imprint its evil past on a person occupying its soft cushion. A young Englishman got married, and he and his wife moved into a cottage on the coast of Devon. Two weeks after the honeymoon, the groom returned home from work drunk and in a vile mood. The young wife was shocked, since her husband had a reputation of being a sober and reliable person. The next morning he showed contriteness for his behavior and vowed that he would never drink again. Within a month, the same thing happened; this time a meanness glazed his personality as he staggered blindly about the small home and was abusive. A few weeks later, he came home drunk for the third time, and the next morning after the husband returned to work with a hangover but no apology, the desperate wife consulted a "wise woman" who came to the cottage and immediately found the reason for her husband's intemperance and ugly moods. It was an armchair that had been given to the couple as a wedding present. When this furnishing was removed from the premises and burned, the young groom became himself again. Later, the chair's history was revealed: it once belonged to a drunken butcher who had killed himself while sitting in it.

A dog, cat, snake and rat were taken to a house in Kentucky which was said to be haunted, and according to Dr. Robert Morris, a psychologist at the Psychical Research Foundation in Durham, North Carolina, their reactions appeared to confirm that past events of horror can saturate inanimate objects for an indefinite period. The dog, when led into the room where violent deaths had occurred, snarled and backed out; no amount of coaxing could persuade the animal to reenter the chamber. The cat was carried into the room, and the moment it crossed the threshold it leaped onto the owner's shoulders and spat at an empty chair. The rattlesnake instantly raised its head in an attack position and had to be restrained. The rat had no reaction; it scampered about and sniffed with indifference. Then the creatures were taken to another room in the house, a part of the building that had no history of violence, and they all behaved normally and showed no signs of concern.

If a crime is more evil than the person who commits it—a murderer may be considered only partially responsible because of temporary insanity—does this mean that evil may have an independent existence? The frequent disparity between an act of criminality and the one performing it has long been regarded as confirmation of the objective existence of evil. A widespread phenomenon that could support this premise is the feeling of despair and horror imprinted on the physical surroundings where a tragedy has taken place: those who visit the scene of the crime are sometimes overcome by the powerful emotions that have saturated the walls and the room's furnishings.

The famous Hope diamond, named after a former owner, Henry Philip Hope, is the most notorious gem in history. This stone has left behind a trail of grief and disaster so visible that few collectors have expressed interest in acquiring it.

The blue-colored Hope, a 112-carat rarity, was mined in India and brought to France in 1668. A gem dealer named Tavernier sold it to Louis XIV of France, who had the stone faceted into a 67-carat heart-shaped setting known as the Blue Diamond of the Crown. Tavernier, on returning to India, became the first casualty associated with the stone— he was killed by a pack of wild dogs.

Louis XVI and Marie Antoinette inherited the French Blue, as it was popularly called, and at the time of their executions, the gem was stolen along with all the other crown jewels. Some of the precious stones taken in this royal heist were recovered, but not the Hope.

Underground dealings and intrigues followed to increase the stone's notoriety. A gem that resembled the Hope was worn by Queen Maria Louisa of Spain when she had her portrait painted by Goya in 1800, and a few years later it was reported that the French Blue was cut to its present size—44.52 carats—by Wilhelm Fals, a Dutch diamond cutter. Fals soon became a victim of the altered diamond: it is said that he died of grief after his son stole the gem from him. Son Hendrick later killed himself.

In 1830, London's foremost gem experts examined a deep blue oval diamond in an unusual setting, and the majority opinion was that the stone had to be the French Blue. Henry Hope owned it for a time—long enough to give the gem his name—and sold it to a Russian prince who gave it to an actress of the Folies-Bergère. When the prince learned that she was unfaithful to him, he shot her and gave up the Hope while in prison. A Greek merchant had the stone briefly; he and his family died when their automobile plunged over a cliff. To continue this series of disasters, Abdul-Hamid, a Turkish sultan, was toppled from his throne in 1909, only a few months after acquiring the gem.

The next owner of the Hope was Evalyn Walsh McLean, a wealthy American socialite. Her son was killed in an automobile accident, her husband died in a mental hospital, and her daughter overdosed on sleeping pills. After Mrs. McLean's death in 1947, Harry Winston, a New York jeweler, bought her jewels, including the Hope. In 1958, he sensibly gave the diamond to the Smithsonian in Washington, D.C. where it is now safely on display.

Many people are convinced that some tragic events can imprint themselves on inanimate objects. (The wife of a Norway, Maine mineral collector told this author that her husband died the day after acquiring a collection of stones from an out-of-state source. I later learned that two previous owners of the stones had died unexpectedly—one under suspicious circumstances. A tourmaline in the collection had been found at a mineral site in Newry, Maine by gem hunter Dick Nevel who was killed in a dynamite explosion at that mine. The Norway woman is no longer listed in the telephone directory, and one is left to wonder what has happened to her and what fate awaits the next owner of these stones.)

BOB ATER'S ODYSSEY

Bob Ater was raised in a religious family, and at the age of sixteen he decided to become a missionary. "I felt a call to go to Paraguay," said Ater, "and preach to the wild Indians." After seminary studies, he spent six months at the New Tribe Mission, a school in California that prepared young people for missionary work in the jungles. But his first assignment was at a Mexican mission in San Antonio, Texas, and before he got the chance to fulfill his South American dream, Bob was asked if he would accept the pastorship of a church in Maine that had only a few parishioners.

The job was a challenge for the twenty-four year old. "I started preaching at the little place," he recalled, "and was their pastor for more than ten years." Membership increased, a new chapel was built, and his involvement in community life absorbed him with the turning of calendar pages. Bob married a local girl—they had six children—and then his world slowly began to crumble around him.

Most people try to hide the downside times in their lives, but not Bob Ater. When he stands at a podium and faces an audience, he gives a full reckoning of those troubled years. "When I got to be about forty years old," he begins, "I had a nervous breakdown and didn't want to live. I was very sad, very depressed, and everything just fell apart. My wife divorced me, and the church decided that they didn't need me anymore."

Ater got into his vehicle one day, drove to the state hospital, committed himself, and stayed there for ten days. But it wasn't enough time to heal the lacerations of his shifting emotions and plummeting moods; he had to go back. "Life wasn't important," he admitted, "but I didn't have the courage to do away with myself. I remember one doctor saying to me, 'You don't want to hurt yourself because your children will have to pay for it.' " Somehow he had to survive his dilemma.

Bob got a night job in a Brunswick, Maine doughnut shop but kept to himself when he wasn't working. "I was quite antisocial," he recalled. "All I wanted to do was to be alone in a room and cry." (In a video recording before an attentive and sympathetic audience, Ater displayed a composed acceptance of that bygone predicament.) "Whenever I speak to groups," he went on, "I always tell them about this. I'm not ashamed of it. It's just part of living."

He realized that he must be with people more and not hide from himself. The solution came unexpectedly one night at work when he heard on the radio that a group of dowsers were having one of their meetings in

Portland, and the public was invited. Bob went and immediately felt at ease with the members, especially with Gordon MacLean, a chemist who was one of the organizers of the American Society of Dowsers. "I saw all these people doing psychic things—they were using their minds in ways that I never thought possible," Ater recalled. "I just threw myself into it and became so excited that it gave me a reason to live."

He gradually became aware of his extraordinary talent with dowsing devices: not just an ability to locate a source of water but to find oil, minerals, and buried treasures. Ater's demonstrations of dowsing seem so effortless. A simple coat hanger cut and bent into the shape of an L becomes alive, a pendulum begins circling its *yeses* and becomes motionless for its *noes*. (He also learned subtleties concerning water: a rod driven into the ground above a vein and then angled a bit with blows from a sledgehammer would set up a vibration and cause the water to flow in a different direction—a useful technique in keeping cellars dry.) Bob soon discovered that he could find things by holding a pencil over a map, and as he progressed he was able to detect energy from plants and inanimate objects with his hands. "I've had so many dowsing experiences," he admits. "It's kind of hard to remember all of them."

One night at work, Ater began a different kind of divining. Whenever a doughnut was placed on a tray, he and the woman working with him heard a clicking noise. Sensing a paranormal presence, Bob picked up his two dowsing rods made from coat hangers—he preferred having one in each hand—and began experimenting. "It really started as a kind of game," he recalled, "and I never was fearful of the spirit." The entity began moving about the shop, and once it brought him up to the woman filling the pastry. When she turned, her face had a stony expression—as if she were dead—and Ater was convinced that the spirit had "manifested itself for a few seconds."

"Maybe I was out of place," Bob told a church gathering in his video *Some of My Spiritual Experiences*, "but I was curious and followed this entity. Quite often it would take me out of the building to a wall—as if it were running away from me. In the back storeroom we had a lot of flour and big buckets of jelly, and one day I chased it into one of those containers. All of a sudden, there came an energy from that bucket of jelly and just filled me. He—or whatever it was—didn't like it in there and came back at me. I had a feeling of being possessed, but not for long: I don't think it was a mean spirit—just a spirit."

The game now was becoming more serious. Ater owned a small Cape Cod house with fifty acres of land on Westport Island near Wiscasset, and he spent his daytime hours there. Bob soon realized that something was different about the house. "I felt a presence; someone was standing in the doorway watching me—I couldn't see it, of course, but I sensed it was there." He also began to feel a spirit in the car when he was driving from work. "One day, partway home, it started to attack me from the backseat by pulling my hair, and I was really terrified while driving down that road. I learned that prayer was the best thing in the world when you are dealing with something like this, and I prayed hard."

Bob didn't know whether it was the same spirit on the island as at work, but the incidents increased with his involvement and became more pronounced. Once, when he was going through his method of dowsing for a friend who was visiting him, Ater's L-rods began swinging in a different direction. What is this? he said to himself, and then realized that something was watching him again from the doorway. "I would like to ask you a few questions," he said as he approached the presence. "First of all, I want to know if you have any intentions of harming me?" The rods remained motionless, suggesting a *no*. "Do you want to help me in some way?" *No*. Then Bob Ater asked the question that he had been turning over in his mind for days: "Do you just want to be here and be left alone?" The wires swung frantically in a vehement *yes*!

It became a challenging game. Often, when Ater was rocking in his chair downstairs, he would hear a squeaking sound coming from the second floor—squeaks that were keeping time with him as he rocked. Then there was a more graphic incident in the kitchen: he was map dowsing when the L-rods over the paper began to misbehave by pointing behind him. "So all of a sudden," he remembered, "this apparition appeared in front of me, like smoke, like a haze in the form of a person—not the complete shape, but there it was." When it moved, Bob dowsed it to an open flue of a chimney and saw cobwebs flutter all by themselves—there was no draft as the top of the chimney had been waterproofed with a sheet of plastic.

The activities gradually became less playful. Bob had insisted that the spirit leave him alone. "Hey," he said crossly, "I own a piece of this place, this is my house, and you get out of here!" But when the entity was treated this way, it showed resentment. "One time when I was sleeping," recalled Ater, "it tried to push me hard into the bed." Another testiness of paranormal temper occurred when Bob had just returned home. A squirrel was running frantically back and forth on the limb of a big tree. The little creature was terrified—Ater earlier had given the presence another eviction notice and the summons rankled. "Then I heard a pounding on the tree. *Bang*! *Bang*!—as if someone was taking a baseball bat to it. So I went into the house and paid no attention."

One treasure hunter made a startling discovery while searching for Indian artifacts along the shores of Spirit Pond near Popham Beach, Maine. He turned over a rock and found some strange markings on the underside, and a short distance from this find there was a second specimen. These runic stones, believed to be Norse in origin, electrified archaeologists worldwide.

Bob Ater lived only a few miles from the site, and having an interest in history and ancient treasures he decided to explore the general area. Map dowsing led him to a ledge not far from where the stones had been picked up, and his L-rods reacted positively as he pinpointed the location. At a depth of four inches, Bob uncovered handwrought nails, bird bones, clam shells, and a wrought iron tool that had been broken at one end. "The strange thing about this small cache of artifacts," wrote Ater in *Treasure* magazine, "is that there was no charcoal found with it. If the birds and clams had been cooked here I would suspect that there should have been some indication of a cook fire."

Bob picked up the L-rods and asked his subconscious mind to point out the exact place where the birds and clams had been cooked. The coat hanger wires led him on a decided course. "Six inches down I found charcoal remains. I can't prove that this was a Norse site, but I certainly suspect it was, and it was totally located by dowsing."

Ater met White Nichols, a man who had been involved in archaeological work for many years, and their friendship led to a memorable dowsing excursion. Nichols had found a book published one hundred years earlier which contained a description of some pictographs seen on an island off the Maine coast, though no specific site was mentioned. Nichols and several others had spent more than 900 hours searching without results.

Using his method of pencil dowsing on maps—this is when a writing instrument becomes a divining rod as described in Bob's booklet *Dowsing With a Pencil*, published in 1970 by the American Society of Dowsers—Ater marked a spot where he believed the pictographs could be found.

Later, on the island, the search was conducted with a rod. "It turned in my hand and steadied," the report stated, "pointing in a northeasterly direction." Nichols and the dowser walked along the shore and within ten minutes the pictographs were found. "The map dowsing had indicated the same location," said Ater. "White became very enthusiastic about dowsing after that success. It is our belief that the writings may be of Phoenician origin."

One of Bob's treasure adventures on an island off the coast was mentioned in this writer's book, *The Buried Treasures of Maine*. An acquaintance asked Bob if he would map dowse the site. The man and a companion had taken three metal detectors with them and all their machines somehow fell into the sea before the shore was reached. Earlier, the two were in a rowboat fairly close to the island at dusk and had seen roughly a hundred people around a huge bonfire—it must have been some sort of celebration, they concluded, for everyone was singing and dancing and shouting. But when they landed their boat, nobody was there. They did find a rock close to shore with an arrow chiseled into it and there was a brief encounter with a ghost.

"So I decided to go out there with one of my sons and a number of people to see what we could do," recalled Ater. "We were all standing around when suddenly my son—he was about twelve years old at the time—literally rose off the ground and turned a complete somersault in midair, very slowly and calmly before landing on his feet. We all stood around and wondered how he could do this. I said: 'John, what happened to you?' And he replied: 'Well, I heard this treasure hunter tell about meeting a ghost, so I said to it without speaking, if you are here, *show me.*' Apparently, the ghost took him up on it."

Ater was sharing this story with a Spiritualist Church group and a look of discomfort clouded his face. "When I talk about these things, very often something comes over me and says: 'Don't tell that! Leave it alone!' This is happening to me right now," he said lamely, and with momentary faltering, clearly anticlimactical, he looked down at the papers on the podium and declared: "So I can't really tell you the rest of that story— because it is just leaving me." But the dowser in Bob Ater couldn't abandon the tale entirely—he had chased too many water veins, and felt so clearly spirits rising around him after his breakdown; he had to relate more, even if it seemed a sort of transgression.

"I could add this," said Ater. "That treasure hunter was out on the island one day, lying on the beach, and he decided to talk to the spirit. 'If you are here,' he said, 'just show me.' " So the treasure hunter claimed he was stood on his feet like a board and the sky grew dark and crows started flying around and screaming. The two friends with him took off into the woods—they were terrified. "It was this story that gave my young son the idea of talking to the spirit."

Bob's map dowsing for treasure on the island led to another excursion. "The pencil kept going up to the mainland, near Boothbay Harbor," he recalled. Ater, and the two men who couldn't land a dry metal detector on the island, made their way to the location. "I held an L-rod in my hand," said the dowser, "and asked: 'Where is it?' " Immediately, the bent wire swung toward an obstacle of dense brush. The three pushed their way through and found a flat stone, about five feet long and four feet wide. Deep coastal waters two hundred feet away seemed a likely place for a mariner to drop anchor. "So we got to reaching around that rock," continued Ater, "and pulled out a heart-shaped stone about an inch thick—this was a pirate symbol (Blackbeard had a heart-shaped emblem on his flag) and it had to do with some Mediterranean religions and was a symbol of life. This heart was similar to stones found in Nova Scotia and Haiti, so we figured this had something to do with a system of buried treasures."

Maybe the two treasure hunters were overly enthusiastic in their quest for caches; again, the ending is anticlimactical. One is left with the feeling that all is not being told—there remains a mystery. "Get me out of here," Bob tells them. " 'This is private property and I don't want to create any trouble. Take me home.' So we put the heart back in the ground and lowered the rock over it. The two went back later with a metal detector and it reacted strongly. I have dowsed the area by map and think there are more of these, not just one heart."

There were reports that a pirate's cache had been buried near Ater's Westport Island home, and he decided one day to map dowse the property. "Where is something of value buried within my fifty acres?" he asked. Though Bob had gold or a treasure chest in mind, his question was couched in such a way that it could encompass almost anything of value. The reading pinpointed a location and Ater verified it with his two L-rods. He dug two feet into the loam and found three stones. "Two I discarded," Bob recalled, "because I didn't realize what they were until I saw the same things illustrated in a book on ancient stone tools." The one he kept was a stone knife probably used by the "Red Paint People" of Maine centuries ago. There had been no surface indications that a site could be in the area; his dowsing question was answered by two wires turning in his hands, and the dowser got what he asked for—something of value.

A mineral hunter interested in beryl crystals took Bob to one of the old mining excavations in Topsham, Maine. Upon arrival, Ater dowsed the dump site and got a response. He brought to the surface a rock about six inches in diameter but there was no visible beryl embedded in the stone.

They decided to break the stone open, and when it was split a small green beryl revealed itself—the crystal had been shattered by the hammer blows but it had been in the precise spot where the rods pointed. "Flushed with success," Ater recalled, "I decided to try dowsing another location. This indicated that a beryl could be found at six inches. I pushed the spade into the soil, spread the contents out on the ground, and there was a beautiful three-quarter-inch beryl. I dug around randomly for a while but no crystals were found by that method. Apparently, the dowsing had worked two times in a row."

Bob has had some success with map dowsing for gold in Maine. A friend asked for a reading and the location was pinpointed on the south side of a stream near a campground. When the enthusiastic prospector returned from his outing, he proudly showed a number of gold specimens found in the exact spot suggested. Probably one of Ater's most striking accomplishments with a map occurred when he dowsed at the request of a miner in Michigan—this was done from Bob's home in Maine—and gold-bearing material was found. "I was more amazed than the person for whom I was dowsing," he recalled. "It is always a thrill when you see that it works."

Bob frequently dowses for oil, and one time he was asked if there were commercial quantities of gas on a large dairy farm in Pennsylvania—no petroleum deposits of value existed but an excellent source of water was located. "While looking at the map," recalled Ater, "I decided to take a psychic look around the farm and see what I could view from ten miles away." Geese appeared in his mind, and when he asked whether the owner of the adjoining property had such birds he was told that these were the only creatures on the farm and there were no other geese within a hundred miles.

A belief that simplicity should be the rule when dowsing has led Bob to adopt hand reactions. This method proves particularly effective when he is in search of commercial deposits of petroleum. Imagine this scene: Ater is in the front passenger seat of an automobile; he is holding both hands in front of him with palms down; he is visualizing oil and expects his fingers to move up and down when passing over a productive area. Once past payload, the trembling abruptly stops—his way of defining the outer edges of a field. Gas deposits may produce a feeling of lightness, and he sometimes can taste a sweetness or sourness in his mouth as he envisions the presence of oil or gas. There can be other body reactions: he may become nauseous when passing over a field and can only find relief when entering the nonproductive area.

Depth is an important factor in the reading of an oil or gas site—a driller needs some idea of how far down one must go in order to estimate the expense of paying the crew and meeting equipment costs. Bob Ater has adopted a successful routine by having a tape recorder going while he recites his feelings about a deposit, and the driver (driller) comments on local landmarks; it is a way of drawing two lines on an imaginary and complicated map—X marking the spot. Then the car is parked over the promising location as Ater relaxes into a light trance and the dowsing/psychic procedure begins. Bob or the person with him can ask questions, and hand responses indicate a yes or no. All kinds of queries are acceptable, even those intricate enough to stumble a seasoned driller, and usually the accuracy rate is excellent to moderately good. Much depends on the mood of the dowser and the mutual confidence of the participants.

Rods, pendulums, forked sticks, bent coat hangers, stainless steel chambers attached to sensitive springs—the tools are endless if one has the urge to dowse. Bob has been map dowsing with a pencil for many years: a procedure in which he holds the writing instrument over the map, clears his mind, and allows the subconscious to take over. Ater claims he can feel the pencil following the lines of least resistance (unseen topographical easements), much as it would slide along a crack in a board. In one of his video presentations, *Dowsing for Water and Treasures*, he traces the forces surrounding one, two, and three pennies placed on a flat surface; as he is a sensitive, his pencil can transmit to him the auras of energy and their interactions.

Ater's video, *The Tactual Detection of Subtle Energy*, clearly shows his versatility as he traces lines and vortices of energy projecting from plants and even inanimate objects—at a Bath, Maine playground he outlines swirls and push-pull forces emanating from a metal pole and a children's swing. It is something he has been doing for more than twenty-five years. "Some people feel a tingling in their palms," he explained, "a kind of programmed response. After being around other dowsers for a long time, I realized that there was a way you could feel energy between your hands." A simple method of detecting these energy fields was by extending the hands, palms facing, and slowly bringing them together. "There is a projection from your palms," said Ater, "and when you get to a certain spot you will feel a ball of energy." With practice, he learned how to touch the forces coming from a variety of objects—a sort of "tuning it," not unlike radar—and in time he increased his sensitivity.

Bob Ater's commentary while tracing the flows of energy up and down a tree is delivered rapidly in his video—he is completely at ease and confident as he follows these invisible forces: "You clear your mind and ask your subconscious to cause your hand to flow along with the energy," he begins. "We have a flow going downward here like that....We move down and feel counterclockwise another line going this way about there....Over here are vortices....This is a line going in a zigzag fashion....This force is clockwise....What is this vortex doing? There's a different speed, moving rapidly....This one isn't projecting; it's just going around and around....That one isn't moving—maybe it's a third kind of energy."

A sensitive is drawn into the unexpected; if one has a dowsing involvement with archaeological rarities and buried treasures, there is a better chance of communicating with spirits—a claim made by a number of dowsers. "I was visiting a person one day," Ater recalled, "and halfway up his front stairway I could smell camphor. There were several people with me but they couldn't smell anything. I told them there was a lady who once lived in a bedroom upstairs and she used camphor." (Forgotten names and faces come to Bob Ater momentarily before fading away; presences that call out in some need of recognition.) "The owner took me to a back stairway where there were a lot of things going on, and before I got up the stairs I bumped into something—it is like going through a wall—and there was an entity. I find this a lot in old buildings and on stairways." The lady who used camphor made an appearance at a later date in a photograph of the house taken by the owner—a female form could be seen standing at one of the windows, yet there was no woman living in the house at the time.

Ater has had many adventures in communicating with spirits, and possibly his most impressive encounter came when visiting a friend who had a home on the coast of Maine. The man's grandparents had once lived in the house and there was now much paranormal activity. Bob sat at the dining room table, where the grandfather used to sit, and took on the personality of the deceased. Then Ater sat at the other end of the table, and to the host's astonishment, the grandmother's mannerisms emerged. "I said things she would say," he recalled, "and there wasn't anything frightening about it." A tour of the house followed, and when Bob and his friend sat at the kitchen table, an object on a tall cupboard fell to the floor—perhaps a reminder that grandpa and granny still lived there.

Bob and a son attended a dowsing convention in Vermont, and on their way they viewed a beautiful waterfall by the road. The two decided to take the same route back after the meeting for a second look. "I was telling some people at the convention about my spiritual adventures," Ater reminisced, "and all of a sudden I thought there was an entity in front of me. I put my hand over it and started to describe the presence and was told that the spirit was John Shelly, one of our past presidents of the American Society of Dowsers." On the way home to Maine, Bob and his son could feel Mr. Shelly in their car. "Then we got lost," recalled Ater, "and drove for a while and came to the most wonderful waterfall you would ever want to see! It wasn't the one we had seen first—this was more beautiful. Apparently, Mr. Shelly had gone with us to show a better one. And after we saw that, we were no longer lost."

"I didn't go looking for any of this," Ater reminded an intrigued audience when revealing some of his paranormal encounters, "but I ran into it. And for anyone to deny that these things exist, hey, they just haven't had the experience! I believe in entities, and being a Baptist minister for twenty years I have had an interest in the spiritual side of things."

AT A PSYCHIC READING AND MESSAGE CIRCLE

(During the summer of 2000, while gathering material for this book, Stella and I attended a psychic reading and message circle at a Spiritualist camp on the Maine coast. Since the program was sponsored by the Spiritualist Church, I wondered whether there would be attempts to convert my wife and me to the fold. Members greeted us warmly, showed us around the camp, and not once were we proselytized.

Spiritualist camps date from the late nineteenth century when the movement was hugely popular. At the present time, there are a dozen camps in this country, in 10 different states, with Maine and Michigan having two each, and all are affiliated with the National Spiritualist Association of Churches. Most of these camps are seasonal, although some have year-round residents and activities.

The program had been announced as a séance, but the person conducting the meeting, a middle-aged woman who was highly regarded, impressed us as being more of a psychic than a medium: I mean that it didn't seem like a séance because many of the spirits she supposedly had contact with weren't recognizable to the recipients. At times, looks of bewilderment passed over the faces of the two males and eleven females present.

Looking back on that evening—we were there for about two hours—I am still in awe of this Spiritualist minister who strolled from one person to another and with more accuracy than error gave detailed résumés. It was a superb performance; one-on-one is startling enough, but thirteen different personalities silently waiting to hear descriptions of their quirks and ordinariness struck me as a challenge. One could tell by the nods and startled looks on faces that when she talked about their lives they all were caught in the cross fire of her competence.

Stella's reading preceded mine. "I see poetry," the psychic told her. How interesting, I thought, the lady has us mixed up: Stella has written some fine poems in her life but I've made a career of it. "You are very family oriented," my wife was told. "Many people depend on you and your steadfastness." I felt this remark uncanny—she is constantly unsnarling the soap opera tangle that friends make of their lives. "You are a very good person," the psychic plunged on, "and you are needed and loved." Then extensive past travels were seen. [Stella was born in Berlin, started school in Vienna, went to Holland, then England, served with the Dutch forces during World War II, came to America, and after our marriage we resided in eight states and five countries.] Music was also mentioned in her background—her father had a Caruso voice and was known throughout European music circles. Then, suddenly, the reading went awry; a picture from a past belonging to another individual was staged vividly. "I see a person in your life who loves to cook and make jams," the psychic told her. "She is there in her apron kneading dough for bread and she means so much to you." Stella told me later there was no such a person. Perhaps I would have seen a look of recognition if I had glanced at the woman sitting near my wife.

The only other male present was in his mid-forties with a likeable face, probably a pot-smoking escapee of the seventies, and from his reading it was easy to see that he was a mama's boy. Not once did he shake his head—the man seemed to be dangling on a puppet string of affirmatives. "You could do so much more for yourself in life," the psychic blurted as she stood before him. He nodded amiably as if a compliment had been placed in his casual care. Immediately, the reader of his life took one step back and made a halting gesture with her hands: the psychic obviously was nagged by what she had said; no rudeness was intended; she had seen him with a clarity that overpowered politeness.

The next several recipients of messages from the spirit world and life profiles are a blur as I look back on that evening. They didn't seem to stand out enough to achieve any real identity. In a way, I felt they were there unfairly: it was just something different for them to do and could

be talked about later with family and friends. In spite of this, the psychic breezily did her readings with a grace and humor that exhibited
professionalism.

   A plump girl in her early twenties was next to receive attention, and I
wondered how much was necessary to bring her life into focus. An unhappy love affair was my guess as I watched her facial expressions in
the half-light. Soon there were tears, and as the psychic leaned forward
to whisper encouragement, one clear moment from my past surfaced: I
recalled seeing myself reflected in the window of a night train; there was
an unwritten face in the glass—life hadn't performed its tricks with
gravity and wrinkles. How much of ourselves do we reveal by looks and
gestures? I was asking. Could it be that prophesy is partly the ability to
read another person's thoughts through an osmotic process of interpreting demeanor and body motion?

   Near the door of the room sat a blonde girl in her late teens—Botticelli
would have painted her. Stella and I were drawn to her profile. She seemed
to distance herself from everyone, stared straight ahead, and when the
psychic held her hands and asked her name there were tears. Something
had happened to this lovely creature; something bad and powerful. A
raped soul, I guessed, and it was obvious that she was on a collision
course with an early death. The minister instantly was aware of the girl's
vulnerability and tried to bolster her waning spirit with a long hug. It
startled me when I heard the reader say: "You will live to see Christmas."
This wasn't cruelty, but optimistic prophesy; something the girl could
cling to after the hug was over. I turned away because it was just too
painful to watch. Good God, I thought, she has her Christmas, and all
the others in this room have the rest of their lives!

   On my right was a plump lady in her late fifties, a cheerful soul whose
baton was probably a spatula. The Spiritualist minister had no trouble
reading her, and all went smoothly until another confusion with the spirits
occurred. "There was a person in your past who stuttered," the psychic
told her. "Someone you were close to and knew well." The woman looked
puzzled and kept shaking her head as a lifetime of years was ransacked.
She didn't know a soul who filled that description, but I did. My Cousin
Sidney and I had been very close—he was more like a brother—and Sid
stuttered badly all his life.

   Could there be just too many people in one room; too many lives and
memories jumbled together? If there is such a thing as a spirit world,
were presences from that sphere projecting themselves too eagerly and
hurriedly, causing this tangle of messages? I wondered about myself

and the lives of all of us.

It was my turn next. As the psychic approached me, her first words were, "You have a lot of money." Stella was the one who inherited; to use a one-liner my father favored: I was "born poorer than a church mouse." But the woman must have found something in my face that life had placed there. "I see a lot of books," she told me—we do have hundreds of paperbacks and hardcovers scattered about in our two homes, and one bookcase in Maine is six feet high and twenty feet long.

Then my reading fell apart temporarily—another person's past invaded her vision. "You are sitting in a hammock with someone elderly who is very important in your life. It is night, and together you are looking at the stars." The only hammock I remember belonged to my Aunt Kate, and the one time I sat in it I fell and bumped my head. A woman, three chairs to my left, had her eyes closed as a smile softened her face.

"You have written many books," the psychic told me as she held my hands, "and have done so much during your lifetime. Those spirits close to you are proud of your accomplishments." The mask I wore was stony, but inside I was grinning and childishly pleased.

She paused for a moment and then unloaded what I had been dreading all along. "You will live long enough to complete your trilogy." One of the things that made me feel uneasy when beginning this writing project was the knowledge that I had to interview a psychic or two for the book. They'll probably look at me, I thought, and say, "Sorry, Buster, but you're on your way to that early grave." I didn't like the idea of someone spooking my plans for a long life and immediately decided that this trilogy would be slow in coming. When I later told an acquaintance what the psychic had said, he reminded me that I already had written *two* trilogies—my three Maine treasure books and three biographies.

The Spiritualist minister further raised havoc with my hypochondria. All my life I've been shy of doctors and tried to avoid them as much as possible. "You must be careful this coming winter," she warned me gently. "Don't catch a chill—just make sure you bundle up when going outside." So I can finish that trilogy, I thought as she freed my hands and moved on to deliver messages to the remaining recipients.

Do I really believe everything I am seeing and hearing? I asked myself as we stood mingling in the entryway. Maybe there is something; *something* coming from ourselves to sustain us in the dilemma of being human. A table-tipping séance was one of the programs scheduled for later that month, and before leaving the camp we made reservations.)

PRESENCES IN PUBLIC PLACES

Some residents of Harpswell Harbor still tell the tale of the phantom schooner *Sarah*. The ship was built in 1812 at the Soule Boatyard in South Freeport. During construction, George Leverett, the owner and captain of the vessel, fell in love with the shipbuilder's daughter, Sarah Soule. They were soon married, and he proudly launched his schooner with her name. But a jealous Portuguese seaman, Charles Jose, also loved the young woman. Jose took command of the *Don Pedro* and shadowed Leverett's ship as it departed on the maiden voyage.

In a fierce battle at sea, all the crew of the *Sarah* were slaughtered except Leverett. He was tied to the mainmast as his schooner was left to flounder in heavy waters. According to legend, the ghosts of the dead crewmates rose to take command of the drifting ship. Weeks later, the *Sarah* sailed down an unmarked channel and docked at Harpswell Harbor. The townspeople untied George Leverett and took the unconscious captain ashore to be reunited with his wife. Immediately after this unleashing from the mast, the ghost ship sailed out to sea. The final sighting of the vessel was in the late 1880s when several guests at the Harpswell House saw the phantom ship enter and leave the harbor.

A specter known as Pitcher Man haunts the Goose River Bridge in the coastal town of Rockport—it is not a pitchfork he brandishes when approaching terrified witnesses, but a pitcher of beer. This ghost is believed to be William Richardson who had been killed by three Tory militiamen on the bridge in 1783. The soldiers felt insulted when Richardson offered them beer in celebration of the Treaty of Paris which ended the Revolutionary War. After the building of a new bridge in the 1920s, people began reporting the apparition, and in 1953, two observers clearly saw the ghost holding out a full pitcher of beer before vanishing.

At a point of land on Appledore Island, one of the Isles of Shoals, the apparition of a young woman with long golden hair is sometimes seen in the early morning light on a cloudless day. She appears to be anxiously searching the horizon for an incoming vessel, and nearby witnesses have heard her murmur: "He will come again. He will come back to me." Some islanders speculate that she awaits Blackbeard's return—that the young woman was one of the pirate's many lovers. Locals think she may have been taken ashore to guard buried treasure and is unaware that her lover was captured off the coast of North Carolina and beheaded.

When Captain Asa Clapp died in the mid-1800s, obituaries described him as the foremost ship and house builder in Maine. The ghost of Captain Clapp is believed to be haunting two buildings: one that his son Charles constructed shortly before his father's death—at 97 Spring Street, now the premises of the Portland School of Art—and the place next-door built by merchant Hugh McLellan in 1800—known as the McLellan-Sweat House, now part of the Portland Art Museum and once owned by Asa Clapp.

Joshua Wingate, another sea captain, purchased the McLellan-Sweat House, and when his daughter married Charles Clapp, the newlyweds built on the adjoining lot. Consequently, Captain Clapp has the ghostly distinction of haunting a house he never lived in and one where he was never more than a guest.

Oddly, when Charles Clapp's widow died in 1920, she left instructions that the Clapp House be demolished. Among several items she wished destroyed were a four-poster bed and the family's Pierce-Arrow automobile. These last wishes were never honored, and some believers in the paranormal suggest that her request to have the mansion torn down was in order to prevent her own ghost from returning; others feel that Mrs. Clapp's requests may have forced the captain's ghost to come back just to guard the family's assets.

On High Street in Wiscasset, the Museum Wonder House, which features old music boxes, is believed to be haunted by the shadowy figure of a young man in his twenties. This specter has been seen moving about the kitchen and in an upstairs hallway. One of his favorite lounging spots is the couch in the sitting room. He is described as a "serene sort of ghost," and some locals think he once lived in this home built by a sea captain in 1852.

Situated along the coast, above Camden, Mount Megunticook was the scene of a tragedy on May 6, 1865. Thirteen-year-old Sarah Whitesell was attending a picnic with her family when a gust of wind blew her off the edge of a cliff. Her parents erected a white wooden cross in her memory, and the area became known as Maiden Cliff. Sarah's spirit often returned to Mount Megunticook during warm weather—mostly in the late spring and summer months when a gentle breeze caressed the footpath up the steep slope. Sometimes, Sarah hovered over nearby flower beds. Her apparition appeared frequently during the 1930s and 1940s, and she was last seen in 1976.

Several Boothbay Harbor residents insist that a second-floor room in the town's opera house is haunted. The building was constructed in 1894, and for a number of years this chamber that now shelters an unknown presence was headquarters for the benevolent and secret fraternal order, the Knights of Pythias. It was in 1949 that a player piano in one corner began turning itself on. Witnesses to this mystery speculate that the ghost is Earl Cliff—a musician for opera house programs in the early 1900s. Sierra Abbey and her husband became owners of the property in 1988 and had several strange experiences before they read of the building's haunted past in a listing of Maine supernatural occurrences.

Swans Island, located just off Blue Hill Bay, is considered to be a place of unrest. For more than two hundred years, mariners have seen mysterious balls of fire, some of these flares with distinct faces, drifting over the dark shores of the island, and several people claim to have witnessed the ghost of a woman with a baby in her arms. It is a troubled spirit taking no notice of the living; the specter walks slowly into a mudflat and disappears. In daylight, after a sighting, her footprints have been found in the soft earth.

Nordica Auditorium on the campus of the University of Maine at Farmington was named to honor the town's most famous daughter, Lillian Nordica. She was born Lillian Norton in 1857 and came from a musically talented farm family. After graduating from the New England Conservatory of Music in Boston and having her name Italianized to Nordica, she stormed the operatic centers of Europe and soon achieved international celebrity.

Lillian Nordica never forgot her origins and returned to Farmington several times to give concerts. Her last appearance took place in 1911 at Merrill Hall, in a second-floor auditorium with high ceilings and gilded fretwork—later to be renamed in her honor.

Nordica Auditorium is now the music department's center of activity with a full schedule of concerts. But there are people who claim to have heard unscheduled recitals late in the evening, usually around midnight when lights are out and the five hundred seats in the hall are empty: a soprano voice echoes faintly in the chamber. Those acquainted with this prima donna's mellifluous resonance on the scratchy records of long ago insist that the voice belongs to Madame Nordica.

Another haunting on the Farmington campus occurred in Mallett Hall, a women's dormitory. Students began hearing mysterious noises behind locked doors in the empty attic. When the commotion became so loud that two students were unable to sleep in the room just below the attic, campus police were called. These incidents were no college pranks, the police noted, since it would be impossible for anyone to gain access to the upper level of the building. Shortly after this investigation, two women on the third floor were jolted awake by a loud crash—it sounded as if someone had lifted the heavy study table in the center of the room and dropped it.

A few nights later, when only one of the students was in the dormitory room, the occupant was awakened at 3:30 a.m. by the sound of someone stirring in the bunk bed above her. Looking up, she realized that the upper mattress was not sagging—there were only the restless sounds of tossing and turning. Too frightened to move, the woman decided to close her eyes tightly, hoping that whatever was happening would somehow stop. Then she heard hushed tones coming from the upper bunk and suddenly understood that her name was being whispered. Finally, in a panic, she turned on the light by her bed and fled from the room without looking back. She stayed with friends the rest of the night, and had to be coaxed by her roommate not to change rooms.

When a rocking chair in the quarters began rocking by itself, the two students decided to seek the help of Kaimora, an Oquossoc, Maine sensitive who had taught two courses in psychic awareness at UMF. A dozen or more spectators crowded into the dormitory room, and within minutes there were results. The medium told her audience that the spirit was present but it didn't like being with so many people. She persuaded the ghost to stay for a short time in order to establish communications.

Through telepathy, a picture of events began to emerge and the identity of the spirit was revealed. Her name was Edith, a student at the school long before it became a university—then known as Farmington Teachers College. The girl had died in an automobile accident, and at the time was engaged to be married. Kaimora suspected that the betrothed was still alive and living somewhere in the Farmington area. The medium told her witnesses that Edith had many happy memories of student life at the college, and this was her reason for staying at Mallett Hall. The girl was unable to accept the fact that she was dead.

After several minutes of conversation in which she utilized her long experience of helping ghosts "get to the other side," Kaimora persuaded Edith to leave Mallett Hall forever. Campus police records confirm that there were no more disruptive incidents in the dormitory.

(Kaimora's psychic powers were confirmed when I interviewed Roxbury gold prospector and gem hunter Harvey Packard for my book *Maine Mining Adventures* in 1992. Harvey and I felt that one of the "hot spots" on the East Branch of the Swift River in Byron, Maine was just below the campsite of gold hunter and recluse Carl Shilling. "I called Kaimora during a radio program," said Packard, "and she told me that I would find what I was after just beyond a log where the river bends." We both had found pennyweight pieces of gold in the area. "I went back," he began grinning, "and this is what I found." Into my hand he placed a vial containing two sizeable nuggets and a glittering spoonful of gold flakes.)

Janitors at the old Brunswick High School call her Mimi, but no one knows who she really is or why she haunts the building. Her footsteps can be heard in hallways, and there are innumerable incidents of doors being slammed and objects moved. There have been three perplexing deaths on the school grounds, leading some people to wonder whether Mimi's behavior as a ghost is all playfulness.

In 1978, Bob and Joanne Perry decided to convert an upstairs section of their Skowhegan cinema into an apartment. Shortly after renovations were under way, Bob sensed that he was being watched. Sharp drops in temperature were noticed along the aisles, and there were unexplained noises. Finally, the Perrys contacted psychic Leslie Bugbee who lived in the nearby town of Cornville—they hoped he would be able to provide them with some answers.

(This author remembers the movie house very clearly. I went there to see films at least once a week during the early nineteen forties, and as a young child I frequently visited an aunt who had a house just behind the theater—her driveway was no place to play after dark. If I recall correctly, seats in the balcony cost ten cents, and downstairs one paid a nickel more. Velvet curtains onstage hid a giant screen, there were several wall murals, and one could slouch in comfortable chairs.)

In the November 1984 issue of *Yankee* magazine, writer Michael Kimball noted Leslie Bugbee's bewilderment. "It first started with the wiring," said the psychic. "Bob was working on the ceiling upstairs and got a real bad shock from some wiring there. The power was off—an electrician had shut it off. They called the electrician back and then *he* got shocked, even though the power *was* off."

There were other incidents, including the time Bob Perry was plastering a ceiling. The trowel began shaking and spun from his hand. The tool came down with such force that it dented a Formica countertop, a surface difficult to penetrate.

During construction, Mrs. Perry left an unopened can of wood stain in the middle of the floor while going downstairs to welcome a visiting friend. When the two women entered the upstairs apartment, they saw a roll of masking tape unwind on the floor in their direction, and it was then they both noticed splattered wood stain on a freshly-painted wall. What mystified both Perrys and the friend was the sealed lid of the can. Joanne Perry's impression was that a child had just thrown wood stain at the wall during a tantrum.

Bob Perry kept two stacks of firewood in an enclosure behind the theater, and one day when entering this back room he found the front stack of the wood still in a neat pile, but all the logs from the rear had been taken out and laid, end to end, across the entire floor.

The Perrys continued to show movies in the theater during renovations, and most of the disturbances took place in the upstairs apartment, but on one occasion a large section of plaster above the balcony dislodged itself from the ceiling and landed near several noisy customers. It was as if the resident spirit wished to express displeasure because of the audience's rowdy behavior.

When freelance writer Thomas A. Verde decided to include these puzzling events in his book *Maine Ghosts & Legends*, published by Down East Books, Camden, Maine, he noted that both Bob and Joanne Perry were unwilling to talk to him about their experiences. (Reluctance to speak of hauntings in a place of business is understandable—nearly a third of the businessmen contacted for interviews in this book preferred to remain silent.)

Bugbee suggested that perhaps the spirit haunting the cinema resented the renovations. The ghost could have been a person who had worked in the theater or who had lived in a house that once stood on the property. There were several spiritual communications during the investigation: the psychic sensed that Bob Perry's deceased mother was in the movie house, maybe just visiting her son.

Bugbee attempted to communicate with the spirit or spirits by using a tape recorder—he felt that it was possible to record messages by "tapping, breathing and whispers"—a process called "electronic voice phenomenon." On one reel, Bugbee and the Perrys detected knocking noises that weren't heard when the tape recorder was running.

Before concluding his investigation, Bugbee had a photographer accompany him to the cinema. The two men entered the theater and found their equipment didn't work. When they went back outside to get an-another camera, the faulty shutter behaved beautifully. Both men felt that a trickster was still roaming the aisles, and when they returned the camera failed again.

ON THE MAP OF THE HAND

The human hand is a map of the moment and is capable of reflecting the changes in a person's life. For those who have confidence in this cartographic wonder, it is a way of knowing themselves and understanding their potentials and limitations. People who have only a momentary interest in palmistry, perhaps pausing long enough to look apprehensively at their hand's life line, usually regard this fleshy instrument as a useful contraption for lifting food to their mouths and outwitting stubborn zippers and broken shoelaces. They might be surprised to learn how the general shape, swirling lines, bumps, crosshatches, and tiny discolorations take on significance when the map is interpreted.

Humans began studying their hands early, and this awareness is illustrated in a number of prehistoric cave drawings where handprints accompany the creations—an artist's way of leaving a signature before the development of letters. The first known book on palmistry appeared in 1448, and during the Renaissance many Italian and French scholars wrote about the science of chiromancy in depth. During the Middle Ages, the legitimacy of the practice was rarely questioned; in fact, its ability to reveal the intricacies of an individual was taken for granted. Gradually, however, a stigma was cast on this practice, and with the advance of science, chiromancy began to wane. A brief resurgence of interest in the subject occurred during the late 19th century, and it is largely from texts published at this time that modern palmistry was founded.

A retired general from Napoleon's army, Casimir d'Arpentigny, traced the history of palm reading to the Kabbalah and ancient Hindu texts. His scholarly observations gave palmistry increased respectability and led to the publication of *The Laws of Scientific Hand Reading*, in 1900, by William G. Benham—he is considered to be the father of modern chiromancy. Benham also furthered the awareness that the human hand can reveal the state of a person's health.

Because of frequent appearances at carnivals and the way they sometimes advertise their skills, these readers of the hand often are envisioned as outsiders: one sees some dark, goateed stranger in a turban, or a gypsy lady with dangling earrings and gold bracelets crowding her bulky arms. "You will live a long, long life," you hear them tell you, "and you are about to embark on an exciting adventure."

A palmist studies the hand's size and shape, as well as the fingers and their three sections. Short, square hands are associated with hardworking folks, while conic hands with tapering fingers belong to those of artistic inclination. The most closely scrutnized lines in the palm are the life line, which runs up from the base of the thumb; the head line, going across the center of the hand; and the heart line, located above the head line near the base of the fingers. These prominent creases are often connected by smaller lines running to and from them in every direction.

One hand is active, or dominant, and the other is passive—depending on whether we are left- or right-handed. What if a person is ambidextrous? skeptics ask, and the answer is surprising: true ambidexterity is rare, though people often claim such ability. On one occasion, Maine dowser Bob Ater used a pendulum to identify the dominant appendage. Another method is employing one hand to *sense* the other's energy—this is done by holding the two in front of one, palms facing each other, about six inches apart, and slowly nudging them together.

Lines are the first thing people think about when they have their palms read, and *quality* of these grooves and the shapes they make along their routes are what palmists consider when interpreting the hand. Heart, head, and the life line are the three principal markings: the heart line maps a person's emotional nature, the head line reveals how one thinks, and the life line views the past, present, and future—length of this line may have little to do with longevity.

Each area of the hand is named after a Greek or Roman god, and the names were assigned to be used in a storytelling mode and for easy identification. *Mercury*, the Roman name for the Greek god Hermes, is the little finger and the mount below it. This was the most versatile of the gods in commerce, speech, and manual dexterity. It is the part of the hand that covers communication and capacity for healing. *Apollo*, the Greek and Roman god of sunlight, represents the ring finger and the mount below it. Apollo is the area of vanity and creative potential. *Saturn*, the Roman name for the Greek god Cronus, is the middle finger and mount below. How one responds to rules, assumes responsibilities, and interacts with law and order is determined in this area. *Jupiter*, the Roman name for the Greek god Zeus, ruler of heaven and earth, is the index finger and the mount below. This is the territory of leadership potential, optimism, and governs close relationships. *Venus*, the Roman name for the Greek goddess Aphrodite, goddess of love, is the mount below the thumb. The heart chakra is found here, and one's capacity for giving. *Mars*, the Roman name for the Greek god Ares, god of war, is represented with three mounts on the middle plain of the palm—these are areas of temperament, assertiveness, and resilience. *Uranus*, the most ancient god and ruler of the sky, is a small mount located on the palm well below the little and ring fingers and is the area of inventiveness and ideals. *Neptune*, the Greek god Poseidon, ruler of the sea, is found at the lower region of the palm. This mount determines the urge to build, potential for travel and a career. *Pluto*, Greek god of the underworld, really more a mark than a mount, is located near the wrist. Here one can view relationships with siblings and possible changes in life. Finally, the "lunar mount," representing the goddess of the moon—Diana, Artemis for the Greeks—whose domain includes maidens, chastity and childbirth, is the mount located on the heel of the hand. This is where imagination and the subconscious are viewed, along with romanticism and curiosity.

All the fingers of your hand tell tales about you, and a palm reader studies them separately and together. The thumb reveals your stubbornness, and it governs your logic, love, vitality, and strength of character; the index finger discusses in a language of lines and shapes your sociability; your middle finger will gossip about your conformity; your ring finger describes your creativity; and that baby finger becomes a tattletale of the way you communicate with others. Any noticeable peculiarities may indicate areas in your life that should be accentuated or avoided: you may prefer to deal with these issues privately but fingers can't stop telling stories about you.

Fingernails also reveal aspects of you by shapes—rectangle, square, oval and almond. Palmists believe the rectangular nail suggests that here is a forceful subject, but one who doesn't always consider all aspects of a situation; this person can be impulsive in the drive to succeed. A square nail indicates strength of character, though there is sometimes a lack of foresightedness. The wider a nail, the greater the physical stamina. An oval fingernail is the most common, and this signals good overall balance in functioning and making compromises in complicated situations. The almond-shaped nail, pointed at the tip, denotes a person who needs a protected environment in order to flourish. By temperament this individual displays fragility and is vulnerable.

Rising lines, which begin in the lower or center portion of the palm and point toward specific fingers, reveal tendencies and inclinations: the one running toward the Apollo finger suggests a talent in art or music; the rising line pointing toward Mercury holds energies associated with communications, commerce, and medicine; the one going toward the Jupiter finger deals with leadership, idealism, spirituality, and charisma.

Inclinations can be read by observing variables; for example, a person is not overly emotional if the heart line is short, and a break in this line may point to some severe trauma. Carried further, if there are a number of branches of equal strength running from the heart line, this may indicate a person of broad tastes, and rising lines from this thoroughfare suggest an optimistic tendency or a mild interest in a given area. Black or blue dots on the heart line sometimes are interpreted as emotional loss, and the configuration of a red dot may signify an overwhelming release of pent-up energy. Some palmists decipher red dots on the heart line as warnings of coronary or pulmonary problems, while other readers feel these spots indicate that there has been a violent struggle between family members.

Handshakes reveal more than the formality of greeting a fellow human. Sometimes the flesh feels cold, warm, dry, or damp. The grip can be weak or more hearty than desired, and the texture of the skin may seem silky or have a lizard roughness. The hand is a good diagnostic part of the body for the physician: areas of redness could indicate a circulatory problem and yellow patches a disorder of the liver; if the skin is shiny and has a slippery feel, there may be a mineral deficiency. Good signs are when the hand is pink, firm in its squeeze, and warm—these features usually indicate a healthy constitution.

Hands change at different rates of speed. One palmist recalled the hand of a widow—her life was in transition and her sorrow so intense that the palm was altering noticeably while the reading was being conducted. Other causes for such immediate alterations can be rage, acquisition, and desire. Good days and bad are duly noted on these fleshy premises, and even humor leaves its indelible mark. One noted palmist, Robin Gile, takes a long look at the head line of his client's palm—this helps him to determine how much explaining he'll need to do during the session. Gile claims he can tell a person's IQ by using this approach.

A test to illustrate how closely the hand reflects your larger self can be conducted by observing the mount of Jupiter—this is the pad just below your index finger on the active hand. A small blue, red, or black dot appears in this area when you have a headache, and the tiny imperfection quickly vanishes when aspirin relieves the pain.

If a person photocopies both hands, dates the copy, files it away, and looks at it a year later, even the most nearsighted interpreter will see differences. Lines can and will change, palmists tell us, because we're not creatures of destiny but beings created by our own cumulative choices. Just as our inner and outer lives are entities apart, the lines of our active hand will not be the same as those mappings of the passive member.

Palmists believe that what occurs in a person's life is reflected in the hand—even a momentary encounter with rudeness will leave its imprint. You see an empty parking space, but before you can maneuver your vehicle into the slot, someone is there ahead of you. The next time this happens, look at the fleshy pad where your thumb joins the rest of your hand; you may find it swollen and red. Major events also are recorded as they happen: marriage, children, death in the family, career change; hands never rest or become forgetful as life progresses.

Many people think of palmists as tellers of fortune, and when there are consultations clients expect glimpses of tomorrow. Perhaps the real value of having the palm read lies in the momentary access to the entire landscape—past, present, and future. One of the givens of a reading is that you won't see in your hand what you can't find in yourself.

SUPERSTITIONS

Superstitions are rituals which can be performed without apparent rationality—they have served as protection against the arbitrary events that happen to all of us. These beliefs are not based upon fact or reason, but are upheld by those who fear that unknown forces are controlling their lives and that they must protect themselves.

Early man's deepest fears concerned the ever threatening destruction of his livelihood and the annihilation of his species. These apprehensions ran so deep that they might be termed instinctive—fear of tempting fate, disobeying old taboos, of darkness and its denizens—and they did surface later in most societal settings: for examples, many superstitions show that the farming population feared that a witch would steal the milk and butter by casting some spell, and young couples soon to be married worried that a witch might tie knots in their clothing to frustrate their hopes of progeny. The persistent dread of witchcraft necessitated many superstitious rituals, such as the way of combing one's hair, hiving bees, selling eggs, and doing things after dark when "evil crones" were believed to be abroad and working their spells. If someone was suspected of being such a person, thorough precautions and fierce countermeasures had to be taken to ensure safety.

When human beings lived in closer proximity to nature—before industrialization—it seemed logical to stir one's food in the same direction as the course of the sun, to accept the belief that plentiful berries in summer are a provision for nonmigratory birds during a coming hard winter, and to hold the comforting assumption that a housefly which lives until January is lucky, not because it is unusual but because the insect seems to be under some kind of divine protection which one might share. Written into the laws of survival were symbolic rituals. A token burial was believed to forestall death and cure the patient, newborn babies were carried upstairs to signify that they would rise in the world, and in a mariner's cottage all bowls were kept upright—an overturned bowl was seen as an invitation for a witch to attempt through magic the overturning of a ship.

Any power but that of God was deemed superstition by the Christian Church in eleventh century Europe, and alien practices, such as divination, charms, spells, magic cures, omens, rituals, and taboos, were condemned. Equally deplored from the pulpit were a multitude of "evil beliefs" also termed "vulgar errors," as the clergy attempted to save parishioners from opinions which "produced heathenism and inventions of the Devil." Bibles fanned in sick patients' faces, communion wines prescribed for whooping cough, and sore eyes bathed in baptismal waters were commonplace actions endorsed by the Church. Yet in spite of these options, many people clung to the notion that it was more effective to cross fingers for the prevention of bad luck than to make the sign of the cross.

In folklore, spitting prevents evil and protects you from ghosts and witches. When you encounter a ghost, all wisdom departs, and to save yourself you must spit on the ground in front of the apparition and sternly demand: "In the name of the Lord, what do you want?" The spittle supposedly prevents the ghost from harming defenseless humans.

Many people were awestruck by coincidences, and when a fortunate chain of events transpired the general reaction was that these happenings were "meant," thus assigning serendipity to fate, rather than to the will of God. Whenever there were freakish occurrences, man, the selftormentor and bad-omen cataloger, was quick to believe that such things forecasted destiny and usually for the worse.

Some psychics believe that thought can travel away from ourselves and influence other people and events that come into our lives—positive thinking attracting good luck and negative producing bad. If misfortune hits us twice, superstition reminds us that bad luck usually runs in threes—though not inevitably. Runs of good luck sometimes occur: once at Monte Carlo, red came up on the roulette table 28 times in a row. The odds of this happening are 270 million to one.

Though the number 13 has a reputation of being unlucky—one rarely finds a motel room or floor in a high-rise designated as such—it is given prominence on our one-dollar bill. At the back of the note, there are 13 stars symbolizing the original colonies; elsewhere on that side one finds the same number of steps on the pyramid, arrows in the eagle's claw, bars on the shield, leaves on the olive branch; and to further this numeration, there is the 13th Amendment for minorities, and the signers of the Declaration of Independence numbered thirteen.

Magic was employed to serve good or evil. Witch knots tied to lengths of string became spells that could cure a sprained ankle or hinder a birth. The black cat had imposing powers—its blood was thought to cure all kinds of diseases, but having the animal cross in front of one was an unlucky sign. Some believers were convinced that magic could be converted from a potentially lethal force to a beneficial one: a white horse brought luck after one had spat at it, and the chimney sweep (when smudged with soot he was thought to resemble Satan) brought good fortune if kissed.

In Indian lore, the ghost of a little girl, known as an *Acheri*, lives on mountaintops and comes into valleys at night for the purpose of revelry and to bring diseases to young people by casting shadows over her victims. Children who wear amulets of red thread tied around their necks are protected. (I remember a classmate of mine in the second grade who came to school with a piece of red thread tied around his neck—he said it kept him from getting nosebleeds. I took his explanation for granted, but in retrospect I wonder if his Native American mother had other reasons.)

Since ancient times, the candle has been used in most rituals and rites of passage, including those pertaining to the dead and spirits of the dead. A custom from Ireland, and brought to New England by Irish immigrants, was the burning of twelve candles in a circle around a corpse until burial. This compass of light prevented evil spirits from carrying off the deceased's soul. The Irish also burned three candles at wakes, and the ends of these tapers were later used to treat burns. A guttering candle foreshadowed a death in the family, and in American folklore, a tallow left burning in an empty room would cause the demise of some family member. Wax producing a dim light meant that a ghost was nearby—the same when the flame burned blue. (In researching my book *The Buried Treasures of Maine*, I read somewhere that seventeenth-century lore advised treasure hunters to carry consecrated candles in their lanterns; this would confuse the ghost of a dead man guarding the buried treasure. Captain Kidd, and other pirates of his time, supposedly killed a crewman at every site where loot was buried. Reliable guards were the dead: if the ghost caused an intruder to react—as such a grisly watchman invariably did—the treasure would vanish from sight.)

Halloween became more enthusiastically celebrated after the Irish potato famine of the 1820s and 1840s when thousands of starving immigrants came to America, many of them settling in the Boston area and northern New England. Flames roaring in fireplaces replaced Celtic bonfires, there were parlor games instead of reenactments of ancient rites, and young people played tricks on neighbors. The Irish had a Halloween custom of carrying lanterns made out of hollowed-out turnips and beets, called jack-o'-lanterns or jacky lanterns, which were used to scare away spirits in the night. Since pumpkins were more readily available, the immigrants soon used these as substitutes.

There are many ways to discourage evil spirits and to prevent them from taking up residency in houses. Some of these charms against unwanted presences are ordinary, and often executed with quick gestures; there is the belief that making the sign of the cross or throwing a pinch of salt over the left shoulder will bring good luck. (When asked why the *left* shoulder, Adam Galuza, a Woolwich, Maine resident replied: "Because one's heart is on that side.") Another precautionary gesture with salt is to strew it across a threshold—do this and a ghost or demon will think twice before entering. Silver amulets and jewelry are worn for protection, and crucifixes are popular weapons when investigators arm themselves for hauntings. Objects made of metal are effective: nails taken from a coffin and driven into the threshold of a door will prevent nightmares, and an iron rod in a grave will prevent an evil spirit from rising out of the ground.

Deathbed superstitions abound: if the dying is "hard" and the deceased finds difficulty entering the afterworld, the caring relatives may want to unlock all doors, cupboards, and windows so the departed soul has free egress from the house; the knots in the shroud must be untied before the coffin is nailed shut—if this isn't done, the spirit of the deceased will wander about and visit its former abode; pins stuck into gateposts where funeral processions have passed will keep away evil spirits; and if the funeral party takes a different route back after the burial, the corpse will remain in its grave. Most important, survivors must never speak ill of the dead—this rule has brought about the clichéd saying "God rest his (or her) soul."

("One needs a good leaf tea," I recall a woman telling my mother, "for a proper reading." The neighbor's hobby was fortune-telling—this was during the 1930s when there were no tea bags in the pantry. Mother was addicted to the brew and rarely made a fresh pot; she just added new leaves to the strong residue left in her kettle.

Reading tea leaves, interpreting cloud formations, and pulling a variety of signs from that bulging grab bag of superstitions were popular methods of alerting one to the coming attractions of sicknesses and deaths in the neighborhood and family.

A teacup with a wide mouth, one with gently sloping sides, was preferable and the recipient of the reading was instructed to leave just enough liquid in the bottom of the cup so the grounds could be swirled freely. This was serious business—not a parlor game—and most of my relatives paid as close attention to tea-leaf procedures as lightning in an August thundershower. Tea grounds that clung near the rim of the cup involved present events, those of the future were further down, and at the very bottom of the cup lurked signs of the remote future. If I recall correctly, a clogged mass of grounds after a brisk swirl spelled troubles ahead, a thin trail of tea bits meant a journey, and leavings resembling bird shapes indicated good news—there seemed to be an omen for everyone's fate in the bottom of a cup.

"If you don't go to sleep, the Boogeyman will get you." This was a warning hurled at me by exasperated grandparents and parents when I made a general nuisance of myself after being tucked under the covers at night. Many of us carry such threats with us into adulthood, and perhaps these reminders tint our reaction to the supernatural.)

There are so many hobgoblins loose in the adult bag of tricks to get an unruly brat to settle down. Bug-a-boo, Boo, Bugbear, Bogeybeast, to begin a list. The Boogeyman idea surfaces in many cultures and countries and with different names—sometimes synonymous with the Devil. In Wales, for example, it is called a Bug (ghost); in Germany a Boggelmann; and in Scotland a Bogle. No matter where it looms the *bogey* is big and threatening, does its work at night, and is mostly used to frighten children into good behavior.

Amulets have been cherished since ancient times for protection against misfortune, evil spirits, witchcraft, illness, and every imaginable calamity. They are worn or carried on a person, and some are placed in homes or among possessions. It is not uncommon to find them painted on houses, barns, and ships. Any object can serve as an amulet, and personal items frequently used include pieces of jewelry, mineral specimens, gems, and even common stones with unusual shapes. In occult lore, these charms can be imbued with supernatural power through magic ritual. (It is no accident that an enterprising businessman made a fortune when he packaged ordinary stones and advertised them as "pet rocks"—they were in an odd way, *friendly* amulets for a Topsham, Maine man who declared that he felt "luckier and safer" since the purchase of his stone.)

Superstition declined as rationalism grew during the early 1700s, and by the middle of that century some followers, unable to sever their beliefs entirely, viewed the apparent demise with nostalgic regret. Today, the origins of most superstitions have been forgotten. Omens that once foretold death are now mere signs of bad luck. The ritual of throwing wheat over a bride "in tokenyng a plentie and fruitfulnesse" has become a postnuptial frolic with rice or confetti. Many people, however, still are aware of the lucky signs and grim warnings shared in childhood—often by grandparents who served as custodians and who were better acquainted with folklore. "One of granny's favorite sayings" and "grandpa used to tell me" usher familiar fables snagged from the past. Some superstitions have become part of our language: "Touch" or "knock on wood" and "cross fingers" are said without thinking—it is just something we had better do...just in case. Spilling salt, crossing knives, walking under ladders, opening an umbrella in the house, hanging up horseshoes, and dreading the 13th of the month when it falls on a Friday are fragments of an antique faith that we still carry with us.

HAUNTED INNS ALONG THE MAINE COAST

A dozen or more inns along the Maine coast are reported to be haunted, but sometimes when one telephones and asks for spooky accommodations there is confusion or irritation. Innkeepers do their utmost to attract tourists, and having a token ghost on the premises isn't always looked upon as the best kind of advertising. "We are not haunted," said an assistant manager with a chill in his voice. "That was a promotional idea of a former owner."—Actually, the legend predated that owner by many years. (One employee at a seasonal lodge left the line for about three minutes, probably to confer with her boss on what to tell the weird man who said: "My wife and I would like to reserve room 22 for this coming Saturday night—you know, the one that has the ghost." When she came back on the line, this caller was told there was nothing available; they were "booked for the season.")

Other innkeepers are delighted that their business is sheltering a restless spirit, and many of the guests feel such presences give prestige to the surroundings. The ghost of a nineteenth-century woman has long held residency at the Captain Lord Mansion, now a bed-and-breakfast establishment in Kennebunkport, Maine. The Lincoln Room, originally called the Wisteria Room, seems to be her favorite bedroom haunt. Seen in clothing of the early 1800s, the spirit floats across a chamber and suddenly disappears. On one occasion, an intrepid guest followed the apparition up a spiral staircase which leads to an eight-sided cupola. Many believe this specter to be the wife of Captain Nathaniel Lord who had workers from his shipyard build the mansion in 1812. Lord died before he could move in, but the property was owned by the family until 1972. Not long after the inn opened, in 1978, a young bride's honeymoon was discourteously interrupted when the ghost wearing a nightgown drifted through the bedroom and vanished into a wall.

Another bed-and-breakfast establishment in Kennebunkport that shelters a ghost is the Captain Fairfield Inn. This Federal-style mansion is believed to be haunted by the spirit of Captain James Fairfield who was captured by the British during the War of 1812. After his release from prison in 1815, he settled in Kennebunkport with his wife Lois and built the mansion. Fairfield died of pneumonia five years later, at the age of thirty-eight. During the restoration of the inn, Captain James's ghost was seen lingering in a dark corner of the basement, and several guests have sensed an "affable presence" wandering about in rooms.

(This writer and his wife made overnight reservations at an inn for a room believed to be haunted. These lodgings—which must remain anonymous at the request of the management—overlooked a postcard panorama of Maine coastline, fishing boats, and islands. We arrived early and were armed with a 35mm camera and flash, two tape recorders, and a motion sensor; the sort of equipment we felt might be useful if we were fortunate enough to have a meeting with some spirit.

Up front, let me say that Stella is more receptive or susceptible to the supernatural. I realized long before starting this book that I am inclined to side with those who believe an explanation can be found for most mysterious happenings, and when I find myself uncertain as to the veracity of an incident, I prefer to leave it up to my readers to decide for themselves.

Shortly after checking in, when descending a stairway, I stumbled badly and nearly fell; "pushed" was the word I used at the time to excuse my clumsiness. Not once, but twice it happened that evening and on the same flight of stairs. That's most unusual, I thought, particularly for a person known to be steady on his feet.

We lounged in our room for several hours. Our conversation centered on ghosts, with an occasional invitation directed at the spirit that frequented this particular chamber to manifest itself—I'm sure our efforts at ghost busting were comical and amateurish. Before retiring, I took photographs of the room from every conceivable angle, set both the motion sensor and tape recorders on automatic, and turned out the lights. The bed was too small and lumpy, the night long, and our sleep fitful.

Stella woke the next morning with a headache. "I've never had one this severe," she said. "I feel as if somebody struck me with a hammer!" I rose slowly from the bed and turning saw my pillow: it was covered with blood, not spotted, but saturated. A close inspection of my scalp revealed no scrapes or cuts.

Tired and disoriented—I guess the better word would be discombobulated—we left the inn and drove north on Route 1 to Bucksport. I used the four remaining frames on the roll in my camera to photograph Jonathan Buck's gravestone—the memorial that bears the image of a woman's leg.

Two weeks later, when I picked up the developed photos, the woman who waited on me said: "Better check your camera. You have only four prints that are good." I knew without looking what I would find inside the envelope: all the gravestone pictures in glossy black and white were there—the last four on the roll. It seemed as if the haunted room never existed.)

The East Wind Inn which overlooks the sea at Tenants Harbor is another haunted site. This sprawling and graceful building constructed in 1860 was part of a shipyard complex. Until the death knell of the three-masted sailing vessels, one of the most active yards in New England was Armstrong & Keane. Shipbuilding gave Tenants Harbor bustle and economic boom during the decade from 1864 to 1874. It was a time when docks teemed with goods, and schooners were busy freighting cargoes up and down the Atlantic seaboard.

Gilbert Armstrong and Harry Keane complimented one another; the former was a shrewd trader and businessman, the latter a talented builder of vessels. The one thing both lacked was luck—seven powerful ships were launched and all were lost at sea. This, and the invention of steamers, broke the company. Keane moved to Camden, Maine to work for another yard, and an embittered Armstrong lived out his days as a janitorial putterer in an empty complex of buildings.

The third floor of the inn, where several ghostly appearances have been reported, was used by the local Masons as a meeting place for more than thirty years. After being unoccupied from 1954 to 1974, the building was renovated to serve the tourist trade. It was at this time that the owner and guests saw a figure climbing the main staircase and looking out of a window facing the sea.

Guests who have stayed in rooms 12 and 14—now one unit after the removal of a partition—claim they have been held down in bed by unseen hands. There seems to be some dispute over the sex of the ghost. (When making reservations for rooms 12 and 14, I received a letter from the inn confirming the accommodation with the comment: "We hope the lady will visit you and Mrs. Stevens." I regret to say, she didn't, and we went home early the next morning.) The figure seen on the staircase and at the window is identified as Armstrong by Carol Olivieri Schulte in her book *Ghosts on the Coast of Maine*, Down East Books, 1996: "He stops to gaze out across the waters that once harbored the likes of his grand fleet of ships."

Guests on the third floor have heard crying sounds and have felt "cold spots" shifting about in rooms and along corridor. The owner of the inn woke from a deep sleep one night and heard loud footsteps in the lobby. When he went to investigate, no one was there, but the swinging door leading to the dining room was still moving back and forth. On another instance, a frequent guest called him on the phone and said: "Tim, you'd better come up and take a look at this." There was a broken window and glass littered the floor. "Jenny," he asked, "why didn't you hold the window when removing the stick that propped it?" Her reply startled him. "I never touched the window." She was given another room, and two nights later she telephoned him again. This time there was glass all over the room, as if someone had smashed the window from the outside with great force—which wasn't possible because a storm window was in place and unbroken.

The ghost was last reported in the winter of 1987. A doctor and her husband were staying in a room on the third floor overlooking the harbor. She felt a chill while in bed and decided to get up and fetch an extra blanket. This, she realized after stirring, was impossible: there was a pressure, two unseen hands pushing down; hands that held her flat on the bed. "Please go," the doctor told the presence. "You are making me very uncomfortable and I can't deal with this right now." The pressure slowly eased and she no longer felt the chill. "The unfortunate soul that had been trying to break through his dimension barrier," wrote Carol Olivieri Schulte, "was Gilbert Armstrong in a different time, a different place."

The Searsport Area Bed and Breakfast Association designed an unusual poster when sponsoring a 1999 Halloween visit of historical inns. "Hystorical Hauntings House Tour" the placard began. Since three of the ten lodgings were reportedly accommodating ghosts, the membership decided that an appropriate addition would be "Come Meet Past and Present Owners." Two of the three haunted sites, The Watchtide B&B by the Sea and Thurston House Bed & Breakfast Inn, are Searsport, Maine establishments, and the third, Hichborn Inn, is in nearby Stockton Springs.

Nancy-Linn Nellis, president of the association and owner of The Watchtide B&B, recalled her first sighting of a ghost in April 1994 when she and her husband were renovating the inn. "I came out of my first-floor bedroom and I saw Jane, my dear friend who was staying with me," she told Corinne Vaccaro, reporter for *The Republican Journal*, "or at least who I thought was Jane." What Nellis saw from the door of her room was an apparition two rooms away. The ghost stood with its back turned, had bobbed hair, wore a long jacket, and was looking at a print of a painting by Winslow Homer. Nellis recalled saying something and thought she heard an answer. It was only later that Nancy-Linn learned that Jane had answered her, but not from two rooms away on the ground floor—her friend had spoken from an upstairs bedroom. The apparition quickly disappeared and Nellis, though startled, soon regained her composure. Her friend was unable to ignore the encounter—she decided to end her visit and return home. Later, the person who had sold them the stately residence asked if she had met Connie Banks—this was a former owner who had died in the house. "If you mean the ghost," Nellis replied without hesitation, "yes I have indeed!"

There are other spirits inhabiting The Watchtide B&B by the Sea. Three months after the sighting of Connie Banks, a female guest asked Nellis if there were ghosts in the house.

"Why do you ask?" the innkeeper inquired.

"Because they were in my room last night," the lodger replied.

The guest had seen a man and woman dressed in old-fashioned clothing—the two were standing at the foot of her bed.

"They just stood there gazing down at me," she told Nellis.

At the time when the house was being renovated as a guest establishment, Nellis and her husband, Jack Elliot, heard horrendous noises, as if "the place was falling apart." These unexplained commotions have lessened since 1994, partly, according to Nellis, because of the merchandise she sells in her gift shop "Angels to Antiques" which is attached to the house; she has also placed an angel in every room of the B&B. It is her belief that these statuettes have a soothing affect on the ghosts and serve as a kind of protective influence.

The Kennebunk Inn was built in 1791, and until 1928 it served as a private residence for a number of occupants. After they had renovated and expanded the inn to twenty-two rooms in 1980, the new owners, Arthur and Angela LeBlanc, began hearing noises at night. There were grumbling sounds that came from the cellar. A "cold, chilling breath of air" often could be felt sweeping into the bar area, and some mornings Arthur LeBlanc would find spilled bottles and bits of debris on the bar-room floor. This was disconcerting for the owner since that part of the inn was swept and made tidy before closing for the night.

"Maybe one of your guests or an employee is a lush," a friend suggested.

"It's more than that," replied LeBlanc. "One of our waitresses was carrying a full tray of our crystal stemware from the dining room the other day, and a glass from the middle of the tray popped up into midair, hovered for a few seconds, then dropped to the floor. The waitress almost went into hysterics, and our luncheon guests, who saw it happen, were awestruck."

Another waitress at the inn, Pattie Farnsworth, had "a strange sensation" whenever she entered a food locker in the cellar. The name "Cyrus" kept buzzing in her ear. Farnsworth was the only waitress who dared to venture into the lower regions of the inn. The ghost's favorite hangout seemed to be under a set of stairs that led to the cellar's ceiling—a former owner had changed his mind and built a second set of steps.

Cyrus, the ghost, enjoyed playing pranks on the employees and had an active dislike for Dudley, the bartender. Behind the bar, there were four hand-carved wooden mugs from Germany. On an August night, one of these mugs picked itself up, spun in Dudley's direction, and struck him on the back of the head. There were no witnesses, recalled LeBlanc, but the bartender "had one hell of a lump on his head to prove it."

"I just stopped by for a drink," an elderly stranger said to LeBlanc. "I lived in this place for awhile—some twenty-five years ago. I heard you talking about Cyrus to those people at the bar."

"Cyrus is our ghost," said an embarrassed LeBlanc. "We just made up the name."

"Cyrus was the night clerk when I lived here," said the stranger. "And he was getting along in years. He used to have his desk in that room."

The man was pointing to the spot where the unfinished staircase rose to the ceiling.

("When I operated the Kennebunk Inn," said Alex Pratt in a telephone interview with this author, "there was one story that the ghost was a man who passed away in 1950—a person who worked at the inn and who also had seen a ghost there. So the question became: Was there one, were there two, or none? It's hard to say. Strange things did occur, but it is an old building, and the way it was constructed anything could happen.")

BIGFOOT SIGHTINGS

For most people, the word "Bigfoot" or "Sasquatch" brings to mind a fictional monster loose on the front cover of a supermarket tabloid. What is not generally known is that stories about these animals have been told since the dawn of language. (Indian tribes of this hemisphere have had a number of names for the creatures, such as Windago, Boqs, Rugaru, Tsiatko, Yeahoh, and Omah. Even pioneers in various parts of the country labelled these wood giants as Skookums, Swamp Boogers, Mountain Devils, and Skunk Apes.) Nevertheless, the possibility of such a species existing today is dismissed by a majority of scientists because no physical remains have been found. A frequent question raised is why with the thousands of credible sightings there is so little photographic documentation. Often, anyone who claims to have seen Bigfoot is ripe for ridicule, even from close family members.

Indians of the Pacific Northwest and Western Canada have a special regard for Bigfoot because of its close kinship to humans; they believe the species is endowed with a borderline human-style consciousness which gives it special power. Animals are never looked upon as inferior to people in Indian culture. Bigfoot exists in the same physical dimension as we do. "He eats, he sleeps, he poops, he cares for his family members." Ralph Gray Wolf, an Athabascan Indian from Alaska, gave this summation: "In our way of belief, they make appearances at troubled times to get more in tune with Mother Earth." Bigfoot brings "signs or messages that there is a need to change, a need to cleanse."

Here in the Northeast, the Iroquois, a six-nation confederacy, view Bigfoot in the same way, though mentioned just as frequently are "the little people" who inhabit the Adirondacks. There is a rush of stories about hunters who see small human-like beings. (This brings to mind Washington Irving's "Rip Van Winkle" in the Catskills; this character met several little bowlers and slept for 20 years.) There are Iroquois who insist that little people are present today—in Maine and all of New England—seldom seen because there is less hunting along deserted ridges of mountains and foothills. For hardy believers, Bigfoot and the little people are regarded as "interdimensional beings" who enter or depart from our physical dimension as they please.

Whether you believe in Van Winkle's games of ninepins, dwarfs with pointed and belled caps, and shiny pots of gold, could there be after all the stories to bolster such improbable sightings, one actual encounter? Our imagination is heightened. The existence of Bigfoot is taken for granted throughout the Native American hemisphere and so are this creature's psychic abilities. In Indian culture, the plants, rivers and stars are all family—so is Bigfoot, the elder brother.

The word cryptozoology was squeezed into dictionaries and became identifiable as a science in 1969 though there was a hint of disparagement—"the study of the lore concerning legendary animals (as Sasquatch) esp. in order to evaluate the possibility of their existence" states *Merriam Webster's Collegiate Dictionary*. When a given is called "legendary" legitimacy is questioned and zoologists are compelled to ask for evidence that such a critter exists. Cryptozoologists and other Bigfoot proponents assert that physical proof is found every month and in most areas of the Western Hemisphere: tracks that don't match those made by other animals, droppings that are totally different, and alien hair samples scuffed into trees. Then why have no remains of these creatures been found? ask scientists and Thomases of doubt—didn't some Sasquatch die of natural causes? Defenders reply that fossilization is rare and most bones get reabsorbed into the ecosystem. If carcasses didn't disintegrate completely in time, the littered woods would be an unpleasant place for hiking.

Based on 407 sightings, some interesting testimony emerged: half the observers stated that the animal was black, 27% thought there was some shade of brown, 15% described it as being light in color, and 8% recalled some shade of gray. There were 56 reports of glowing eyes—23 glowed red, 11 green, 9 yellow, 1 white, and 12 not specified. Only 14% of observers in Florida (supposedly home of the skunk ape) noted an odor, compared to 5.6% nationally. The smell of this elusive wood dweller was called "putrid, rancid, awful, sickening, rotten eggs, skunk putrid, overpowering, intolerable, rank, dead, old outhouse, foul, terrible, vile, rotten, powerful, horrible, dead fish, and nauseating." Did it just stink or had it been rolling in some excrement?—there was no report of a *mild* odor. 64 witnesses stated that the animal was eating or carrying food, and the Bigfoot diet included grubs, apples, oranges, berries, leaves, water plants, sheep, cattle, fish, roots, rodents, and garbage.

Signs, sightings and encounters have been taking place throughout Maine—there seems to be no favorite campground for a Sasquatch. One

report came from a witness who grew up in an unpopulated area of Oxford County: "My Mom always had an irrational fear of us going outside at night," recalled the contributor. "When I had to feed my horses it
was to be done in the light." Their father was away frequently and the
lonely setting caused anxiety. The mother claimed that a prowling, lurking "something" often screamed at her when she was hanging clothes on
the line behind the house—this was in the early 1960s. "We had a large
German shepherd who would not go beyond a certain point in the field,"
the informant continued, "and he left one day and never came back. We
never did find his body." The mother couldn't suppress her fears: "I
often heard her mention the animal she saw crossing the hill below our
house, but she never said much more to us than to stay away from the
swamp and get home before dark." Sometimes, "it" made a noise outside
at night when all the curtains in the windows were drawn. "We often
heard screams, but my Dad said they were bobcats and to not be afraid.
My Mom is 78 now, and she finally told me what she saw. It was large,
hairy, and walked on two legs."

Among numerous sightings, this report came from an unidentified
observer who was gathering firewood near Acton, Maine and Highway
109: "I heard a noise behind me and turned around expecting to see a
moose as I was in moose country. At first I saw nothing and resumed my
gathering. Again, I heard the noise. I turned to look, and there it was
about 30 feet behind me. Male or female I do not know. It was just
standing there watching me. Needless to say, I split. This happened in
the summer of 1985."

Two sets of 20-inch footprints in snow, both going west and not joining,
were found in a wooded terrain near Litchfield, Maine on February 3,
2000. Two weeks later, under similar ground conditions near the
Winthrop and Manchester town lines a 16-inch track was followed for
some distance. These were personal field notes submitted by Richard
Brown to the Gulf Coast Bigfoot Research Organization.

This organization also carried a netscape report of two sets of tracks
that were discovered on February 15, 2000 in Richmond, Maine. These
were a mile apart with one going east and the other west. Both bipedal
prints measured 16 inches in length and were visible for some distance
in snow.

Two sisters were driving to school one morning on Route 46 near
Bucksport, Maine in 1996 when they saw "straight up ahead" a creature
"standing there in the road on two feet for sure, staring at us as we
approached." It was the size of a human and covered with very dark,

shaggy hair. The animal was "hunched over" and its arms were long and "hanging down." As the vehicle drew nearer, the hairy figure quickly disappeared into a roadside grove of fir and hemlock. The girls mentioned the sighting to a few close friends at school and told their parents but didn't think of reporting the incident to a game warden or the police. "Since most people don't believe in Bigfoot," said one of the sisters, "we kept it pretty much to ourselves. I do know what we saw was real, and it wasn't a bear—bears are not shaped like humans and rarely walk around on two feet."

The *Boston Sunday Globe* and six Maine newspapers carried Bigfoot activity in Durham, Maine during late July 1973. On the 25th, a "chimpanzee-like" animal was seen by Lois Huntington, 13; George Huntington, Jr., 10; Scott Huntington, 8; and their friend Tammy Sairo, 12, as they were cycling along the Brunswick-Lisbon Falls Road. Lois's mother, Meota, told reporters that her daughter "fell off her bicycle only three feet from the creature."

"I fell right down in front of him," the girl told a *Maine Sunday Telegram* correspondent, "and all he did was look at me. I would have known if it were a hippie or something. But it had a regular monkey face. You have seen a monkey before, haven't you?" Lois's sighting was further substantiated by James Washburn who claimed to have seen a gorilla-like figure on its hind legs in the same area that day.

On the 26th, Mrs. Huntington was driving home from a baseball game when she saw the "ape" twenty feet from the Durham Road. It was lurking in bushes and made a hasty retreat into the nearby woods. She estimated the animal to be five feet tall, it had a shaggy coat of black hair and must have weighed about 350 pounds. Later that day, Mrs. Huntington returned to the same location with neighbors for another sighting. Authorities were called, and several deputies from two sheriff departments, the Maine State Police, and game wardens searched the woods. Meota Huntington sat in her car during the hunt and again saw the animal: it was peering at her from the crotch of a tree.

On the 27th, a helicopter unsuccessfully joined the chase, but several Durham residents again saw the creature. Tracks were discovered behind a cemetery—the area where most of the activity occurred—and these footprints were described as being about five inches wide and "rather deep." "Whatever made it weighs 300 or 350 pounds," said an Androscoggin County Deputy Sheriff, "and I can't tell you more. It's definitely not a bear track. I don't know what's going on here and I'd rather not express an opinion."

One curious detail surfaced while newspapers were investigating the sightings: It was a report of a gorilla suit being rented at a Portland area costume shop in March 1973 and it never was returned. This provided a reasonable explanation to some disbelievers but not to most Central Maine authorities at the scene and other eyewitnesses.

A young man and his girlfriend were returning from a motocycle rally in the spring of 1974, and the two decided to camp for the night in a thick pine growth about one mile from Route 95 near Kennebunk. "An hour or so after camping," the man informed BFRO—Bigfoot Field Researchers Organization— "I heard movement near the tent but was not concerned. Then the sound got closer and there was this really pungent odor. I thought 'uh-oh it's a bear' but was still not concerned as black bears are mostly just curious and usually will not bother you." The cyclist had spent much time in the woods since both his parents were Maine guides, and he was acquainted with the habits and sounds of wildlife in the different seasons.

"Then it happened. Whatever it was let out a scream that made every hair on my body stand straight out and nearly gave me a heart attack." The noise woke the girl and she became hysterical. The creature was near the tent, and they could hear it breathing. The sound of something heavy prowling about the campground continued for more than twenty minutes before fading into the darkness.

"After a sleepless night and at first light," the witness stated, "I crawled out to investigate. I looked for tracks but there were no clear imprints, only impressions in the grass and some broken ferns. The impressions were about half again as big as my own shoe and I wear a size 11."

Later that year, the couple saw a Bigfoot television documentary, and in the film there was a recording of a scream. "You guessed it," the man concluded, "hair straight out and an exclamation from both of us of 'Oh sh—!' If that was Bigfoot then we have been very close to him."

Jean Williams was driving on the southbound lane of Route 95 just north of Bangor when she had her July 1973 sighting. Her husband and two children were asleep in the car, and it was early evening though still bright enough to drive without headlights. Then suddenly, up ahead, she saw a huge, hairy creature, either black or dark brown emerging from the wooded median. It then marched swiftly across the highway and disappeared. Her first thought was that an escaped gorilla was on the prowl, as she immediately realized the arms were too long for a bear and it didn't move like one. At the time, Mrs. Williams was "utterly perplexed" and unable to provide a rational explanation for what she had witnessed.

"I did not hear of Bigfoot," she communicated to the Bigfoot/Sasquatch Database Network, "until several years later when some photos were televised and I realized that this looked like what I had seen. I did stop the car and attempt to look across the low traffic barrier and into the woods where the being had gone but I could see no trace of it."

Frequently, tracks in the snow can be as informative as a sentence on the white page of a book, and if these footprints are followed, entire paragraphs may be revealed. Reports sent to the Gulf Coast Organization in January 2000 indicate that traffic is relatively heavy for so few in number: Sidney, Maine, 1/20/00, 18" tracks going into the Sidney Bog; North Topsham, 1/20/00, many 16" and 17" footprints going north; Northeast Portland, 1/25/00, 16" and 17" tracks followed several thousand feet and all going north; and again North Topsham, 1/27/00, footprints in the direction of Bowdoin; as these ascended a 45-degree incline the stride measured 54".

Loren Coleman, a Portland writer, college professor and consultant, has been researching Maine's animal legends since 1975—these include black panther sightings, sea serpents in the Gulf of Maine, and Indian devils around Mount Katahdin and in the hills of Franklin and Oxford Counties. Coleman is the author of a number of books on cryptozoology and is a frequent guest on radio and television programs. His field investigations and interviews with people who have seen giant snakes, lake monsters, phantom kangaroo, mystery feline, thunderbird, and Sasquatch have prompted visits to 45 states, Canada, Mexico, England, and the Virgin Islands.

"Belief is a thing for religion," replies Loren Coleman when asked if he believes in the existence of the animals he studies. "Among zoologists, naturalists and cryptozoologists, there is an acceptance of the evidence, or a nonacceptance. I accept that in 20 percent of the reports, there seems to be some actual evidence for an undiscovered animal. In the majority, it's misidentification, hoaxes, mistakes." Coleman, who has a background in anthropology and social work, looks upon the search for a Bigfoot as an activity of intellectual curiosity. "I'm not interested in ghosts or UFOs," he concludes. "I'm interested in tangible biological species. These are not wisps of smoke that I'm pursuing."

Some cryptozoologists are convinced that Bigfoot has blood ties to a giant ape assumed to have become extinct several hundred thousand years ago. Coleman, however, believes these "Big-foot-Sasquatch types (and their relatives in China) are related to the fossil apemen, found from fossil, in Africa and Asia" and probably migrated to this hemisphere across the Bering Strait.

It isn't known how long the legend of "Cassie," the sea serpent of Casco Bay, has flourished among mariners, but one of the earliest reports describes how Ensign Edward Preble, a Portland, Maine naval hero, fired at Cassie with a cannon. Throughout the 19th century there were sightings, particularly between 1817 and 1830, and often the monster was seen by groups of ship passengers and sailors. A recent encounter with this creature was experienced by two Norwegian fishermen.

Transcripts from Coleman's 1985 interview with Ole Mikkelsen, one of the fisherman, provided this version: "We were five miles off Cape Elizabeth. We saw an object coming toward us out of the haze." At first the two Norwegians thought they had sighted a submarine, but as it drew nearer they realized that this was different— "some live thing, light brown like a cusk, with a tail like a mackerel's. It looked well over 100 feet long. Its head stuck out of the water and was broader than the neck it was on."

When asked for a detailed description of the head the fisherman replied: "I was not sure of the ears or eyes but it could hear. Every time the foghorn on the lightship Portland sounded, she turned her head in that direction." The two Norwegian fisherman had more than a glimpse of the sea serpent; Cassie could be seen for 45 minutes.

There have been few reported Bigfoot sightings along highways, which may tell us that this creature by nature is both cautious and shy. According to reported encounters, it is a deep-woods animal and not likely to become a roadkill statistic. Hundreds of collisions and near misses occur annually on Maine roads with moose and deer—rarely with bears—but when Bigfoot is seen lingering in the shadows of a tree line it is probably waiting for traffic to subside before crossing. Since the driver's attention is centered on what lies ahead, rare glimpses may have been missed.

In Maine, as in some other states, there are thousands of acres that have never been visited by sportsmen, campers and hikers. Should these untrampled grounds be invaded, a hunter wearing bright fluorescent clothing would probably capture attention as quickly as a group of boisterous vacationers; also, coon hunters and their dogs can he heard for miles, and even well-trained bloodhounds are programmed to follow particular scents and ignore others. All this, compounded with the Sasquatch tendency to nocturnal feeding, nomadism, and shyness, preserves and protects the species.

Richard Greenwell, Secretary of the International Society of Cryptozoology, readily concedes that Bigfoot "attracts more crackpots than, say, astronomy." This, however, makes what his society is attempting to accomplish all the more important. "We're trying to produce better evidence," observes Loren Coleman, "and not take everything that comes along."

A CONVERSATION WITH TAMARANDA

Jean Laier (Tamaranda) is a published poet, gifted artist, actress, songwriter, and storyteller. In 1972 she took up transcendental meditation and became a member of the Spiritual Frontiers Fellowship. Major surgery and a near-death experience in 1974 changed her life. "It moved me from being community centered to being more universal," she explained. In 1976, while in California, Tamaranda became involved with The International Cooperation Counsel of the Unity Diversity Center of Los Angeles and three years later was ordained as a minister. On returning to New England, she began working at psychic fairs in malls, and in 1980 Tamaranda moved to Hiram, Maine where she organized her "Rainbow Caboose," a study group that concentrated on metaphysics and the counseling of human spirits. After travels in India, Sri Lanka, Ireland, and England, she returned to Maine to continue her workshops in healing, storytelling, the Seth concepts, UFOs, and her lectures on Native Americans.

(This author visited Tamaranda in her Stockton Springs, Maine home and the following conversation was recorded on tape.)

Q: I think you have an unusual name. Does it have a particular meaning?

Tamaranda: I remember saying to friends: "Don't call me Hattie or Jean anymore, call me Tamara." But a voice in me said: add an nda, and it soon was Tamaranda. Later, somebody told me what the name meant. The "ta" is the yolk, "ma" is for the feminine, "ra" is the masculine, and the "nda" means the joy of becoming complete, which I am working on. I can tell when I am with a group what time period I am missing; I may be with people who call me Jean or Hattie, and others know me as Tamaranda. I don't mind; it's all the same for me.

Q: When did you begin readings?

Tamaranda: I started doing readings in 1972 and probably have done over a thousand. For a while, I was working with a group that did them in malls several days a week, twelve hours a day. I didn't enjoy that—I was linking with people who were confused about their roles in life. I also was a part of the First International Parapsychology Conference in San Juan, Puerto Rico in 1979.

Q: Do you have a particular method of communicating, such as through Tarot cards, crystals, or palm reading?

Tamaranda: What I do is have people draw a mandala with magic markers. My belief is when you have the smallest amount of a color you have access to the total power of that color because everything is connected.

Q: How do you begin such a reading?

Tamaranda: I put on some music and lead them into a meditative state and tell them to decide on what they would like to put in the center of the paper for a simple symbol. It can be a star, heart, cross, diamond, circle or square. Then I ask them to add to it—anything they want. I leave the room, and when they feel they have done enough they call me back.

Q: Then you interpret it?

Tamaranda: I hold the paper in one hand, close my eyes, and move my other hand slowly in a circle over what they have completed. Everything we touch provides vast amounts of information—we have in our palms a sensitive sensor. That's why people should wash their hands more often! Hands get cluttered up with so many things. When I finish, I say: "If you have any questions now, ask me and I'll tune in for you." But usually I have already told them everything they needed to know.

Q: What do you think of the Ouija board? Do you use it at all?

Tamaranda: I have used it in the past, and I don't have any problem with a Ouija board as long as the people who are going to be using it encircle themselves with protection and insist that only positive things be allowed to come through. A person can be taken over by spirits on a Ouija board. This is something to be cautious about.

Q: When were you first aware that you were a sensitive?

Tamaranda: When I was about three years old. I tried to ride those beams of sunlight that came through the window—I was sure that I could sit on them, and I got so upset when I couldn't do it. Mother didn't understand any of this.

Q: There were no other sensitives in your family?

Tamaranda: My father probably was one—he died suddenly when I was nine.

Q: You grew up in Maine?

Tamaranda: No, Massachusetts. But my father's family was from Kennebunk and Houlton, Maine, and we do think there is some Native American in our family.

Q: A woman recently told me that she had a friendly ghost in her house. How can you tell if you are dealing with an *unfriendly* one?

Tamaranda: I will smell a very unpleasant odor. At first, I won't ask: Is that a spirit around me? I'll think: What is this? Then all of a sudden it occurs to me—not only will there be the odor but I will be very tired. I'll feel that something is attached to me; something is draining my strength.

Q: Do you experience a temperature change?

Tamaranda: Temperature changes, yes. They are usually cold, and you sometimes feel a breeze.

Q: Why are some ghosts more earthbound than others?

Tamaranda: Because they either went over suddenly or someone they love is still on earth. Spirits also may be earthbound because they fear hellfire and brimstone for the bad things they did. There could be other reasons why they are still around and at different levels. This reminds me of one of our speakers at an annual Spiritual Frontier Fellowship conference who had lost his wife—they had been married a long time and both hoped they might communicate with one another after death. When she passed over, he waited hopefully but there was no message from her. Then one day, several months after she died, he got a call from a young couple who really knew little about him. They wanted him to visit because they had something unusual on their computer. It was a message from his wife. After that she began communicating regularly through his machine.

Q: I would be interested in having you share some of your adventures with spirits. Do you mind?

Tamaranda: Not at all. One night, around Halloween, a few years ago, I got a call from a young man—I don't remember his last name but his first name was Jeff. He wanted me to come over to his house in Frankfort, Maine and see about some ghosts that were there. So I asked a friend of mine, Linda Seekins (a sensitive) if she would like to go with me. Jeff met us at the door, and we had coffee with him. He told us that he was aware of a spirit in the cellar when he was cutting wood down there—and a lot of sadness. He also had another ghost on the second floor, in the hall outside his bedroom. This one didn't bother him as much as the one in the cellar, but Jeff felt the upstairs spirit kept looking in on him whenever he left his bedroom door open and this made him feel uncomfortable. So we went to the cellar first. Linda and the young man were in front of me, and as I started down the stairs, I saw this young woman with a kind of grey shawl, a white blouse, she wore a long skirt, and she was carrying a baby in her arms. Suddenly, she tripped on her skirt and the baby fell into a cistern which was at her right. The woman had stayed in the cellar after she died because of the child's death and her feelings of guilt. So Linda and I worked with her, and we told her that it was an accident and there was no need to feel guilty, that the baby had gone on to another dimension, and she could let go of her sorrow and her guilt. Then all of a sudden, Linda started to shake with grief—she cried and cried until there were no more tears. Usually, when the spirit leaves, you just take a deep breath. So ever after that, Jeff never had any problems in the cellar.

Q: And the ghost upstairs in the hall?

Tamaranda: Jeff showed us around, and I saw this wonderful gentleman, kind of thin, and he had on one of those old-fashioned shirts that they wore with a buttoned-on collar—he didn't have the collar on—the man was wearing suspenders, and had a strawhat. He was shaking badly. We asked him why he was there, and he answered that it was the only home he had cared about. He had been a surgeon in a town above San Francisco and had developed Parkinson's disease. No longer able to work, he had come by train to Frankfort to live with his brother for the rest of his life. So we said to the young man: "Would you like to send this gentleman on his way or let him stay a little longer until he feels comfortable about leaving?" Jeff agreed that the man could stay since he now better understood the spirit, and Linda and I told the man not to stand by Jeff's open door because it made him feel uncomfortable. The ghost didn't realize that, and he said he wouldn't.

Q: That was it?

Tamaranda: No. A few months after that, Linda and I were in Hampden, Maine with a circle of friends who got together for meditation and healing. Kenny, who was a strapping young fellow—I don't know his last name—was a really good healer and channeled wonderful energy. He was quite late getting there, and when Kenny arrived he was shaking. We asked: "What's wrong with you?" "I'm sorry I'm late," he told us. "My grandparents weren't doing too well when I stopped by to see them, and my grandfather has Parkinson's disease." One of us said: "You must have picked up some of his energy because you're shaking just like that." "I know," he said, "and I can't stop." "Come into the living room," we told him, "and we'll do a healing on you." So Linda put her hands on him and said a prayer and all of a sudden *she* started shaking—uncontrollable shaking—and she couldn't stop. It was that gentleman spirit from Frankfort—the surgeon—who had come through Linda to work with Kenny. After a few minutes, the young man stopped shaking and so did Linda. The spirit said that Kenny would be all right. The gentleman now was able to leave the house in Frankfort. It was powerful! Powerful! I think sometimes that's why people linger here after they die: they want to be of service to others.

Q: Are there any haunted houses in this vicinity?

Tamaranda: There is a beautiful house here in Stockton Springs called the Hichborn Inn, and the original owner was a shipbuilder who had his hands into everything. Some friends of mine bought the place to open a bed-and-breakfast. Their daughter was given a bedroom on the first floor, but she was restless there—she felt there was some spirit present and a lot of sadness. So her mother asked if I would come and talk to this spirit—tune in and see what it was about. I did, and what I saw was a casket laid out with flowers and people dressed in black funeral attire. The name of the woman in the casket was Harriet Hichborn, one of the shipbuilder's three unmarried daughters. Harriet was a photographer, and the chemicals she used for developing film affected her mind. She also was involved in an unfortunate love affair—I believe the young man hung himself and she had a nervous breakdown and was committed to a mental hospital....I didn't know, at the time, who was the woman in the casket when I went to clear the Hichborn house, but earlier I had been asked to go to Beal College for several weeks to be a resident chaperon and to conduct workshops.

Q: What kind of counseling?

Tamaranda: I do workshops in healing—using color and sound and poetry. Well, when I went there I felt this overwhelming sadness in the building where I resided and didn't know what to make of it. I later learned it was because this building linked with Beal College had been a mental facility for a number of years. All those spirits were clamoring to be released, and among them was Harriet Hichborn. So if you meet spirits in one place, you may encounter them in another until you become aware of their needs.

Q: Have you ever attended any of the UFO abduction meetings held in the Bangor, Maine area?

Tamaranda: No. I have thought of it, but they usually are held in the evening and I don't drive at night.

Q: Have any of your friends or acquaintances been taken aboard a UFO?

Tamaranda: I have a very dear friend who was abducted but she didn't want to talk about it for the longest time. Finally, I got her to let me regress her to the incident, and she hasn't been the same since. She used to be very shy and inhibited, and now she's entirely different with lots of high energy.

Q: You hypnotize people?

Tamaranda: I regress them—yes. To their past lives.

Q: I was going to ask if you believe in reincarnation, and you have answered the question.

Tamaranda: Yes. I do. However I think it can be termed many things. It's multilayered and dependent on your vibrations at a given point in time. It depends on where you are; whether you have a fast vibration or one where you are dragging.

Q: Since you believe we live more than one life, have you had examples to substantiate this when doing mandala readings?

Tamaranda: Let me tell you about a little girl. Her name is Megan Kelly, and her mother and I had been in a community theater in Massachusetts. She and her husband moved away overseas, and I later connected with them accidentally in Florida. Meanwhile, they had had this little girl, and she was a delight. I did a reading for her parents, and of course she wanted to do this herself. Here is this bright child, and she told me that she had lived a lifetime on another planet. I said to her: "Megan, do you remember what your name was when you were there?" And she replied: "Oh, I didn't have a name; I had a number. I'll write it down for you so you won't forget." She took a piece of paper and wrote 6361. I almost went right up the sky because when I was in California I had heard that number given to me several times—6361. It was almost as if I was being told that I was going to connect with this little girl.

Q: Your readings must give you the opportunity of meeting unusual people.

Tamaranda: I met the most wonderful man that I did a mandala reading for in Orange, New Jersey. He had taken on a big challenge in this life. Number one, he was black; number two, he wanted to be a doctor—that's quite a bit; and number three, he had such a gifted voice that he was involved with a community group that put on some operas that were very professional. So he had all these challenges, and he was handling them beautifully, but so many people who are gifted are unsure. What I like to do more than anything is to mirror to them the wonders and beauty that is in them. Then they go away with a lighter heart—so many gifted people are put down.

Q: Have you ever had an out-of-body experience?

Tamaranda: Yes, all the time! (The tape recorder registers laughter.) A very vivid one was when I was recovering from an automobile accident. I was in bed sitting up and talking with someone who was in the room with me. All of a sudden, I began to feel myself becoming large, like a balloon swelling up, and I found myself becoming weightless—it's very difficult to explain. I went through the walls and the roof of the house, and I felt myself not only staying up there but moving out, out, out of Maine, and across the ocean. I traveled through several countries and observed what was going on. Then I came back to my body in the bed and resumed talking with the person who was in the room with me.

Q: Before this interview, you mentioned a near-death experience.

Tamaranda: When I had surgery in 1974. I was up there on the ceiling and looking down at them working on me.

Q: Did you experience going through a tunnel and being subjected to a bright light?

Tamaranda: Yes, I did. And there was such an overwhelming awareness of love that I wanted to stay. You just feel there is nothing more that you need—so there is no reason to return.

Q: Did someone tell you that you had to go back; that it wasn't your time yet?

Tamaranda: My grandmother told me that I had more to do.

Q: You saw her?

Tamaranda: Yes. And after I came back, that's when I began the work I have been doing for the last number of years.

Q: I'm told that lifestyles and outlooks frequently change after near-death experiences.

Tamaranda: That's right. I went from being a community person—you know, the Camp Fire girl mother, Boy Scout mother, League of Women's Voters—to being more connected with the universe. It was then I started teaching classes to help people grow in consciousness and to become more aware of their spiritual gifts and how important it is to see the wonders; to realize that if you do something unkind to one person, you are doing it to yourself.

Q: No regrets in the direction your life has taken?

Tamaranda: I remember going to a community theater in another city, and afterwards there was a big cast party. Many of my friends were there and I looked at them and thought: Well, they are nice people and I know them but we really don't connect anymore. I was more like an observer— there were many changes going on in my life. I remember my oldest daughter, Frieda, said to me one day: "Would you please tell me where my mother is?" And I replied: "What are you talking about?" She said: "Well, I know that you are not my mother. Where is my mother?" I said: "Maybe we could say that I am another aspect of her. I went and gathered some more of my stuff and came back in again." I think that is what we do.

AT A TABLE-TIPPING SÉANCE

(A sheet on what to expect at a table-tipping séance was shared with Stella and me upon our arrival at the Spiritualist camp. We were informed that such gatherings usually took place in darkness or in a room lit by a dim red light. Some phenomena were luminous and could only be distinguished in the dark, and subdued lighting offered less distraction. The procedure was to form a circle with five or six people placing their hands very lightly on a table. A prayer asking for the highest and best vibrations was recommended, and one could call out the names of people in the spirit world. "A throbbing sensation is felt pulsing through the table," the sheet informed us, and went on to explain that the wooden surface of the furnishing acted as a reservoir of externalized nervous energy. "The table may jerk, tilt, and move about, you may hear raps, footsteps or things moving, ectoplasm may form, and the table may become entirely levitated."

We are still shaking our heads in amazement when recalling that evening of table tipping. There were nineteen people attending in a twenty- by twenty-foot room—six of them males—and we all gathered in a circle as the lights were dimmed. A round table, about three feet in diameter, rather heavy with four circled legs, was selected—it looked ordinary to me as I stared at it in the half-light.

The Spiritualist minister conducting the séance, a lady from Florida, explained that our questions for the spirit world must be phrased to accommodate yes and no answers—one tip of the table would be a yes and two tips would be a no. Five people at a time, and the pastor who served as group leader, sat in chairs with palms lightly placed on the table's surface.

Probably the dim lighting made me more susceptible, yet while I accepted what I saw happening, part of me resisted. When I later discussed this confusion with Stella, she recalled a comment made by Jules Peters, an acquaintance in Holland, who had attended a séance. "I saw a grand piano fly through a small window," Peters told her, "and I said so what! I still don't believe it."

When the table tipped its first yes and no answers, I was asking myself: How does she do it? The muscles along the minister's bare arms aren't flexing; she's not pressing her hands firmly on the surface; the table sometimes tips away from her; and standing back, I could see that her knees didn't touch the underside. I also carefully observed the five with the pastor and soon was convinced that she had no accomplice.

The questions asked were often banal and some downright tedious. One young man kept asking his grandmother in the spirit world if he should buy a particular model of a Toyota automobile or a Swedish import. The table trembled in confusion—no clear yes or no. It was obvious that the departed old lady didn't know or care a damn about the different makes of vehicles.

A woman who was obviously devastated over a departed loved one—some young man who had either killed or hideously injured another person before passing on—kept asking questions that got negative responses; one could tell that she was praying for some positive reply. If the group leader were prone to fakery, I told myself, this poor suffering woman would have been given better news.

The table rocked violently at times, tipping and tilting its way all over the room. Looking back, I am gripped by a feeling of unreality. Once the table fell over and had to be stood upright. When my turn came to join the circle, I could feel a vibration as the wood came alive under my bare hands. I do recall the pastor saying to me: "You are very spiritual."

What Stella and I couldn't understand was the lack of interest most of those present displayed for the departed ones on the other side. No participant worriedly asked: Are you happy Aunt Mabel? Are things better for you, Grandpa Mosher? The living were more concerned with their own time and position; too many seemed mired in details that cluttered their lives.

At the end of the séance we all stood in a knot talking, away from the table. While no one was looking, Stella carefully inspected that once hyperactive arrangement of wood and varnish. Innocently motionless in the half-light, it was again just a piece of furniture—used only moments earlier as a conduit for God knows what had transpired among us and beyond.

Stella, a firm believer in more lives than one, and I clearly leaning that way, were interested in a workshop on past-life regression led by the same person who had conducted the table tipping. Before we left that night, reservations were made to join the group two weeks later. Maybe under hypnosis we could learn more of who we once were before all this happened.)

BUCK'S GRAVESTONE

Jonathan Buck's gravestone can be seen on the left as one travels north on Route 1 in Maine. It is located behind a locked gate on a slight rise, across the road from a shopping mall in the center of Bucksport. The memorial has a clear, smooth surface, and one can tell by the quality of the monument and cut that this marker must have been selected with care by the deceased's family. It is an appropriate tribute to a regional Revolutionary War hero and founder of the mid-coast community that carries his name.

Buck's role as first citizen of Bucksport and valiant soldier isn't what draws people to the stone—it is the flaw below the chiseled lettering of his name: a dark discoloration two feet long and six inches at the widest point in the unmistakable shape of a woman's leg from the knee down. Had the leg been more masculine and the lines coarser, the tales about its mysterious appearance might be fewer and briefer. Some residents are casual when asked to explain the phenomenon: "It's just a witch's curse," they tell one, something that "came over the stone years and years ago."

Jonathan Buck was born in Woburn, Massachusetts on February 20, 1719 and grew up in Haverhill. He married Lydia Morse in 1742 and the couple had nine children, six of whom survived childhood. Buck became successful as a merchant and shipbuilder, and in 1762 he joined a group of settlers who had petitioned the Massachusetts Court for land in the area of the Penobscot River. This territory in Maine had been taken from the French and declared open for settlement by the British. Six parcels were surveyed which led to the construction of Plantation No. 1 two years later. A fort was built in what is now Stockton Springs, near Bucksport; Fort Pownall it was called, after a governor of Massachusetts, and Buck would become its last Colonial commander.

When the colonists severed all ties with the British and hostilities began, Buck was commissioned colonel in the Fifth Militia of Lincoln County and Justice of the Peace. He participated in the disastrous siege of Fort George, and in 1779, when refusing to swear loyalty to England, was forced to flee Maine. The colonel was a man who possessed an indomitable spirit: he walked the entire 200 miles from Plantation No. 1 (Bucksport) to Haverhill—an extraordinary feat for a person suffering from gout.

Jonathan Buck's grandson, Rufus, described his grandfather as being "thin...with an expressive face, Roman nose, black arching eyebrows, and dark, penetrating eyes." This was an individual who had convictions and "an iron will, not easily changed."

After the revolution, the colonel and his sons rebuilt Plantation No. 1—the settlement had been destroyed by the British—and in 1792 it was renamed in his honor. Jonathan Buck lived to the age of 76 and died on March 18, 1795. Decades later, in 1852, his grandchildren set a larger marker on his grave, a stone that would weather into a legend.

There are several versions of the way this image of a leg came to disfigure the gravestone, but one common theme can be found in every telling: it is a curse, the condemnation of an innocent victim. The first rendition was published in the March 22, 1899 issue of the *Haverhill Gazette*. Buck, the article claimed, was a Puritan who loathed witchcraft, and when a woman was brought before him accused of practicing the dark rituals, he sentenced her to be executed. "Just as the hangman was about to perform his gruesome duty," offered the *Gazette*, "the woman turned to Colonel Buck and raising one hand to heaven as if to direct her last words on earth, pronounced this astounding prophecy:

> "Jonathan Buck, listen to these words, the last my tongue shall utter. In the spirit of the only true and living God I speak to you. You will soon die. Over your grave they will erect a stone that all may know where the bones of the mighty Jonathan Buck are crumbling to dust. But listen, all ye people and may your descendants ever know the truth. Upon that stone will appear the imprint of my foot, and for all time long after your accursed race has perished from the earth the people will come from afar

to view the fulfillment and will say: 'There lies the man who murdered a woman.' Remember her well Jonathan Buck. Remember well!"

Another version is introduced by Oscar Morrill Heath in his *Composts of Tradition: A Book of Short Stories Dealing with Traditional Sex and Domestic Situations*. What he renders may be too coarse for some straitlaced readers. Heath writes that the doomed woman has a deformed son who was fathered by Buck. Though at the time of her execution the colonel had impregnated her again, he is not deterred by sentiment—in his role of Justice of the Peace he condemns her for witchcraft. The woman is tied to the door of her house and she is set on fire. The son rips off one of his mother's burning legs and uses it to cripple his father with telling blows. The leg becomes a gruesome souvenir, and when the colonel dies, and this dismembered part is held to his corpse, he rises from his casket to confess all. The concluding moments of the yarn find Buck returning to the coffin and saying to his deformed offspring: "Close the lid, boy."

A further twisting of the leg and foot legend is offered by A. Hyatt Verrill in the 1930s. Now the tale centers on a "half-witted" man who is brought before the puritanical Justice of the Peace. The poor simpleton, accused of murdering a woman and stealing one of her legs, is quickly sentenced to death and vengeance follows its predictable path.

Maine poet Robert P. Tristram Coffin's romanticized account, "The Foot of Tucksport" (with a T instead of a B), introduces Ann Harraway, a paramour of Jethro Tuck, who bears a son by him out of wedlock. The bastard is a nightmarish-looking creature who lives with his mother on the outskirts of town at the edge of a wood—Coffin's story line may have been influenced by *Beowulf's* Grendel and his witch-parent. Despite his features, Tuck's illegitimate son has the same color of hair and handsome brow as the father. Jethro tries to bribe Ann into leaving town but she refuses. This is too much of a risk for a man of his stature; the woman is brought before the local church magistrate and Tuck. Ann is sentenced to be burned, and as the flames engulf her, the son suddenly appears, pulls one of the cooked legs from her body, and runs into the woods never to be seen again. The image of the leg, which "no scrubbing could erase," wrote Coffin, appears on Tuck's stone shortly after the burial.

There have been many attempts to prove or disparage the stories of the gravestone curse. Did anyone have justifiable reason to disfigure a prominent man's memorial with such an image? Researchers point out that there is no record of a person being executed by burning in Maine, and the New England witch trials occurred more than 25 years before Jonathan Buck's birth. As a Justice of the Peace, the colonel had no authority to sentence a person to death, and as to his veracity and character—he was respected and admired by townspeople and the soldiers who served under his command. At the library in Bucksport are several letters addressed in Buck's cramped handwriting to his wife Lydia, all confirming his everlasting affection.

There are residents in Bucksport who believe that the monument was replaced once and the leg returned in the same location on the new marker. Others insist that this never happened and the foot can be explained: it is a knot, an imperfection within the stone, an inclusion on the surface. "Oh yeah," said a man mowing the cemetery grass. "Then how come the stonemasons didn't notice all this when they cut that slab?"

Did Buck have a relationship with this woman who threatened to ruin his reputation? Coffin dramatizes this in his "Tucksport" poem when he drops reference to the "Red Whore of Babylon." If there were such rumors adrift at the time, the Buck family would have displayed indignation publicly. On file at the Bucksport Library is an undated piece on local legends by Ester E. Wood. The composition has this observation: "Kenneth Roberts wrote, 'Local tradition spits on truth and tramples the gown of common sense.' It could well be said, 'Local tradition feeds upon lies and flies far and fast on wings of nonsense.' "

More than a century of scrubbing has passed and still the image of a leg on this memorial remains and will be there for the unborn to see. This is a special kind of blessing, not really a curse at all; it is a mystery that enlarges our vision of the wonders around us, not something that can be cornered and diminished by gossip, fiction or science.

UFOs

UFO investigations have prompted more laughter than serious attention in the past, and traditionally scholars and scientists have greeted the hypothesis of visitors from other worlds or dimensions with scorn. There was a time when magazines with garish covers at local supermarkets did much to undermine the credibility of authenticated sightings. But a 1987 Gallop poll revealed a change in public reaction; an increasing number of Americans believe that UFOs are real, and the more educated one is the more inclined one will be to believe such things exist. Nearly nineteen million people in this country alone claim they have seen lights and objects in the sky that they could not explain.

Why then the shift in thinking? Most likely because in the past twenty or thirty years (gradually at first) media coverage has broadened. The chuckle has been take out of reporting and a more open-minded attitude prevails. Such respected newspapers as *The Washington Post* and *The New York Times* are no longer hostile—both have published in-depth articles on the subject. Television also has thoughtfully explored UFO issues in such programs as *Nightline* and *20/20*. Philanthropist Laurance Rockefeller has advanced credibility by donating substantial grants to several UFO and alien-phenomena researchers and financing a 169-page document detailing "the best available evidence" on UFOs. This report was prepared as a briefing for heads of state and other influential world figures in an attempt to quickly diffuse the atmosphere of secrecy that arises whenever there is an incident or sighting. Rockefeller also urged President Clinton and national science advisor John Gibbons to publicly acknowledge the existence of alien presences in the skies.

An ambiguity exists in the UFO phenomenon, in the sense that sightings never seem to get out of control; like a thermostat the temperature is kept within certain limits. Sometimes the skies appear crowded with objects, but before the general public becomes aware of this increased activity, the numbers diminish.

Aberrations are more common occurrences than hoaxes, and some sightings may be due to hallucination or misinterpretation. Photographs are useless as proof: it's easy to fling a metal-tinted Frisbee in the air and click the camera; yet some photographs are too convincing to be labeled frauds. How often hoaxing occurs is impossible to determine, but probably less often than the debunkers of UFOs would like to believe.

There have been countless reports of UFOs seen by pilots. As witnesses, they are clearly more competent than the average person—aviators are totally familiar with their terrain of clouds and vistas and they are not easily excited. Pilots also are unlikely to be hoaxers, particularly if they work for an airline. Undoubtedly many of these encounters go unreported when the pilot is alone in a plane and there are no other aircraft in the general area.

Most sightings of UFOs suggest that they have solidity, leave burn marks and other physical traces when landing, and seem solid when observers are able to get close enough to touch them. There are reports, however, of glass-like and translucent objects capable of changing shape in mid-flight, and sometimes disappearing instantly. Such exploits lead some viewers to identify them as "time machines" or apparitions from another dimension.

There are reports from witnesses who have been close enough to touch UFOs. The most publicized encounter, featured in the April 1954 issue of the *Flying Saucer Review*, occurred in France. Two men were cutting logs when they heard a loud noise and saw three cigar-shaped objects coming towards them. Two passed overhead, but the third hovered in the clearing where the two men stood. The craft had a smooth metallic exterior and was estimated to be 600 feet in length. One woodsman fled, but the other walked up to the ship and placed his hand on the smooth surface which felt cold. Then, to see what would happen, the forester foolishly raised his axe and hit the gleaming metallic surface with all his strength. Immediately, a mysterious force hurled the attacker twenty feet back and he lay on the ground totally paralyzed for several minutes. When he staggered to his feet, badly shaken but uninjured, the UFO rose from the clearing and disappeared.

Scientists point out that they have little to work with in their attempts to prove the existence of UFOs. The above adventure could be a complete fabrication, or the two woodsmen may have been hallucinating. Ufologists, however, are convinced that American authorities have kept under wraps one or more crashed UFOs for decades, and there has been an ongoing campaign to prove this assertion. Until the mystery is solved, the general public and untold thousands who have seen objects at close range or in the skies must wait. When solid evidence cannot be provided to substantiate incredible claims, an encounter has no scientific value— that resounding blow of an axe on the skin of an alien craft must remain in the province of storytelling.

There are nearly a hundred agencies worldwide which are active in alerting a curious public. The largest is MUFON (Mutual UFO Network), an international organization whose members are interested in studying and researching the phenomenon. This network sponsors and conducts conferences, trains field investigators, and publishes reports of unidentified flying objects.

At the time of this writing, Maine ranks 13th in the nation for the number of sightings—New Hampshire 6th in frequency, Vermont 14th, Massachusetts 21st, Connecticut 29th, and Rhode Island 50th. When reminded of these numbers, Leland Bechtel, State Director of the Mutual UFO Network, responded that Maine might well be first if his organization had more trained investigators. One possible reason that fewer sightings are reported in the lower three New England states than the upper three could be city lighting coupled with industrial haze. Cool, crisp evenings out in the country with limited smog give sky watchers a better chance of seeing a UFO.

Credibility of the person who reports seeing a streaking light or an unusual craft in the sky is established by trained investigators. This is followed by painstaking research. Were there any natural causes, such as a comet or optical illusion that confused the observer? A warm mass of air, light bouncing off a car windshield, perhaps a Stealth plane flying low—these are among the frequently misidentified occurrences.

The Mutual UFO Network in Maine assembled a chronology of sightings around the state, and the first recorded viewing occurred in 1812. A Camden woman wrote in her diary that she saw an unusual light in the sky that couldn't be identified. This report also noted a frequency pattern of lights and objects seen in such locations as Mount Desert Island, the town of Franklin, Blue Hill peninsula, and Rangeley. Balls of light have been observed in various forms and colors throughout Maine. They often have been associated with thundershowers and minor earth tremors. Another manifestation is meteoric lights which sometimes evince aurora-like discharges. Some of these displays can be larger than beach balls—either opaque or translucent—and remain stationary, float slowly across the sky, or suddenly plunge to the ground. Under certain daylight conditions they can appear metallic. To further complicate sightings, and often used as an explanatory tool by dubious officials to pooh-pooh the allegations of a concerned witness, there are such easy props at hand as water towers, electrical installations, and fault lines.

Many of the sightings from Kittery to Fort Kent go unexplained, and the bewildered sheriff or airport worker who answers the telephone is not always qualified or equipped to solve the mystery. A policeman can conduct an on-site inspection—this is usually done long after the incident—and an airport control tower can pinpoint by radar all aircraft operating in the area.

For UFO investigators, one of the difficulties in achieving accuracy is the general public's reaction to a sighting. A person who sees something unusual in the sky is eager to share the experience but soon learns that it is wiser to say nothing. Leland Bechtel estimates that nearly 90 percent of all sightings go unreported and too often participants regret having made such disclosures. A typical example is the story of a deputy sheriff and his wife from the Farmington area who had an encounter with a mysterious light in the nearby town of Industry, Maine and later regretted reporting the incident when their experience was fully publicized by the press.

It was night and the two were returning home after having dined out. At the bottom of a long hill, they were stopped by several men in a car coming from the opposite direction. "Don't go up there," they were told. "You're not going to like what you see." Why should a light in the sky discourage him from going on? thought the deputy as the men drove off. Besides, they would have to detour an additional 10 miles to reach home. Up the hill they went, and as the couple neared the top a bright light came out of the sky and faced them. They stopped and it stopped. When they started the brilliant object drew nearer. After the third attempt to get through, a troubled sheriff told his wife: "I've got to turn back—I can't see!" Later that night, in the same hilly area, a woman died when her car went off the road and sideswiped a tree. The smashed instrument panel indicated that she was traveling 93 miles an hour at the moment of impact. It was 10 o'clock, totally dark, and the victim was wearing sunglasses.

When the man at the local Agway store laughingly asks Bechtel if he has seen any flying saucers lately, the state director for the UFO network isn't offended. "I just laugh along with them. We don't have any explanation for these flying objects, and people are very helpful when they report things to me."

Bechtel's background would surprise many a scoffer—UFO investigators are sometimes looked upon with derision, particularly by those who are convinced that an alien presence in the sky is hysterical nonsense. A graduate of Eastern Baptist Theological Seminary in Philadelphia, he assisted two pastors and had his own church in Camden, New Jersey before deciding to become a teacher. Bechtel taught psychology at Bates College for 33 years. Now retired, he spends much of his time investigating sightings around the state. He has never seen a UFO and is envious of those who have—which includes his son who was totally skeptical of their existence before an incident. "I believe he can't talk about it without biting his nails. I'm dying to see one," Bechtel added, "and I keep a camera in my car, just in case—I scan the skies daily."

A listing of all the UFO sightings in Maine since the mid 1940s would take up a large portion of this book. People from all walks of life have seen lights and mysterious objects in the skies, but many have not reported their experiences to authorities for fear of being ridiculed. Lois Palches, the wife of a highly-respected minister, felt obligated to alert police when she and her husband watched a huge disk-shaped craft hovering near their home. The desk sergeant who answered the telephone

was quick to give advice: "Lady," he said, "I think you and your husband had better stop drinking!" A young and agitated couple, who had a
close encounter with a UFO, was told by police in the Augusta area "not
to make a fuss" and "to forget all about it."

There is diversity in the incidents reported over the years—enough to
suggest that several kinds of craft are being seen. Are these UFOs operated by aliens from other planets, could they be visitors from a different dimension right here on earth, or are they machines controlled by
our great-great-great-grandchildren's children? It is anyone's guess.
Perhaps there is validity in the assumptions that we are seeing advanced
military aircraft, polar reflections, marsh gas, and yes, there is a possible explanation that we are in the grips of mass hysteria. Sightings and
circumstances vary, though there are often familiar patterns within the
frameworks of these incidents. The following listing attempts to give an
appreciation of the variable range.

In March of 1945, near Belfast, Maine, a man out hunting saw a cigar-shaped object flying very slowly and at a low altitude. It seemed to
crash into some trees at the edge of a clearing, but the enormous ship
was undamaged and soon rose from the ground. There was a humming
sound as it started to spin. A shower of "fine silvery threads" was released as it climbed straight up and "disappeared in seconds."

A silver, disk-shaped UFO flying at 23,000 feet was spotted by a crew
in an F94 jet over Millinocket in 1953. A chase ensued but the crew of
the jet soon gave up. Two pilots from a different squadron also saw the
object, and one of the flyers was heard by ground control to say, "I'll
never admit I saw the thing."

Ralph Berg of Corinna, Maine recalled a night in 1953 when he and a
friend were sitting in a canoe on remote Big Houston Pond, above
Brownsville Junction. The two boys, barely in their teens, watched as a
full moon streaked rivulets of silver on the water. Then they noticed
another moon, three quarters of it showing over a distant ridge of trees.

"Finally, we got a little smart," declared Berg—they decided that this
moon "slightly orange in color and brighter" was something else. "But
the second we looked at it and said, 'that isn't the moon,' it went out,
just as if it were listening to us. Then it appeared again, about three miles
away."

The object made no sound, and before the two could get a better look,
the light went out and three seconds later they saw it again, but fifteen
miles in the distance. Then another disappearing blink and seconds later
it was seen mingling with the stars before vanishing entirely.

"We didn't report it," said Berg. "If we had, probably we would have been put in a cage."

Astronomer John Cole of South Brooksville, Maine observed ten very light objects, with two dark forms to their left; they moved like a swarm of bees to the northwest near Harborside. A loud roar was heard as they quickly passed. Jets? Nobody confirmed it. This was in July of 1947, a time when such air technology was in infancy.

It was an August night in 1954 and stars were crowding the midnight sky as Glennis Gardner sat on the sunporch of the couple's Augusta, Maine home. Her husband, Glazer, had just gone to bed, and as she looked out the window she suddenly noticed a white light in the distance—it stood out among the stars and seemed to be coming directly toward her. Glennis called her husband and together they stared at the object in disbelief.

"It was as big as a house," she told a reporter for the *Central Maine Sentinel.* "We didn't know enough to be scared. It was shaped like a traditional wedding cake with three tiers. It had tall white lights—there were lots of lights—shaped like long, florescent bulbs coming from the bottom tier up to the top."

The Gardners went outside to get a better look at the craft as it passed over the rooftop of a house across the street, barely missing a TV antenna.

"There weren't any lights in the middle," Mrs. Gardner remembered. "At the very top was a rounded, closed-in space. Its lights were yellowish-orangey, and the whole thing seemed transparent. There seemed to be shiny instruments inside the thing. We watched it for about five minutes as it spun counterclockwise, very slowly, without a sound." Then, before their eyes, the object disappeared—*vanished.*

"My husband wouldn't let me call anyone," said Glennis Gardner. "He said people would think we were crazy. About five years later, we started hearing about these things, and then we talked about it."

Also in 1954, near Pittsfield, Mr. and Mrs. F. E. Robinson watched for more than four minutes a silver object with a dome and flashing light. The craft made a sound "like a swarm of bees" as it hovered and tilted, then flew horizontally and rose without tilting.

"I was never so scared in my life, and my heart was in my mouth," said Sharon Hurd of Freedom, Maine. The date was October 30, 1973.

Sharon, 23, and her husband, David, were watching a moving light in the sky, which was not on the usual travel course for air traffic. Suddenly, the blinking light changed directions and slowly descended toward them. Within 100 yards from their home, the object became a huge "ball of fire" while it hovered in a spinning motion. An upper and lower row of "lighted windows" were seen, and there was a "central rim-type structure" which didn't appear to revolve as a shaft of light flooded the ground below.

The couple opened a window and heard a "woo-woo-woo" kind of humming, similar to a child's top. Then this noise rose to a scream, and the ball departed so rapidly that the Hurds were unable to tell its direction of flight or locate it in the sky among the stars.

Unidentified craft have been seen over a number of Strategic Air Command bases, particularly during late October and November 1975, including Loring Air Force Base in northeastern Maine. "Strange sightings" were reported in the Rendlesham Forest of England, an area located between two sensitive military installations. In Russia, where the press was usually muzzled, several newspapers featured a July 28, 1989 incident when a UFO was hovering for nearly two hours over a missile base. The KGB file on this episode detailed testimony from seven military witnesses and there were drawings of the craft.

In 1975, Loring Air Force Base was part of the Strategic Air Command with a storage site for nuclear weapons. A number of small huts covered with earth for camouflage had been constructed, and this highly sensitive depot was fenced and patrolled night and day by a military police squadron.

At 7:45 p.m. on the 27th of October, patrol guards saw an unidentified aircraft approaching the facility at a low altitude of about 300 feet. The object was viewed on radar, and several attempts by radio, both civilian and military, were made to communicate with the invaders entering the perimeter of Loring. There was no response as the craft circled within 300 yards of the restricted area. The base immediately was placed on a security alert and the air commander requested assistance from Hancock Field, New York and North Bay, Ontario, Canada. For some unexplained reason, both bases refused to send air support, and finally the Maine State Police and local airport flight services were enlisted in an attempt to identify the craft. For more than forty minutes the UFO circled before heading for Grand Falls, New Brunswick where it disappeared from the radar screen.

The next night, again at 7:45 p.m., the visitor returned. This time it began to circle three miles from the restricted area. A flashing white light and an amber or orange light were spotted by ground crews. Several observers saw "an orange and red object shaped like a stretched-out football hovering in midair." Suddenly the craft turned off its lights and hovered about 150 feet over the end of a runway. It was described as "about four car-lengths long, solid, reddish-orange, with no doors or windows, and with no visible propellers or engines. It was totally silent." By now Loring was on full alert, but a sweep made by security failed to gather helpful information. One moment visible and then gone from sight, the craft was again picked up by radar as it streaked away in the direction of Grand Falls.

The activity of the previous two nights was now troubling the military brass in headquarters of both countries. Permission was granted for an American National Guard helicopter to cross the international border and a Canadian Mounted Police officer was sent to Loring to accompany the pilot as an observer. The UFO appeared on schedule that evening, and the helicopter, a Huey, took off to give chase. However, the pilot, Canadian Mountie, and several Loring security officers aboard could see nothing from the air, even when they were as close as 100 yards from where ground observers perceived the craft. They were chasing a phantom ship; nothing was being detected on radar.

The following night several lights and objects were again seen over and near Loring—this time the prowlers were viewed by radar. During the remainder of 1975, unidentified craft were seen on numerous occasions in the skies between the air base and New Brunswick. But for security reasons or to silence those who voiced concern that a nuclear dump was under surveillance, U.S. and Canadian agencies became cautious and edgy when questioned by reporters. No more reports of lights and reddish-orange invaders hovering over runways were made public.

Shalel Way, a Skowhegan psychic, tells of three UFO sightings. Way was headlined in newspapers around the world in 1984 after she did a Tarot reading for Barbara Walker whose former husband, John, was serving as a communications specialist in the U.S. Navy. The reading revealed Russian espionage activities, and Way convinced Mrs. Walker that it was both a moral and patriotic duty to report her ex-husband's involvement to authorities.

"I first saw a UFO outside my bedroom window in 1967, at the age of 12," recalled the psychic. There was unhappiness in the home and the young girl found comfort in looking at the stars and meditating. "I saw this orange orb and received a message that I would have a role in world peace." An "elongated face" in the sky communicated telepathically, and Way learned that she was psychically gifted. "It told me that I was being protected for a role bigger than just my personal life." Later, when she revealed to her mother that a presence in the sky had spoken, the child was rushed to a doctor and medications were prescribed. In the fall of 1975, Way saw a circular orange disk hovering over Wesserunsett Stream, in Cornville, Maine, and in 1977 she saw a similar craft in the same location. Both objects appeared to be metal and had the dimensions of an average-sized room. "Between these two sightings," said Way, "I got inspired for a book involving a study of the Old Testament—that the 12 tribes of Israel are psychological/psychic character typings." She is convinced that UFOs are spacecraft from another star system, and the entities operating them are trying to save humanity. "They are intent on the preservation of the species," declared Way. "That's why they're being sighted so frequently now."

Robert, a college student, and his friend, Carol, left her home in rural Detroit, Maine for a dinner engagement in Pittsfield. The couple had traveled only a mile when they began their two-minute encounter with a UFO. It was 9:05 p.m. on July 15, 1984 when they first saw the light—estimated to be twice the brightness of the North Star—directly above the road in front of them.

Suddenly, the light made a perfect vertical dive, and Carol, who was driving, stopped the car and began backing up. Both saw the object parallel them moments later at a low altitude of 150 feet. The glow had subsided to a gray color with red and white lights, a craft that was immense in size, larger than a 747 airplane, and it made no noise when streaking past them.

Carol stopped the car and Robert opened his door to look back. To his astonishment, the object had also stopped; it hovered momentarily and then began slowly moving toward them. Worried, and feeling that perhaps it would be safer, Carol backed into the driveway of a nearby farmhouse and both got out.

A cat-and-mouse game was underway: when they stopped, it stopped; when they moved, it moved. Robert remembered having the feeling that they were being "contained." The object was now almost directly above them and slightly to the left side of the car at an altitude of no more than 100 feet. The thing was triangular in shape with a red light at each corner and there was one very bright white light. They were unable to see what the top looked like, but there was a dome under the craft.

A car was seen coming down the road, and Carol asked Robert whether they should stop it to get help. He advised her not to as the object now was moving away from them. It traveled about 200 feet and then vanished, not into the distance, but "before our very eyes."

A control tower employee at the Bangor Airport said that two 747 planes were in the area at the time of sighting but both were flying at 6,000 feet. Robert and Carol did not see or hear them.

The following day, Robert's mother telephoned the family residing in the farmhouse to learn more about the incident. They had been alarmed "by all the commotion" outside their home and with "people running up and down their driveway." They did look out the window but not up at the sky.

A well-known, highly-respected Maine attorney and two companions had an unexpected adventure when driving on Route 142 between the towns of Phillips and Weld. The three women were returning home from a fishing trip when they saw a beam of light "which looked at first as though somebody was opening up a new car dealership in a big field." Initially, they concluded the source of light was from the ground "going upwards," but when the beam began to move they realized it "was coming from an object a great distance away in the sky." All three had the distinct impression that some craft was engaged in a search.

"After a few minutes," recalled the attorney in a report sent to this writer "the light lifted up away from us, but we could still see it between the silhouette of Mt. Blue (located in Weld) and ourselves." The beam seemed to be coming from some nearly stationary object in the sky as it shifted back and forth only slightly before disappearing into the "clear crisp late autumn evening."

One of the women in the group had had a similar sighting the year before at her lakeside cottage. She awoke in the middle of the night to witness a beam of light originating from the sky and ending on her wharf. As the woman watched, she saw "the outline of a being inside the beam. The object was not scary, but rather pacific." The first explanation that came to mind was that "the beam and its authors were looking for water." After several minutes of glowing the ray disappeared. This dockside viewing was never reported to the police or UFO authorities.

The July 27, 1989 issue of the *Bar Harbor Times*, along with other coastal newspapers, reported a UFO sighting by two experienced pilots over Blue Hill Bay. Randy Rhodes, a dispatcher with the Ellsworth Police Department, was flying with Somesville, Maine lawyer Bill Reiff in Reiff's Beechcraft Bonanza V35—they were on their way to attend a sailing regatta in Boothbay Harbor.

It was 3:45 p.m. with no clouds in the sky and at an altitude of 4,500 feet when passenger Rhodes turned and discovered a small plane behind them. He watched it for several moments and then sensed that there was something else in the area. As Reiff banked the aircraft on a ten-degree turn at a slight climb, Rhodes saw to his left what appeared to be an oval-shaped object with distinct edges. In the sunlight, it cast an aluminum shine and was about 25 miles away at an altitude of 10,000 feet. Since there was no vapor trail, Rhodes wondered if what he was seeing was a reflection on the window from some boat in the water.

"On the intercom system," recalled Rhodes, "I asked Bill to look out the window without saying why. He looked and said: 'What is it?' " This was no smudge or reflection on glass. As the two gazed, the object bolted down to their altitude and stopped in midair.

"I've got 4,500 hours flying time as a commercial pilot," Randy Rhodes later told reporters, "and I've never seen anything like this during the day."

Suddenly, the motionless UFO streaked around them to an 11-o'clock position, and it again hovered as if waiting. As they watched, the object's aluminum shine took on what Rhodes described as a rose or pinkish color.

"It was not shaped like any plane I've seen," Reiff remembered, "and it was not generating light but seemed to be reflecting light—a thing that was first silver in color and later gleaming red. Shaped like a disc, it was, and in my 300 hours of flying time I can definitely say it was bigger than anything I've ever seen in the air."

After several troublesome moments of feeling threatened, the two men saw the huge craft, nearly dead ahead at twenty miles, break away in an unbelievable burst of speed; a glowing object that disappeared as it was swallowed in a gulp of sky. The entire encounter had lasted no more than two and a half minutes.

The size of the object was intimidating, and they feared that the craft could be waiting downrange playing a cat-and-mouse game. "What do you want to do?" Reiff asked Rhodes. But already the decision had been made. They would turn back; they had lost all enthusiasm for attending a sailing regatta.

Rhodes remembered an instrument glitch when he discussed the sighting with reporters. The ADF (aerial direction finder) was operational at the time of the encounter but the DME (distance measuring equipment) wasn't receiving. Never before had this device been a problem within 60 to 80 miles of an airport.

There was another equipment breakdown after the two pilots landed at the Bar Harbor-Trenton Field: the radio in Reiff's automobile was dead and several minutes went by before they had sound. A power surge, the announcer apologized to his listening audience—some careless resident had severed a light line when cutting trees.

Air traffic control in Bangor informed Reiff that the only visible objects on the radar screen at the time of sighting were his Beechcraft and the small plane behind them. There were no flights coming in from Europe and no military aircraft in the area.

One detail from the sighting was quickly dismissed by a hydroelectric company spokesman as a cause for the outage; this was when Rhodes observed that the UFO was moving in an on-line direction of the nuclear power plant in Wiscasset, Maine.

A schoolteacher from Belfast saw an unusual UFO in nearby Swansville; an object which she described as being round, about 30 feet in diameter, and with a triangular-shaped system of railings underneath. At one end of the triangle there were two very bright white lights, a single white light at another end, and a yellow-white light at the last point of the railing.

The woman had just entered her sister's driveway when she saw the UFO. She stopped her car, turned off the motor, and waited as the thing approached; it moved silently and steadily at an altitude of no more than 150 feet—"like a boat plowing through water." The object drifted directly overhead with its two bright lights shining down at her, and from the side and rear windows of the car she watched until it disappeared.

A week before this sighting, the woman's sister had heard a faint humming sound as a bright light from overhead illuminated the yard, and the night after the driveway incident, the teacher's husband saw a huge light shining in the distant sky.

Another Swansville resident, a man in his seventies, confirmed the teacher's sighting. Not to be outdone, he declared: "I see stuff all the time but I never tell anyone."

"Yeah," his girlfriend replied sarcastically, "I suppose little green men will jump out at you."

"That's why I never tell anyone," he retorted.

Sightings along the blueberry fields east of Cherryfield, in the vicinity of what is known as the Great Heath, have been reported by several local residents. When a man and his wife were asked by two UFO investigators whether they sensed any ridicule after having made public such an encounter with a strange craft, the couple hesitated only briefly. Though there may have been some incredulity, most people greeted their tale with good humor "because these things are now commonly seen on the barrens." One individual's curiosity wasn't aroused when confronted with such a phenomenon—perhaps it was a temporary loss of imagination: the man was working in an irrigation ditch when a UFO landed only a few hundred feet from him. He looked at it briefly and then continued working. Eventually, the craft took off.

Several sightings have been reported in the New Sharon area along Route 2 where fields offer open views from horizon to horizon. The March 30, 1994 issue of the Lewiston *Sun-Journal* noted one made by three college students driving from Augusta to Farmington.

At first, the object was thought to be a star, but when the three neared New Sharon village it was "the size of a car or pickup truck with a light sweeping the sky." The students parked by the roadside and got out to better observe the UFO as it prowled a field at an altitude of only 150 feet. There was no sound of an engine, and they now could see that the craft was round, had a dome, and there was a circle of red and green lights flashing around the bottom. The threesome stood mesmerized until a sweeping light shifted and was directed at them. Curiosity became terror as they scurried back to their car and made a hurried escape.

Noticeably shaken, they related the incident to campus friends who at first were not inclined to take them seriously. Should the sighting be reported? they wondered, and would such a bizarre tale leave them open to ridicule? Finally, they alerted the local sheriff's office and a deputy was sent to patrol the area.

"UFOs over New Sharon Monday night," began the March 30, 1994 Lewiston *Sun-Journal* article, "turned out to be an encounter of the not-so-close kind, according to Franklin County Sheriff Don Richards." His office had responded to a sighting along Route 2 twenty years earlier with little success, but he didn't discount the possibility that Maine had become attractive to aliens. The unidentified light in the sky probably had a less fanciful explanation: it may have been a helicopter checking the Sandy River to see if the late March thaw had created a potential ice jam, the sheriff speculated. It was that time of year when emergency management workers monitored water levels in rivers. "Personally," said Richards, "I've got no reason to believe that aliens aren't out there—there could be other worlds. Are we the only ones? You've got to think about that."

The witnesses of the sighting gave evidence "of being under considerable emotional stress" when questioned by the Mutual UFO Network. There was that on-the-scene fear of abduction, and the three were having difficulty sleeping soundly at night since the incident. Sharing their encounter with sympathetic UFO officials appeared to give all three a welcome relief.

"As researchers in this field," wrote the investigator filing his report, "we were impressed with the respondents' intelligence, sincerity, and internal consistency. They seemed devoid of pretense or striving for effect. We came away feeling that we had met with some very high quality young people who appreciated being taken seriously."

A November 21, 1995 sighting on the Maine Turnpike between Wells and Kennebunk was one of many received at the National UFO Reporting Center in Seattle, Washington. "There's almost no doubt in my mind," said Peter Davenport, the Center's Director, "this was the most dramatic night in our twenty-one years history." Reports had been coming in all evening along the Eastern Seaboard from Greenville, North Carolina to Maine.

Emmanuel Striligas, a registered nurse, was returning to his home in Biddeford at 10:30 p.m. after completing his second-shift duties at a nursing center in North Berwick. "I was driving north on the turnpike in a dark area when I see this very bright, white light." The glare ahead was uncomfortably close when he pulled over in the parking lane. "I am looking out the windshield," said Striligas, "and I see this object which is about the size of a single car garage." It was moving slowly over the trees from east to west and crossing the highway in front of him. The craft "looked oval in shape, had a shiny surface," and the nurse reported that there were "three rings around it." The first was "white-dusky," the second "yellowish-amber," and the third ring appeared "olive" in color. "It was completely noiseless," he remembered, "and the amazing thing is that the trees are moving as if there was a storm! As it passes the trees on the other side of the turnpike it rockets upward just like a firework and disappears."

Two other reports from Maine reached the Seattle Center that night, and several of the Eastern Seaboard sightings were unusual. One woman described the UFO as being "a triangular-shaped object, twice the size of a football field."

"I know what I saw—it wasn't a plane or a helicopter," declared Striligas. "I can say that I was frightened and quite a bit shaken up."

Not everyone retreats when confronted by an alien presence. There are those who decide to take the offensive rather than to turn back and avoid danger. In March of 1965, John T. King made such a decision on a stretch of highway near Bangor when he came upon a huge domed disk hovering over the road directly in front of him. The craft was only a few feet off the ground, and as he slowed up his lights grew dim and the radio stopped playing. King, convinced that his life was being threatened, reached for a loaded pistol he kept in his car. From the open window he began firing at the UFO. On the third shot the object rose and streaked away at a "tremendous speed." There was little traffic on the road at that time of night, and King was the only one who saw the disk.

UFO Roundup, a website that carries reports of sightings, got an e-mail contribution from a Kathy M. She, her mother and two children were camping in a remote area north of Greenville, Maine on June 13, 1997. The family had driven their travel trailer off Route 15 onto the Lily Bay Road just as it began to rain. "My mother and I decided to look outside to see if there were any stars out after it had stopped raining," wrote Kathy. "It was then we saw this thing flying overhead. It was flaring bright white, about three times the size of a satellite. It was followed by a second object. They crossed from horizon to horizon in six seconds (an estimated 2,400 miles an hour) and would flare bright white and then fade to white. About 30 seconds after they disappeared, we saw a pair of jets following the same path. And the next night, Saturday, around the same time, we again saw the objects fly overhead. One of the lights changed direction, from traveling north, to west. They were followed by one jet that time."

January 27, 1998 was a busy evening for UFO investigators in Colorado, Wyoming, and the state of Maine. A number of witnesses reported seeing fireballs and hearing loud explosions. Pam Pelletier of St. Agatha, Maine, was walking her dog when she heard "a series of explosions, maybe as many as seven or eight," and Ellen Cousins of Millinocket saw a "bright orange thing streak across the sky." The object reminded her of a "gun flare." It was "bright orange with a white tail." Explosions were heard as far south as Oakland in Central Maine. Kelly Sirois and her father, Ron, heard two thunderous blasts "like something hitting the house." This was between 9:30 and 10:30 p.m., and at the same time, Evelyn Robinson saw a streaking fireball which was going "very fast and falling to the ground at a 45-degree angle"—she was driving on Interstate 95 from Houlton, Maine toward Island Falls.

The Federal Aviation Administration stated there were no missing planes, and a spokesman for a Maine planetarium had no reports of major meteor activity. An astronomer, Robert Stencel, at the University of Denver, suggested that the earth may have been pelted with pieces of the Hale-Bopp comet—in January our planet was passing through the part of space the comet had traveled. "Comets are like kids with muddy boots," explained Stencel. "They leave a trail of debris in their wakes."

In the October 14, 1994 issue of the Lewiston *Sun-Journal* an article by Jennifer Sullivan was given front-page attention. "Mainers Report UFO Sightings" the bold headline announced. Vienna, Fayette, Wales and Raymond were among a number of communities where mysterious objects had been seen in the skies over a period of several weeks.

"It was very, very bright, very brilliant," said Lisa Noyes of Wales. She and her fiancé first saw the UFO near her home in late August or early September, and again it was spotted a mile away hovering over Sabattus Mountain at 6:45 p.m. on October 12. Noyes described the light as "almost like a halogen"—crystal clear. "Then all of a sudden it just dropped down out of sight. We did see just a bit of the top of it behind the mountain. It stayed there for probably 30 seconds, then came back up into the same position for a minute before moving off."

The object that the Wales woman saw was described by several other observers in the area as being about "10 times the size of the North Star" and it seemed to be emitting a light which was "diamond shaped." Noyes was initially reluctant to talk about what she saw for fear of public reaction, but a man in Fayette had also reported seeing a light hover and dip below the tree line in September, and a Vienna resident called the UFO Reporting Center in Seattle with a similar sighting which occurred three days later.

Paul Hubbard, a safety inspector for the Federal Aviation Administration in Portland, was asked whether these lights were some type of aircraft. "Very often a helicopter can produce a very strange effect if there's a slight overcast," replied Hubbard. "You'll actually see a glow. But I don't know of any helicopter operations in these areas."

A sighting in Richmond on January 3, 2002 prompted an industrial engineer to contact authorities. The observer was driving on Interstate 95, near Exit 25 in Bowdoin at 9:35 p.m., when he saw a stationary object in the sky. There were blinking green and red lights on each side of a bright center glow of high intensity. At Exit 25, the engineer parked behind two other vehicles where travelers had stopped for a closer look. The lights slowly began to move diagonally to the northeast and then changed directions instantly without forming an arc. There was no sound as they passed over the heads of the astonished witnesses; "it seemed to be a wedge or a chevron," and the underside was "lit with a diffused light which faded at the periphery." It was difficult to determine the dimension of the object which was estimated to be "the size of a quarter when held at arm's length."

Peter Davenport at the Seattle Center believed that Mainers were seeing "something that was very interesting." The unusual flight characteristics of the lights suggested UFOs. "The geographical area where sightings take place is probably not in the least important at all because these objects can move so rapidly," explained Davenport. "They can be in one state and in another state the next minute."

("If I wrote a book about UFOs, what kind of reactions would I get from law enforcement officials, the military, or the government?" It was a question I asked when interviewing a dozen people while preparing this chapter. Four of the contributors echoed what one highly intelligent person told me in confidence: "I think you'd better be prepared for some government intrusion. It's my opinion there is a cover-up the likes of which the world has never seen—a conspiracy. And I'm not talking about our government alone but possibly 50 countries that mislead people into thinking there aren't any aliens out there. You may be dealing with dangerous material.")

THE MARY HOWE MYSTERY

Many mysterious happenings in the distant past have been kept alive by diaries and gossip. One bizarre account is the case of Mary Howe, a young Damariscotta, Maine woman who was an ardent believer in spiritualism and who held séances. Was she buried alive in an unmarked grave? Here is the strange unwinding of events that culminated in the year 1882.

After military service, Colonel Joel Howe, Jr., his wife and nine children, moved to Damariscotta. The Howes were prominent in the Boston area—Elias Howe invented the sewing machine, and one member of the family built the Wayside Inn in Sudbury, Massachusetts, a structure made famous by Longfellow's poem "Tales from the Wayside Inn."

It was an unusual brood of children that Colonel Howe unleashed on this coastal community and not one rooted in conventionalism. The five Howe girls were "freethinkers," and their inventive brothers were active in devising a machine which was "propelled by perpetual motion." The boys also constructed a mold to make counterfeit half-dollars.

After the colonel's death, the family established an inn in town known as "Howe's Tavern" with the eldest son, Joel III, as proprietor. It became a popular stagecoach stop, and among the distinguished names found in the tavern's register was James K. Polk—the U.S. President was inspecting lighthouses along the Maine coast.

Spiritualism was now a family passion, particularly for Mary and two of her brothers, Edwin and Lorenzo. She soon was known as a medium, and the theatrical side of her nature flourished. Mary once conceived the notion that she could fly. Stretching her arms out and whispering unearthly incantations, she leaped into space and landed heavily at the bottom of the stairs with a broken ankle and multiple bruises. Such a fiasco was only a temporary setback; her faith in possessing supernatural powers remained unshaken.

Mary's sideshow antics to contact the dear departed attracted people up and down the coast, and she thrived whenever the lens of attention focused in her direction. She welcomed questions from the audience, and would generously supply them with the voices of spirits from beyond the grave. Some were convinced of her integrity—others had suspicions: the voice of old "Grandpa Snazzi" was too glib; could the croaking sound be Edwin moaning through an amplified setup of pipes?

Mary Howe's reputation as a medium was elevated at one séance. A guest, who had a relative visiting New York City, asked when the family member would be returning to Maine. Miss Howe began mumbling in the tense silence. "I can see him clearly," her voice rose. "I see many lights! Wait! He will not return! When all those lights appear, he will die!" A few days after this gathering, word was received that the man had died of heart failure just when hundreds of gaslights were lit to illuminate the newly-constructed Brooklyn Bridge.

Many mediums of the eighteen hundreds believed that acquiring a state of suspended animation was beneficial in sharpening visionary abilities. After she went into a deep trance, warm stones were placed near the medium to compensate for the loss of body heat. Respiration decreased to a point where no movement could be detected in the chest area while pulses and heartbeat slowed to a near standstill. The reposing figure on the couch was seemingly dead though there was no trace of physical deterioration. For several days—sometimes more than a week—the suspended state held, and after she came out of such a trance there were no adverse reactions. Mary Howe frequently slipped into unconsciousness while her brother Edwin acted as tour guide for the many curiosity seekers who visited the Howe home. He encouraged the callers to feel his sister's wrist for a pulse beat and delighted in giving scientific explanations that stretched into lectures.

For several days in 1882, people in Damariscotta and nearby communities flocked to view Mary. Each day the gossip intensified. Was she really in a trance or had she died? Finally, disturbed local authorities ordered Dr. Robert Dixon to go to the Howe home and give them his medical opinion. After examining Mary Howe, he pronounced her dead.

Dr. Dixon's diagnosis caused much excitement and alerted a number of newspaper reporters to wonder in print whether Mary was still alive. Laura Castner and Everett Dunbar of *The Twin Village Herald & Record*, a Damariscotta newspaper, were welcomed into the Howe home by Edwin. He took the two into a little room where Mary lay on a couch with warm stones surrounding her. The roaring fire in a stove made the small chamber an oven. Dr. Dixon had stated that Miss Howe had been dead for more than two weeks, though there was no indication of rigor mortis and there seemed to be color in her cheeks. Edwin invited the reporters to feel his sister's ankles; they felt warm, and there wasn't the slightest odor coming from the alleged corpse.

It was time now for the authorities to end speculation and talk. A professional threesome—minister, sheriff, and undertaker—forced their way into the Howe home, and over the violent protests of an outraged Edwin, the trio prepared the body and took it away.

The next difficulty was finding someone willing to dig Mary's grave. One thought lingered as people, in distraught whispers, heatedly argued about what should be done: Was Damariscotta, Maine about to bury a woman alive? Finally, a laborer was found and the spadework accomplished, but the undertaker's assistant refused to help lower the casket into the ground. This task, and the filling in of the grave were done by the undertaker, sheriff, and minister.

After the burial, there were many who were afraid to pass the Glidden Cemetery in Newcastle, Maine where Mary was consigned to an unmarked plot. Moans and groans have been heard over the years, all coming from somewhere behind a jumble of tombstones, and late at night some residents have seen a dim light flickering within the cemetery.

MEN IN BLACK

David Stephens, 21, and his friend, Paul, 18, saw a UFO at Tripp Pond in Androscoggin County, Maine on October 27, 1975. It was no ordinary sighting. Both were left with feelings of uneasiness caused by a period of "lost time," and for several hours after the incident each realized that the other had a peculiar orange tinge in his eyes.

The next morning, alone in the trailer which he and Paul shared, Stephens had an unexpected caller. The heavyset man with his crew cut, dark sunglasses, and dressed in a black suit, was no door-to-door salesman or someone there to read the gas meter. Instead of saying "good morning," he glared at David and asked: "Did you see a UFO yesterday?" The young man nodded and before he could speak the scowling stranger told him: "Better keep your mouth shut if you know what's good for you!" With that threat delivered, the man turned and quickly disappeared.

The sighting and missing-time syndrome worried David—there were so many unanswered questions, in addition to the disquieting appearance of an unknown person who knew about the UFO. After several weeks of anxiety and vague physical discomfort, Stephens underwent therapy with physician and hypnotherapist Dr. Herbert Hopkins. These interviews suggested that this was a classical case of abduction, with medical examinations having been performed aboard an alien craft.

Nearly a year after the abduction, on September 11, 1976, Dr. Hopkins was at home alone when the phone rang. The caller identified himself as a UFO investigator and he had certain questions concerning David Stephens. Would Hopkins be willing to see him? "Certainly," replied the doctor. Within seconds after he had lowered the telephone receiver and turned away, the doorbell rang. There on the steps was the person who had just telephoned—the voice with the slight accent was unmistakable.

Dr. Hopkins hesitated several moments before asking the stranger into his home—the investigator's appearance was bizarre: dressed in black with only a hint of white about the throat to suggest a shirt, the entirely hairless man was wearing lipstick. Would Hopkins like to see his trick? Before the doctor could answer, he saw a coin vanish in the palm of a hand. UFOs were discussed briefly, and then the visitor's voice became softer and the words slurred. "My energy is running low....Must go now," the stranger muttered as he fumbled his way to the door.

Two weeks later, the doctor's son, John, and daughter-in-law, Maureen, had unusual company at their home. The callers were a man and woman dressed in dark, old-fashioned clothing who seemed to have some difficulty in walking normally; a sort of uncoordinated motion was perceptible when they stepped forward after having stood still for several moments. They asked the Hopkinses inane questions, such as: "What do you talk about?" Then the male visitor began touching his female companion intimately and asked John whether he was fondling her correctly. When the doctor's son had to leave the room to answer the telephone, the man asked Maureen "how she was made" and if she had any photographs of herself naked. Shortly after John Hopkins came back from his call, the couple announced that it was time for them to leave and did so without saying good-bye. It was then that the Hopkinses noticed that the odd pair "could walk only in a kind of dead-straight line"—like windup toys.

Out of nowhere they seem to come, usually three figures dressed in black suits, hats and ties—the clothes they wear are shiny, not silky, as if the cloth had been cut from bolts of unknown fabric. Later, one learns that they give false names and flash phony identification badges as they make claims of being UFO or government investigators. To reinforce their authority, they bring up embarrassing and intimate details of their host's life. "There isn't a thing we don't know about you," they are quick to inform one, and pausing to strengthen the coming threat, they say: "If you want your wife to keep her pretty face, you'd better...." Their voices have a computerized delivery, battery-powered and monotonous; they are olive-complected with high cheekbones, pointed chins, and eyes that are slightly slanted. Upon leaving, they are seen driving away in luxurious black Buicks or Cadillacs, sometimes Lincolns—usually in vehicles from the 1950s—with headlights off, and eerie green or purple glows illuminating plush interiors. One New Jersey family was visited by a huge man whose pant legs hiked up when he sat down and they saw "a green wire grafted onto his skin and running up his leg." Their entrances and exits are mysterious—they have been known to wallow through mud after a heavy rain and moments later when entering a house their shoes looked "polished with no trace of dirt."

(This author was reluctant to include any material relating to Men In Black; in fact, early in the research for this book I destroyed everything I had on the subject—it all seemed so far-fetched. As writer, I like to be a bystander who imparts rather than validates information, but when one distrusts what is at hand, all chances of flexibility are lost. I got thoroughly disenchanted when I learned that Men In Black were members of a race called Horlocks, a group of aliens known as Draconians, reptilian creatures who have no souls and come from caverns in the Himalayan foothills. Another writer placed their abode somewhere in the Gobi Desert in Mongolia where there have been reports of crashed disks and alien bases. I also resisted the notion that these unsavory weirdos have been known to disintegrate a coin in the hand of a UFO witness and then tell the poor man that they will do the same to his heart if he talks. Other foolishness to plummet confidence was the statement that Men In Black sometimes attempt to purchase soft drinks when doors to vending machines are locked, and that they "sing to birds in trees." I had second thoughts after reading the testimony given by David Stephens and the Hopkins family—all three are curious aftermaths to a UFO abduction in

Maine, but the participants exuded sincerity. I was particularly struck by the doctor's reactions: He didn't realize how bizarre his visitor's behavior was until the man—or it—had left. For Dr. Hopkins, the visit seemed a sort of dream; a meeting with something that had no physical entity but existed in a shadowy place between the world as we know it and the psychic realm.)

Timothy Beckley in his book, *Mystery of the Men in Black: The UFO Silencers*, brought up many situations concerning these ominous beings. He claimed they didn't have their beginnings with the rash of sightings reported in the 1950s. According to Beckley, they have been seen since Elizabethan times; they surface in witchcraft incidents, and many have been observed prowling the countryside as traveling salesmen in the late nineteenth century.

These villains got national exposure in October 1953 when Albert K. Bender placed a notice in his popular UFO publication *Space Review*. Bender stated that he had obtained information which would solve the "flying saucer" mystery but wasn't allowed to reveal it. The announcement concluded with a warning to publishers of other magazines that they must be very careful when writing about any activities concerning spacecraft. This notice was the magazine's swan song; *Space Review* ceased publication without informing its readers. In an interview, Bender admitted that three men wearing dark clothes had ordered him to stop publishing. He complied, Bender told reporters, because he was "scared to death." Later, after having changed his mind, perhaps no longer feeling threatened and convinced that it was important to tell the whole story, he made public his encounter in a book called *Flying Saucers and the Three Men In Black*.

(In closing, I return with another digression. After having written this short chapter, and being somewhat acquainted with my material, what will I do within the next few seconds if there is a hammering on my door? Will I cross the room casually and slide back the lock without giving one thought to the possibility that I may find three callers standing on the steps and all wearing black suits, hats and ties?)

BEHIND THE CURTAIN OF BIRTH

There are those who believe that if you are unhappy with your life, your health, your financial situation, then you must realize that causes exist and these can be traced back to past lives. Such thinking accepts the premise that the subconscious mind survives death, and a new existence is an exchange of one body for another—all the things one does or has left undone in a past life will generate effects in this life and probably future lifetimes. If you react negatively with hatred, jealousy, pettiness, revenge, etc., then you have failed the Great Test and will have to learn the lesson in a future existence.

The Greeks are often given credit for the idea of reincarnation, and they acknowledged that much of what they believed came from the Egyptians. There is now, however, solid evidence that ideas about reincarnation arose simultaneously around the world. This suggests that the concept of past and future lifetimes needed no discoverer.

Belief in reincarnation differs in various regions, religions, and cultures. Some feel that people enter another body immediately after death, and others think there are intermissions of several years or centuries. A representative from one culture might insist that a person always returns as a human, and another believer is convinced that people can become superhumans and no longer have a need to return. Many feel that if one behaves badly the punishment is being born an animal in the next life—some believers in Hindustan have the custom of purchasing captive birds in order to set them free: they do this because the souls of dead people could reside in these feathered creatures. The Hindus conclude that karma from past lives determines the course of the present one, and the returning soul does not choose its parents. The Tlingit, an Indian tribe in Alaska, believe that one has a choice of parents and role in life. Sometimes this conviction is so strong that a tribal member will tell relatives how to recognize him or her in the coming existence.

During the Dark Ages, the doctrine of reincarnation was kept hidden in monasteries by scholars, and limited acceptance was slow to seize Europe. It wasn't until the last quarter of the nineteenth century in this country, largely through efforts of the Theosophical Society, that reincarnation gained widespread consideration. One of the attractions of this belief was that people felt they had greater control over their destinies and a better chance of being rewarded. In an infinite universe there must be infinite possibilities for growth and development. "As you sow, so shall you reap" was an appealing concept based on the laws of cause and effect.

Hypnotists and parapsychologists often point out that the length of time between lives varies greatly. When patients are regressed to the Middle Ages, it can be centuries before another birth. Regressions of the eighteenth and nineteenth centuries average about seventy to eighty years from the end of one life to the beginning of the next. Twentieth century regressions, however, are the fastest: there is a range of only one to twenty-five years between lives.

After experiencing a past-life regression, a person begins to question the truthfulness of the recall. Memories are not as simple as they may seem, and there are no clear boundaries between reality and fantasy. Some parts of the memory can be emphasized at the expense of others, and the sequence of events may be altered in the telling: one only has to listen to eyewitnesses at the scene of an accident to hear different versions—elements of fantasy and real memories frequently are interconnected.

Regressed couples often find that they have been together in many past lives. A husband and wife may be reunited as mother and daughter or sister and brother in a subsequent life. Even an acquaintance may reappear. Therapists theorize that this cycle will continue until all of the life lessons are learned and negativity is balanced by positivity. Forgiveness, we are told, helps to speed up this process, but cooperation is necessary from all who are involved.

Hypnosis as a method of regressing one behind the curtain of birth remains controversial. Nevertheless, many accounts of its past reliability and potency have been passed down to us, including miraculous cures performed by early medicine men, witch doctors and priests. A hundred years ago, hypnotism was looked upon more skeptically than it is today—it has now been taken off the stage as an exhibition and adopted by physicians, dentists, educators, and psychological counselors as a tool. Some decades ago, entertainers tried to give the impression that they possessed remarkable control over their subjects and could force them to do bizarre things—the only real power behind hypnosis lies with the subject and his or her own mind.

A hypnotized person will experience relaxation in every muscle of the body: some people feel a floating sensation, others a warm or tingling feeling. A heaviness is felt in the arms and legs—one is able to move the limbs but doesn't *want* to break the trance.

Hypnosis is a state of increased suggestibility paired with a focusing of concentration on one thought, person or idea. To better clarify its subtle hold, we should note that one is not unconscious when hypnotized—one is *super* conscious: you can be regressed to a time when you were learning to write, and the clumsy handwriting will be of that period in your life, as well as your childish babbling, should you be asked to speak.

Contrary to popular misconceptions, the best hypnotic subjects are intelligent people with excellent memories; individuals who can visualize scenes, express emotions easily, and are not overly critical. An ideal candidate is one who attends a film or reads a story and becomes so involved in the plot that time passes unnoticed. Those who usually make the worst attendants are people with short attention spans, who use logic and never emotions when faced with problems, and who find it difficult to relax.

The stages of hypnosis are classified as light, medium, and deep. Those under *light hypnosis* have their eyes closed and are unable to open them. Completely relaxed and breathing regularly, they cannot move or talk unless directed. *Medium hypnosis* is accompanied by a partial amnesia, and subjects can be made to enact simple posthypnotic suggestions. In *deep hypnosis*, the subjects can talk with eyes open, walk about, and are in a state of complete anesthesia and amnesia. They can be told that they don't see things that are there, or vice versa, and can carry out involved posthypnotic suggestions.

M. Didier, the father of European somnambulist Alexis Didier, was hypnotised so frequently that he developed the habit of falling into spontaneous trances. This sometimes happened at the breakfast table while he was reading his newspaper. The two young sons stared with fascination at their father as he continued to read—M. Didier was unaware that he had dropped the paper on the floor. Sometimes, the boys would sneak the newspaper into another room, but their father would keep on reading as if he still held it in his hands.

There is no proof to substantiate the concept of reincarnation, and how a person responds in a past-life regression could be influenced by what has been heard or read. Still, there are instances in regression sessions that point to the plausibility of many lives: for example, a child using the vocabulary of an adult or speaking in an unfamiliar language.

Ian Stevenson, psychiatrist and noted researcher, found that many children begin to speak about reincarnation at the age of three or four. They talk in a matter-of-fact manner about their past lives until the ages of five to eight when these events begin to fade. It is unclear whether the child continues to think about these memories of another life after the age of eight. Stevenson did observe that even when a past-life story involved a traumatic or sudden death, the child did not display strong emotion in its telling.

Parents often are reluctant to report such a memory by young children, even in cultures that accept the concept of reincarnation. In one study, 25 percent of the parents had initally suppressed such information. One of the reasons for this could be the folk belief that it may prove fatal for children to remember former lives.

Dr. Stevenson came to the conclusion that a child talking about another lifetime experience was not, in and of itself, sufficient proof of reincarnation, though he did find over many years of study that birth defects and birthmarks in children often match fatal injuries suffered during a past life. In the majority of these cases, a child's previous personality died unexpectedly, violently, or at a young age. Stevenson published his findings in a massive 2,300-page report covering 210 cases. Birthmarks resembling injuries such as axe wounds and bullet holes were verified and strengthened enormously the argument that such imperfections were evidence of reincarnation. One of Stevenson's cases was a British Indian boy who remembered a previous identity, and his death by a shotgun blast to his chest. On the boy's chest were several discolorations which matched the location and patterns of the fatal wounds verified by an autopsy report.

Past-life researchers estimate that 1 in 1,000 children under the age of five can remember experiences or people in previous lives, and in the Middle East and northern India there is a frequency of 1 in 450. It is possible that these numbers are low estimates since most parents worriedly discourage discussion when a child shares such memories.

A striking testimony for reincarnation is the case of Shanti Devi, a girl in India who claimed to have lived a previous life in the town of Muttra. Shanti, born in Delhi in October 1926, began to speak of her former life when she was only four years old. The child said she had been of the Choban caste, had lived in a yellow house, and that her husband had been a cloth merchant named Kedar Nath Chaubey. A curious neighbor wrote to the address the girl gave him, and to his surprise, he received a reply from Chaubey himself. The husband confirmed a number of details about life with his deceased wife and requested that a relative of his in Delhi be allowed to talk to the girl. Shanti recognized the man immediately as Chaubey's cousin, Kanji Mal. When learning of Shanti's genuineness, the former husband rushed to Delhi, and the little girl flung herself into his arms.

In November 1935, the nine-year-old child was taken to Muttra by her parents and three respectable citizens of Delhi who went along as witnesses. When the train entered the station, Shanti recognized Chaubey's elder brother who was waiting for their arrival. They took a carriage, and the girl was told to direct the driver anywhere she wanted. Along the way to her former husband's house, she pointed out buildings that had not been there during her lifetime and had the driver stop before a residence that she and Chaubey had once occupied. Asked by a local man where the "jaizarur" was located—the word used in Muttra for privy—she pointed to the outdoor lavatory. Then they all went into the house where she had died. Shanti led them to a spot where coins had been hidden in a metal container. The tin was found empty, and an embarrassed husband later admitted that he had taken the money. As they left Chaubey's house, Shanti Devi recognized in a crowd of curious onlookers her former mother and father.

One popular after-death scenario is the appearance of a guide who helps the deceased through a difficult transition period. The newly dead must be made aware that they have died, and give consent to being led into an intense white light that will take them to an intermediate realm. Here lives are evaluated and choices are made for the next life. It is at this time one sees relatives and friends who have previously died, and communicates with them telepathically. If the newly deceased refuses to enter the white light, the soul remains on an astral plane as a troubled spirit, possibly finding some comfort in familiar surroundings, such as the last house inhabited on earth. This, claim believers, explains why so many houses are haunted.

The intermediate realm, sometimes called "the soul plane," is where one chooses parents, brothers, sisters, and other family members. It is at this stage that plans are made for all the major events in the coming life. Will you be black or white, rich or poor, a member of a large family or an only child, blessed or cursed? Much of this, reincarnation believers insist, depends on your past-life history.

Therapists use past-life regression as a means of eliminating the causes of phobias, compulsive habits, and negative tendencies. Some professionals lead one back to the birth experience and then suggest the next regressive step—the leap into a past life. Since birth is such a traumatic encounter for everyone, many therapists prefer bypassing this event by asking their patients to allow the subconscious mind to go back to the origins of particular problems and relive them.

Beliefs in what happens to the life force, or soul, after death vary greatly: Some say the spirit is judged and rewarded a place in "heaven" or

condemned to dwell in "hell," all based on one's attitudes and deeds
during life; others subscribe to the notion that the spirit continues a similar
existence in a different realm; the more pessimistic humans, often calling
themselves pragmatists, are quick to point out, "when you're dead, you're
dead"; there are theorists who are convinced that the spirit undergoes
many changes in the process of achieving a more lofty spiritual plane;
and then there are those who believe that the soul waits for an eventual
resurrection.

If we have lived other lives, then we may bring with us some of the
capabilities developed during these lifetimes. The word *prodigy* comes
to mind: What was Mozart's occupation in a previous life, this child
who composed sonatas and minuets before he was seven and an opera at
twelve?

SETH

(Madelon Rose Logue was one of eight people attending Jean Laier's
psychic group in Stockton Springs, Maine—Tamaranda thoughtfully had
arranged this meeting so Stella and I could join their circle. Madelon
had brought with her a 30-inch aluminum trumpet, similar to those used
by physical mediums during the early 1900s. I half expected the instrument would emit one or two feeble blasts during the course of the
evening, but it preferred silence. Later, Madelon Logue told me that
during a séance the trumpet might respond by floating in the air and
amplifying spirit voices. "Sitters must be receptive for this to happen,"
she explained, "and truly want to communicate with loved ones on the
other side." I asked if it was human energy that caused trumpets to sound,
and she replied: "Well, it's supposed to be spirit energy. The trumpet is
supposed to levitate and amplify the voices of the spirits of the departed
loved ones called upon during the séance. I'm steeped in the philosophy
of Jane Roberts and Seth. So I know that the trumpet has its own consciousness as well." It was like table tipping—a form of communicating
Madelon had learned to do. "I remember talking with a table. It was
jumping up and down, and I said: 'Hey! Watch out for our knees and
feet! Be careful!' Then it would stop and hover instead of pounding its
legs up and down, and light as a feather it put its feet gently down on the
floor. I'm sure we all played a part in that experience. We, the sitters at
the table session, the energy essence of the departed souls called upon,
the consciousness of the table itself, all cooperating very nicely."

Maine readers who browse the New Age shelves in bookstores have no difficulty finding titles by Jane Roberts or volumes dictated through her by Seth. When Madelon Logue purchased a copy of *Seth Speaks*, an associate warned her: "Don't read that! Burn it! Seth is evil!" The book stayed on her bedroom shelf for three years untouched while she pursued other titles. One day, when her children were away and she was alone in the house, she opened the book and was immediately captivated. "I was so excited," she recalled. "I was shouting 'My gosh! Someone has taken everything currently known about the occult and psychic phenomena, back to the mid-1800s at least, and put it in one book!' Little did I know then how many more Seth and Jane would write. Later, I took a psychic development class and learned to do psychometry. Through reading Rob's [Robert Butts] italicized notes in which I found many Seth quotes regarding Jane's trance state, and from her own books I learned a lot about psychic phenomena and mediumship. The Seth material is in three parts, actually—Seth's books, Rob's notes and Jane's work—they weave in and out and around each other as if mirroring the way the universe works. So many questions were answered." Then Madelon began working psychic fairs and doing Sethian-based readings and met with conflicting reactions. "It's really weird," she marveled. "Some people cannot physically touch a Seth book, while other people have the books fall off shelves, sometimes on their heads, to attract attention!")

Seth appeared on December 8, 1963 while Jane Roberts and Robert Butts were living in Elmira, New York. She was thirty-four at the time and he was ten years older. During their nine years of marriage, Jane sold Avon products, taught nursery school, and then worked in an art gallery. "She was good at selling," recalled Madelon. Rob was an artist at a greeting card company in Elmira, and he also worked on comic books. Roberts had written two science-fiction novels, *The Rebellers* and *Bundu*; she also had published several stories in *Fantasy* and *Science-Fiction Magazine*.

The startling adventure began on a Ouija board with communications from Frank Withers, an Elmira English teacher who had died in 1942. It wasn't until the fourth session that Withers withdrew and the board was taken over by Seth.

Though the Ouija pointer spelled out the same message that Roberts got mentally, she felt impelled to speak it aloud. Entire sentences leaped into her mind, and the words were not her own. By the eighth meeting with the board she shoved it aside, stood up, and dictated while pacing. Six sessions later she no longer used this method even for the first messages. Throughout 1964, Roberts paced the room restlessly while dictating; her eyes were wide open, though she had no awareness of her physical surroundings. Later, she spoke while sitting down, her eyes closed, and in a room that had ordinary lighting. Jane was then so in tune with Seth that she sometimes spoke in a deep masculine voice with considerable volume.

Seth would speak through Roberts for periods as long as two hours without a break when dictating his books, and often the flow of words was so hurried that Rob Butts had difficulty taking the dictation in his own shorthand. Jane's feminine gestures were replaced by the trance personality's masculinity. Into the quiet room came a shrewd old man, radiating wit and humor.

A skeptic might ask whether the medium's bent for writing science fiction had brought forth a Seth from her subconscious. Yet Roberts was not a "born psychic" with paranormal experiences. She and her husband had little knowledge of such affairs, and they seriously questioned what was happening in their lives. "When all this began, in fact," wrote Roberts, "I wasn't at all sure that we survived death once, much less over and over again."

A number of scientists labeled the projections of Seth a fraud, and during the eight years she conducted ESP classes only four or five psychologists and two physicists showed enough interest to join the gathering. It was trickery, skeptics proclaimed; Jane Roberts was hoodwinking her gullible students.

In her ESP class, Seth's coming through was spontaneous, in response to questions raised by students. Though he would sometimes lecture, his was a trance personality edged with curiosity: he also listened. It became obvious to everyone present that this entity enjoyed participating in these sessions. "Seth was mostly very funny while being poignant," recalled Barrie Gellis, one of the students who attended classes from October 1972 to May 1973. Those who crowded the living room were far from being well-behaved witnesses. They hooted, drank too much wine, swore, and challenged Seth. Usually, these rambunctious meetings went on from 7 p.m. till past midnight. After Seth left and the trance was over, Jane Roberts would ask class members to tell her what had happened as she was never aware of the things she said as Seth.

Groups of Sethians have sprung up all over the world. There is comfort in the premise that within us lies the power to bring order to this intimidatingly complex universe—that harmony can be achieved between the inner and outer worlds. Here, in brief, are some of the Seth concepts: All things, even atoms and molecules, have consciousness. Thought has "an electromagnetic reality," and your thoughts and expectations shape your world. Trust your inner self. As the outer self manages the world you see, the inner self is the potter who shapes and transforms psychic energy from the intangible world within into the tangible world of matter. By interacting with our world as we create and perceive it we grow spiritually, and can help others to do so. Be in tune with your inner self, and you are connected to an infinite source of wisdom.

A trance personality is said to manipulate the entranced medium, often superimposing its own characteristics. Jane Roberts was deeply committed to the practical application of bringing forth Seth's philosophical presentations. "Through me," wrote Roberts in the introduction of her book *The Seth Material*, "Seth has produced a continuing manuscript that runs well over five thousand double-spaced typewritten pages, in not quite five years time." This was completed while she pursued her own creativity, which included two books of nonfiction, two collections of poetry, and a dozen short stories.

For nearly fifteen years, from September 1967 to August 1982, private meetings were conducted Mondays and Wednesdays with Rob Butts recording more than 1500 Seth sessions. Roberts also had her ESP classes, held on Tuesdays and Thursdays, with a charge of $2.50 per person. These earlier gatherings drew up to a dozen participants and were later expanded to accommodate three dozen or more students. Classes continued until 1975 when Jane and Rob bought a home and spent their time developing material for the Seth books. As of 1996, 23 books had been published—seven were dictated exclusively by Seth and two were compiled by Robert Butts and published after Jane's death. The Seth and Jane material is now housed in the Jane Roberts Memorial Archive at Yale University.

Jane Roberts was hospitalized in 1982 for severe arthritis and an underactive thyroid gland. During her illness Seth gave suggestions to make her more comfortable, and for a time she showed improvement. Gradually, her condition grew worse, and she died on September 5, 1984.

(When asked if she thought there were other mediums in contact with Seth, Madelon Logue's response was immediate. "You have got to say in your book that Seth only spoke through Jane." There had been imitators: one author channeled three books and claimed that Seth was writing through her in order to save civilization; another worker of words also produced three offerings and insisted that the deceased Jane Roberts had written them. Many Sethians are purists and have little patience for paranormal interlopers. When discussing such matters with one member of the circle that night in Stockton Springs, I was told: "I find most New Age stuff rather trite, and I'm not heavy into flying saucers and pyramids. I came to Seth for his concepts of 'time' and the ability to create reality consciously."

Logue is the editor and publisher of *Black Sheep*, "a networking fanzine," published every other month for those who admire the philosophy of Seth. Madelon has had many adventures, including the exploration of megalithic ruins in Ireland and Wales. Her psychic specialty is practicing psychometry. In 1989, she joined an expedition as a map dowser and psychic to search for a lost city in the jungles of Peru. The highlight of that trip was her recognition of a mountain near the city of Cuzco. "Twelve years before, and sight unseen," she wrote in the December 1991 issue of *Fate* magazine, "I'd painted a picture of that mysterious mountain." This mountain guards the entrance to the sacred Valley of the Incas.

Madelon spoke of an untrained medium who had exceptional talent; a person who could go into a trance and would have no memory of what had happened. "And he wouldn't believe it," she added. "One night we decided to hold a séance, and he set up a card table at his place and said: 'I want to know how my uncle died.' 'No, Jerry,' a friend told him, 'we don't want to know.' 'Yes, yes,' he insisted, 'how did he die?' We had our hands on top of the table, sitting around it in a semidark room. When the table started rocking back and forth, I said 'Makes me think of water sloshing back and forth.' 'Yes, yes,' he concluded, 'that's how my uncle died—he drowned.' "

Seth's messages were designed to turn his audience back onto and into themselves. On my way home, after that evening at Stockton Springs with Madelon Logue, Tamaranda, and the other members of this circle, I recalled these Sethian proposals: "The vitality you feel in my voice is your own vitality," he told his witnesses. "We create our own reality" and "our point of power is the present." It must be understood that "we are not at the mercy of the subconscious, nor are we helpless." As beings we are gods couched in harmony.)

146

EVERY NUMBER TELLS A STORY

Numerology is rooted in the ancient cultures of Egypt, China, and Greece, and was influenced by the Kabbalah—an esoteric interpretation of the Scriptures said to have been passed down orally from the time of Abraham. It has been used for more than 2,500 years in attempts to unlock the mysteries of life. The 6th-century BC mathematician Pythagoras is considered to be one of the fathers of this metaphysical science. Reasoning that nature is balanced by sets of numerical relationships, and divine laws are accurate and can be defined, Pythagoras developed through calculations a workable application of names and numbers. There are no theorems to master: all one needs to do is to accept the premise that a birth name and date can render a portrait and prepare one for the challenges of the future.

In the early 1900s, Mrs. Dow Balliett, an ardent reader of the Bible, Plato and Pythagoras, introduced her own number-based philosophy focused on persuading people to accept themselves as divine beings. Through her spiritual teachings, she is credited with originating Western numerology. Her diagram of numbers, in a circle of 1 through 9 with the Master Number of 11 at the top and a 22 in the center, gave practitioners a foundation for further work.

A group of women in California, led by Dr. Julia Seton who modernized this system of numbers, studied every aspect and nuance of the subject for 25 years. Names and numbers were tested until a manageable formula was established—with the result that every authority on numerology today is grounded to one degree or another on these findings. There are, however, deviates who try to "liberate" themselves from the teachings, and frequently the number values are changed, often when new information has been channeled by mediums.

The number 12, in the pre-Christian Middle East, was associated with harmony because it represented the 12 signs of the Zodiac. The Babylonians were familiar with seven celestial bodies in their sky: the Sun, Moon, Venus, Mercury, Mars, Jupiter and Saturn. Christian tradition displayed similar associations with seven: Earth, fire, air and water—the four material elements—are combined with the spiritual number three representing the holy trinity, thus linking matter to spirit sevenfold.

Some numbers are considered lucky, others are not. 7 is the leading number for luck, and the bad guy is 13 in many countries—Mexicans think 13 a sign of good fortune. In Italy, 17 is believed to do one harm, and superstitious Chinese businessmen have an 8 on their automobile license plates.

There are Japanese and Chinese Americans who believe that the 4th day of every month is unlucky, and when computerized death certificates of more than 200,000 Asian Americans were examined, researchers found that cardiac deaths were significantly more frequent on the fourth than any other day of the month—an astonishing 7% higher. Dr. David P. Phillips of the University of California at San Diego gave these results increased interest when he noted that the word "four" sounded very similar to the word "death" in both the Japanese and Chinese languages.

Perhaps you have a favorite number or one that seems to surface frequently in your life. (Immediately, I think of 3 and 13. My U.S. Army service number ended in 13 and began with 31, my social security ends in a 3, I was married on the 13th, I am one of 3 children in my family, my Maine post office box is 303, my summer address is 193, and the winter number is 1413. Coincidences?—I sometimes wonder. Numerologists tell me that each number has a vibration and distinct energy pattern. Do I attract 3s and 13s?)

One begins with a chart—without it there would be no way of interpreting this alphabet soup of consonants and vowels. To calculate a name or discover the meaning of a word, numerologists have assigned values and established rules. Here is their conversion map of letters and numbers:

1	2	3	4	5	6	7	8	9
a	b	c	d	e	f	g	h	i
j	k	l	m	n	o	p	q	r
s	t	u	v	w	x	y	z	

Some numerologists prefer full birth names while others are more relaxed and allow the omission of the middle. Here is John Doe's conversion in full:

$$
\begin{array}{ccc}
\text{J O H N} & \text{H E R M A N} & \text{D O E} \\
1+6+8+5 & 8+5+9+4+1+5 & 4+6+5 \\
20 & 32 & 15 \\
2+0=2 & 3+2=5 & 1+5=6 \\
& 2+5+6=13 & \\
& 1+3=4 &
\end{array}
$$

Mr. Doe has a base number of 4.

A woman who was later to become an authority on numbers, mentioned to a friend that she was thinking of changing her last name after her divorce was finalized. "Oh, if you're going to change your name," said the friend, "you ought to use numerology to harmonize the new name with your birth date." The divorcée selected a last name which gave her the Master Number of 11: a decision that placed her in the advantageous category of "spiritual messenger"—one who is born to bring spiritual insights to Earth—and with such key words as intuitive, sensitive, enthusiastic, inspirational, and visionary. Numerologists insist that all numbers are good, but if the woman had selected a name giving her the base number of a 1, the summary of the personality traits and approach to life would seem less elevating: "You are full of bright ideas and love freedom and independence. Sometimes you can be a bit stubborn. Beware of arrogance or selfishness. If good luck comes your way be sure to share it with others." Numerologists believe that the naming of a person is never haphazard; they feel that last-minute changes and misspellings are part of the fine-tuning that occurs to create the vibrations of our identities.

Each number has a specific meaning in numerology. For those who wish a brief glance at themselves, the following key words and concepts may prove helpful. Any book on this system will provide readers with in-depth profiles:

1. Independent, determined, ambitious, confident, creative, but can be self-conscious and sometimes lacking in self-esteem.

2. Patient, supportive, gentle and sensitive. A peacemaker. Can be deceitful and fearful of what others say and think.

3. Happy spirit. Often humorous, optimistic, and lucky with money. Enjoys luxuries. Sometimes moody, gossipy, and self-centered.

4. Practical, sober-minded, determined, and hardworking. Known to be stubborn, suspicious, and sometimes gloomy.

5. Adventurous and quick-thinking, has executive skills, enjoys travels, and is unconventional. Exhibits impatience and impulsiveness.

6. Romantically inclined, proud, straightforward, and sympathetic. Can be stubborn and argumentative.

7. Enjoys being alone. Is inventive, intuitive, and eccentric. Sometimes moody, unsympathetic, and skeptical.

8. Successful in business, likes money, has integrity and dependability. Can be demanding, impatient, and egotistical.

9. Strives for perfection, is dramatic, artistic, and highly intuitive. Often accident-prone, displays prejudice, and is too idealistic.

The Master numbers of 11, 22, and 33 share idealism, high creativity, and natural leadership ability. They have special purposes: 11 is the inspirational leader, 22 the master builder, and 33 heals through love.

Followers of numerology think twice before changing their place of residence; they feel the right number can improve a lifestyle or situation. Should one have money troubles, an 8 house or apartment is recommended: such an address encourages organization, vision, and management of financial matters. If the need is to focus on one's spiritual path in life, a 7 house is the perfect choice as this is a residence where one can rest, contemplate, and have good telepathic communications. Linda, a Portland businesswoman, rejected a number 5 house in the Scarborough area—she had enough stress in her life. A 5 house is a hub of activity, movement and change. Variety is the norm with such a number; it is an address leading to hectic living and chaos.

In order to accept this metaphysical science, one must have confidence in the thought that each number has a specific meaning. It also is necessary to exhibit a willingness to follow the rules when working its math. Some people feel more comfortable with astrology and can't get past formula while others swear that numerology is more accurate than a Tarot reading. At best, it is a way for some people to discover themselves—to find where they are heading

THE WORLD OF ALEXANDER TANOUS

Alexander Tanous was born on November 26, 1926 in Van Buren, Maine. He was the oldest of eight brothers from a Lebanese family that was Catholic and poor. The father sometimes worked in construction and sold merchandise door-to-door with a horse and wagon. When he died, his estate totaled $1.28—before the Depression the Tanouses were well-to-do merchants and had one of Van Buren's two automobiles. Ann Alice Tanous insisted that her sons continue their education after their father's death, but they had to find odd jobs in order to survive: the brothers sold newspapers, picked potatoes, scavenged the roadsides for discarded bottles, and gathered bits of coal that fell from passing trains.

Alex Tanous's father and Lebanese poet Kahlil Gibran became friends when both men were living in New York City during the early 1920s. "You will have a son," said Gibran, "a man of exceptional gifts, of great abilities—but also a man of great sorrows." Gibran's prediction was further substantiated when the boy was born with a fetal membrane covering his head and shoulders. This caul, a water bag that protects the fetus, had in the past suffocated many babies at birth. Several Middle Eastern cultures hold that children born with "the veil" possess amazing psychic abilities.

Alex believed that he came into the world with other signs of this power. In the palm of his left hand the fold creases formed a perfect hexagram, or six-pointed Star of David—Dutch psychic Peter Hurkos also had such a network of lines in his palm as did Jeane Dixon. Another remarkable engraving of folds was his name *Alex* spelled backwards. "Before I was born," explained Tanous, "my parents had considered naming me after a grandfather, Alexander. When they saw the palm of my hand they felt my name had been preordained."

Both Alex's father and mother were psychic. The father gave readings and was known in Van Buren as a talented dowser; the mother displayed incredible healing gifts in Tanous's fifth year. She was carrying a kettle of boiling water when she tripped over her son. "Lord, don't let anything happen to this child!" she cried, wiping and hugging him. Later, an astonished doctor found no sign of scalding, only a tiny blister at the back of the child's neck.

The first demonstration of Alex's psychic abilities came when he was eighteen months old. The child loved the song "Mary Had a Little Lamb," and a recording of it was in the middle of a stack of fifty records. The toddler passed his hand over the edges of the albums, and without failure, time after time, he pulled out his favorite. This was something he would do years later with a deck of cards at lectures and on television.

Tanous claimed that his first out-of-body experience occurred when he was five years old. He often amused himself by jumping down a long stairway, but unlike other children who played games on a flight of stairs, he didn't fall; Alex floated down, and when he landed at the bottom he could see at the top an exact likeness of himself—the boy was in both places at the same time. Here was a new playmate, and he remembered the two waving to one another.

At this time, there was direct contact with what he later believed were the spirits of dead children. They wore ordinary clothes and looked real but he was the only one who could see them. Once when his father and mother heard him talking to himself, they questioned him, and he described a set of twins whom his parents recognized immediately. They were children of relatives and had died at the age which he saw them, though years before Alex was born.

His psychic capacities were noticed when he entered school. His third-grade teacher was reading a poem to the class one day and Alex interrupted her. He recited the rest of the poem, a work he had never read, and his explanation for this accomplishment was that he received the lines from her telepathically. On another instance, he startled her by giving the answer to an arithmetic problem before she wrote it on the blackboard.

One out-of-body episode came when he was nine years old and had an emergency appendectomy. Tanous had no memory of being taken to the hospital, but after coming out of anesthesia Alex described the entire surgical procedure to an astounded nurse. He recalled looking at his unconscious body while hovering above the operating table.

At this age, the boy wasn't always tactful when making predictions. A friend of the family visited their Van Buren home, and when Alex shook hands with the man, he asked: "Sir, are you ready to die?"

"What do you mean?" asked the startled guest.

"You're going to be dead within twenty-four hours."

The man laughed uncomfortably.

"What are you saying?" demanded an irritated father.

"Dad, I just can't help it," replied Alex. "That's what I see."

The father apologized to his friend and the embarrassing exchange was dismissed as childish nonsense.

But the boy was not mistaken: within twenty-four hours the man died of a heart attack.

Young Tanous wasn't urged to stop having psychic experiences or to keep his predictions to himself, but his mother did insist that he try to become part of his age-group and restrain himself when faced with visions that forced him outside the circle of small-town social acceptance. It was only then that Alex became aware that he possessed unusual gifts.

High school was a difficult time for him. Several of the teachers were priests, and when listening to lectures on theology, he realized that exhibiting his psychic capacities placed him in jeopardy of violating the canons of his faith. "No priest ever actually told me that I was evil (at least not during my high school days)," remarked Tanous—but the doubts he harbored caused him to withdraw socially while his grades plummeted. This introversion deepened and with it came the realization that it was impossible to suppress the flow of premonitions and psychic images.

Several times he made efforts to rise above his self-imposed isolation by getting involved in school activities. He signed up for an early 1941 classroom debate; the subject was "Will Lend-Lease Involve the United States in War?" Tanous's team was assigned the position that such an involvement would bring about conflict. The debate went well until Alex stood before the class and delivered his bombshell: "On December 8," he predicted without thinking, "the newspaper headlines will read WAR

DECLARED." It was another psychic incident that left him with the feeling of having sinned.

There seemed to be no way of avoiding his dilemma. One day when he was playing football and running with the pigskin a fellow student named Everett Tilley tackled him. Tanous went down hard and when he got on his feet there was anger in his voice. "You're going to die for that!" he roared. Six months later, on Alex's birthday, Tilley died of an appendix complication.

It would be years before the Catholic Church adopted the doctrine of conscience which allowed Tanous to follow the tenets of his religion without feelings of guilt. There were unhappy experiences for him as war raged in Europe and the Pacific. Once during confession with a young priest he admired, Alex learned that Father Duhamel intended to go to Guadalcanal as a missionary. "Don't go overseas," Tanous urged him. "If you do, you'll never see America again. You'll be killed, bayoneted through the throat, and your church will be burned to the ground." On October 14, 1943, the priest was killed, bayoneted through the throat, and his body and the remains of two nuns were buried near the smoldering ruins of their church.

After graduating from high school, Alex served in the army at Fort Bragg, North Carolina, and it would be nine years before he attended college. "The time I spent in the service," he recalled, "was probably the most difficult of my life." He would glance at his fellow soldiers and know who would lose his life in the far Pacific and who would return home crippled. Now that he had left "the repressive atmosphere" of hometown Van Buren, there was an avalanche of visions: he predicted a plane crash at Ford Bragg and startled troops on bivouac by telling them the war with Germany would be over by the time they marched back to camp. "How do you know these things, Tanous?" asked his commanding officer. "Are they lucky guesses?" Instead of answering directly, Alex tried to deflect his commander's curiosity with another prediction. "Sometime in mid-August (1945) an extremely unusual bomb will explode in Japan and, as a result, the war will end there too."

Death often surfaced in Tanous's psychic pronouncements. A woman came to him and asked when her son would be discharged from the army. "He's coming back very soon," Alex replied, "but I want you to tell him not to cross railroad tracks by car. I see great danger to him in that situation." A few days after returning home the young man was killed when going across a railroad track in nearby St. Léonard, New Brunswick. But it wasn't all grimness: he had visions of job promotions, bonuses, unexpected marriages, and children for couples who had little hope of raising a family. Lost objects were found and missing relatives located. Tanous kept no records in these early years, but his predictions attracted a wide circle of followers.

After his discharge, Alex returned to Van Buren to help his mother in raising his younger brothers and seeing that they all got high school diplomas. He held down a number of jobs and was at this time in his life too distracted to think of further education. The *Aroostock Republican* of Caribou, Maine hired him as a newspaper stringer, and shortly after he accepted the position his psychic demon appeared front and center.

"What you'd really like is a murder, right?" Tanous asked the editor—one was about to happen but it was too early to pinpoint.

"I don't expect anything like that in sleepy little Van Buren," replied the employer.

Three days later, Alex sensed that a strange death had occurred the night before.

"There's been a murder," he told his boss who dropped the telephone in astonishment.

Though a verdict of suicide was later ruled, Tanous and many other people in town were not convinced.

Alex started to satisfy a childhood dream: he began composing songs. His first attempt was called "Maytime," which was brought out by Savoy Records—this was a pop song that the recording company made into a successful Western number. But his fascination for music wasn't intense enough for a career choice. His most ambitious composition was a symphony called "America in Jazz." It was later performed at a music festival in France and received an award.

The Korean War further delayed plans of college. Tanous was recalled to service and sent to Fort Devens, Massachusetts where he was assigned to the U. S. Army Public Information Department. He met a number of actors and singers while in uniform, and upon discharge in 1952 enrolled at the Cambridge School of Radio and Television in Boston. Alex had been told that he had a resonant voice, and for a while he thought of becoming a disc jockey. But a persistent interest in religion kept him from his radio career. In the fall of 1953 he entered Stonehill College, a Catholic institute outside Boston, to study for the priesthood.

Tanous found his college courses difficult to follow; his high school background was sketchy and in the first year he failed several exams. Only prophecy saved him from flunking everything—predicting the questions he would be asked was one way of studying. Finally, he tried

Edgar Cayce's method of absorbing a book: after leafing through the pages to get some idea of the contents, Alex placed the book under his pillow and slept on it. When the exams had been corrected, he was called into his teacher's office.

"You must have cheated," the professor told him. "That's the only possible explanation."

"What do you mean?"

"You got your 100," said the bewildered don.

It didn't always work, Tanous admitted, but often enough for him to win a full-tuition scholarship for graduate school at Boston College.

A fellow student once challenged Tanous's psychic powers and he didn't hesitate.

"You have an unopened letter in your purse," he said to the girl, "an important one."

"No I don't," she replied. "You're wrong."

"Take a look," Alex urged her. "I know I'm right."

She opened her purse to humor him and then saw the unread letter she had stuffed there in her rush to be on time for classes that morning.

"Let me have the letter," he said, "but don't open it."

Tanous held the envelope for a moment before passing it back.

"Now, I want you to open the letter," he instructed. "I'll recite it while you read it silently sitting here, and I am at the other end of the table."

She opened the envelope and read the letter to herself while he spoke the contents, word for word.

A sad premonition came to him when he and a brother were driving to Van Buren after learning that their ailing mother had taken a turn for the worse. Alex glanced up at the night sky and saw a shooting star. "Slow down and stop, please." "Why?" asked his brother. "Because Mother has just died." They both looked at their watches; it was eleven o'clock. The two arrived home at five in the morning and were told that their mother had passed away at eleven the night before. Kahlil Gibran's prediction that Tanous would be "a man of great sorrows" was much on Alex's mind at this time of his life—in little more than two years he had lost his mother, three brothers, and a nephew.

Sorrow didn't hamper his studies at Boston College; he completed his master's work in one year, graduating in June 1960. There were more degrees ahead: a second master's from Fordham University in 1964; a doctorate of divinity at the College of Divine Metaphysics in Indiana, 1965; and a master's in counseling and guidance from the University of Maine in 1973.

Tanous began by teaching theology at Manhattan College in New York City in 1965 and then accepted a professorship at St. John's University in Brooklyn. For ten years, with brief interruptions, he taught a variety of courses at secondary schools and colleges until he assumed the mantle of a full-time psychic.

His predictions were increasing his national exposure: Robert Kennedy would be President, Tanous declared, if the Senator from New York didn't get shot; Richard Nixon would be nominated for the presidency—this was months before the former Vice President announced his candidacy; three astronauts would die in an accident; and Thurgood Marshall would be appointed to the Supreme Court—at the time Marshall, though highly respected, was not yet a public figure.

One of Tanous's most controversial readings concerned the Edward Kennedy incident at Chappaquiddick. On WABI, Channel 5, in Bangor, Maine, Alex told his version which baffled viewers. The vehicle that went over the bridge had been tampered with—an act of political sabotage or *assassination*. As Tanous perceived the tragedy, Kennedy was not in the car; the Senator had loaned it to Mary Jo Kopechne after she dropped him off at a party they both were going to attend. When she didn't come back, he went looking for her, even diving into the waters in an attempt to rescue her.

Tanous felt there was support for this scenario: the diver who pulled Kopechne's body from the car found the doors locked—he had to smash a window to get inside. And why didn't Kennedy make this information available to the press? Because, Tanous insisted, the Senator feared what would happen to the country if the public learned that yet another assassination attempt had been made on the Kennedy family.

Publicity generated by his predictions caused controversy within the hierarchy of Catholic circles, particularly a long article published in the Manchester, New Hampshire *Union Leader*, entitled "He Is Able to Predict the Future." In early February of 1969, after the appearance of this publication, he was notified that his teaching contract would not be renewed. With it went his dreams of becoming a priest. "I might still be a teacher today," wrote Tanous, "content with my lot." But the dismissal was a catalyst rushing him into the inevitable. When he accepted a host position on the WGAN, Portland, Maine radio program *Maine Line*, he didn't depend exclusively on psychometry—divination by touching—to provide answers. When asked a question, Alex Tanous would often leave his body and travel to any distance or time point to enlighten his audience.

In addition to his radio program, Tanous gave lectures in theology and psychology at Cheverus High School in Portland. Personal readings were frequent, some involving family tragedies and illnesses, and others less serious, such as locating misplaced house keys or telling parents the sex of their expected child.

("I was pregnant at the time," recalled this writer's daughter, Juanita, "and I decided to test Tanous's powers by asking him the sex of the child. He said it was a boy! I delivered a baby girl, and I remember him visiting me in the hospital and bringing flowers, because, he said, he'd made a mistake. Later, I had him speak to an English class I was teaching. He gave a lecture on psychic phenomena, and I believe he brought along a Kirlian camera so the kids could take pictures of auras.")

Tanous's long record of accurate predictions attracted law-enforcement officers, and he was frequently asked to solve crimes and to find missing children. He did, however, cause a few heads to shake when he offered one explanation: "I am convinced some children who disappear and are never found have not been kidnapped by criminals—or even human beings. They've been taken, I believe, by residents of another planet." He realized it sounded preposterous but there were reasons for thinking this way. Too many young people disappear when they've been left unattended for only a few moments. Also, there were the documented cases of missing children who returned to their homes years later—with no memories whatever of what happened to them while they were gone. "How could an ordinary kidnapping account for this?"

The March 4, 1973 issue of the *National Enquirer* carried an interview with Police Chief Herman Boudreau of Freeport, Maine. The officer credited Tanous with solving the case of a missing eight-year-old boy. Boudreau took Alex through the apartment house where the boy had lived and drove around the neighborhood. Tanous said the child was dead and "the body is wrapped in something and under something."

The next day Tanous came to Boudreau's office with a sketch he had drawn. "This is the murderer," Alex told him. The chief reached into his desk and pulled out a photograph of Milton I. Wallace, one of the suspects. "You couldn't tell the difference—his sketch and the photo, and there was no way Tanous could have known about Wallace."

The suspect lived just down the hall from the missing eight year old. "We went to Wallace's apartment," said Chief Boudreau, "and found the boy's decomposed body under a bed, wrapped in a blanket—just like Tanous had suggested."

Alex's first conscious attempt at healing was in Portland, Maine in

1969. The sufferer had his foot caught in a power mower; the limb had turned blue and amputation seemed inevitable. Tanous assured him that all would go well. "I felt a current from your voice," the subject remembered, "it penetrated my head, went right down through my system. Within days there was movement in the foot—the healing was absolutely phenomenal."

Tanous never was able to explain the interaction he had with those who came to him seeking some cure. He did recognize that the energy he felt coming from him was "universal"—a laying on of hands that radiated confidence. Many of the cures were only partial and some attempts failed entirely, but there were more than a hundred instances which could only be described as miraculous.

Cameras often lost their dependability when Tanous was in focus. "Better not take that," he told a photographer. "It will break your camera." Paying no heed, the man proceeded and his expensive equipment was instantly disabled—such malfunctions were commonplace. At a 1970 psychics' seminar in Tennessee, both the lens aperture setting and shutter speeds kept changing for a frustrated photographer. The Rumford Falls, Maine *Times* on March 30, 1972 reported another incident: "Dr. Tanous informed Pat Milligan backstage that he would make this photographer's flash go off without the trigger being touched and so it did when the camera was being focused." Perhaps the most bizarre demonstration of his powers over equipment came at a lecture when a man in the audience stood up to take a picture. "You don't have to snap the shutter," Tanous told him. "I'll do that, from here." And he did.

Gremlins often were busy when Alex got near microphones, tape recorders, electric lights, and watches. At a Mary Baldwin lecture he warned his audience that the microphone was about to go dead moments before it ceased functioning. A watch he was wearing stopped, ran backwards, skipped forward a day on its calendar calibration, jumped back an hour, and then began running flawlessly.

Once during a fund-raiser for an antidrug program in Machias, Maine, someone in the audience asked him if he could put out all the lights in the high school auditorium. "I don't know," he replied, "but I'll give it a try." Alex stared at a glowing bulb, as if to draw energy from it. "Lights out!" he commanded, and moments later the hall was pitch-black, and so were all the rooms in the school. For nearly a minute, there wasn't a burning light in the town of Machias—a total power failure. "Afterward," wrote Tanous, "I was interviewed by the local radio station. I could not explain what happened. But I was sure I had caused it. This happened on

April 28, 1970."

When Tanous discovered that he could move objects without touching them, he wondered whether psychokinesis was the reason that his presence sometimes disabled cameras and other mechanisms. As an experiment for his Cheverus High School students, Alex placed the cap of a ballpoint pen on a book. After several moments of concentration, he felt some form of energy leave his eyes and the cap moved. The students, not believing what they had seen, insisted on placing a mark under the object for the next demonstration. When the cap was lifted, they found a scorched spot on the book.

There were other curious happenings. In an art gallery, one of the paintings swung back and forth on the wall so violently that Tanous quickly turned away. Heavy drapery reacted to his gaze, the fabric moving as if the wind were blowing it—this in a room with the door and every window closed. But these disruptions of inanimate objects weren't limited to direct concentration—there were aftershocks: a row of big books fell from a shelf when Tanous entered the office of a radio executive, and later when he telephoned the man, the books fell again.

"Challenging myself further," wrote Tanous in his book *Beyond Coincidence*, 1976, "I discovered I could project not only balls of light, but actual images, images which could be seen by everyone in the room." Before a startled group of friends, for nearly two hours, he shot streams of light from his eyes, and pictures appeared on a living room wall in a firework of color—one was a schooner in full sail. These projections were described by Tanous as a "solidifying" of light, and he had limited control over the images. "I cannot turn it off," he admitted at one point. Only by putting his hands over his eyes and turning away was he able to gradually dim the projected band of light.

Dr. Tanous's special relationship with light began when he was in grade school. At this time he learned to bring forth psychic images from flickering kerosene lamps and find visions in the rays of the sun; it was a way of energizing himself psychically. He warned others not to attempt such a technique, but he himself never suffered retinal burns. Tanous could—and there were hundreds of witnesses to substantiate this feat—make balls of light shoot out of his eyes. Lights would dim and switch off when he entered a room. "Well, now we are going to see something," he would tell his audience. "I'm going to get more power." Moments later, the lights would flicker and fade.

After a 1970 lecture in Brunswick, Maine, he absorbed light from a photographer's flashgun and then projected the light in such a way that it hovered like mist over the head of a young priest who was standing a few feet away. First blue in color, and slowly changing to green, yellow, orange, purple, the cloud gradually dissolved from sight. There were more than three hundred attending, among them Reverend Edward O'Leary, later Bishop of Maine. "I don't know how I do these things," Tanous admitted. "They just happen."

Another demonstration occurred a year later before an audience of 150 people in Portland. After gazing into a blinding flashgun, Tanous became mischievous with his projections of light: "Now I'm holding it here," he told the crowd, "and I'm folding it into a square, now it's over your head, it's crawling up your leg, you can see it down by the floor"— he was playing with the light, the way a child would with a toy.

Tanous's psychic achievements were frequently accomplished through out-of-body experiences. Again, as with his ability to project light after absorbing it, he couldn't explain his travels forward and backward in time. For him, the feat was nothing more than exercising his will: "I've done it dozens of times. I've been seen at distant locales while it was verified that I was at home."

He achieved a memorable OBE when someone asked at a Brooklyn Heights, New York banquet what the date October 11 meant to him. "It's the day before Columbus Day," Tanous replied. "But it doesn't mean anything to me outside of that." Then it appeared to him. "I know what you want. October 11—the Russian Revolution."

As the astonished questioner, a disbeliever in OBE, and others registered surprise, Tanous had left the dinner gathering and was dangling in midair over the city of Leningrad—it was October 11, 1917. He saw it all, and gave instant commentary: the Czar coming forward, men falling, blood pulsing from wounds. Then, after a lapse in time, Tanous was back at the banquet table sixty years later.

"Do you know what you described?" he was asked.

Tanous didn't.

"You described the Czar's winter palace, the Hermitage, and its spectacular gate. Have you been there?"

"No," answered Alex. "I've never been to Russia."

"Unless you saw it," his questioner told him, "you could never speak about it. Yet you described it in detail—I know, because I was there only a few months ago."

"Then I read your mind," Tanous offered.

"No, I don't think so," came the reply. "You saw things I never saw. You saw things no one could have seen unless he was there at the time."

Tanous was introduced to Dr. Karlis Osis, Director of The American Society for Psychical Research, as a result of the "trip" to Russia. "In a series of ESP tests given to Dr. Alex Tanous in which he scored very high," wrote Osis, "the law of probability that it was chance was 1 out of 3,000." From 1968 until the time of his death, Tanous was associated with the ASPR as one of their gifted subjects in a variety of experiments, such as faith healing, projecting thoughts on a screen, solidifying light, OBE, and communicating with ghosts.

He and Dr. Osis talked at length about an OBE in which Alex saw himself performing the role of "a tiny ball of light." These trips had brought him closer to religious beliefs. "I have the feeling that I have shared in something divine," wrote Tanous. "When I go out-of-body, I see lights and beauty. Sometimes, I don't want to come back. But I know I have to. I know that unless I return and share this gift with others, I would never be happy."

For a short time, after his brother David's death in 1957, Tanous had joined the staff of the Holy Ghost Hospital in Boston, a medical unit for the incurable. His purpose in taking a job there was to observe people who were dying. "If a living man is able to detach part of himself, send it elsewhere, then retrieve it," he asked, "might not a dying man detach part of himself and not retrieve it, leaving that part to survive him after death?" The dark tunnel and intense light that so many people spoke of when having a near-death experience intrigued him. "On several occasions," Tanous stated when recalling his hospital observations, "I saw a shapeless mist drift away from a patient when he died."

Tanous used his "Mary Had a Little Lamb" skills in many of his readings, though he went further than that on the WGAN *Maine Line* program with Steve Morgan. An ESP test was suggested. Morgan thought of a record and whispered it to another announcer. Alex quickly pulled the selection from a sizeable collection. To test him further, the two announcers asked him to leave the studio while they picked another recording. It made no difference: the psychic returned and breezily pulled their choice from the stack.

He never made claims of being a medium—in the sense of one who holds séances in order to achieve contact with the dead while in a trance— in fact, he was skeptical of many occult practices. Though convinced that the dead twins he had played with during his childhood appeared to him because he was able to slip through some gate in time and space, it took him many years before he felt comfortable with this part of his psychic self; liberated enough to make contact beyond the barrier.

His communications with spirits rose from an awareness of their energy, and he met them on a psychic and highly compassionate level. He felt a deep need to help break the shackles of those whose negative emotions and unfinished business had accumulated during their lifetimes, and were keeping them earthbound. "You are free," Alex assured them. "You are loved."

There were frequent encounters when he allowed himself to be receptive: the ghosts of a woman and her murderer made their presences known in a vacant room in Switzerland—Tanous saw a wealthy old woman being dragged out on a balcony and pushed over the railing; in Westminster Abbey, he recited the concluding lines of Elizabeth Barrett Browning's "How do I love thee?" while standing at Robert Browning's grave—it was a poem Alex had never read; and a dead woman in Alabama used Tanous "as a ghostly-messenger service"—he was to tell the woman's daughter that there were important documents forgotten on a shelf.

Three strange men had been seen near a "sensitive experimental installation" in New Mexico, and Tanous was sent there to investigate. Local residents claimed that the three had been around for years—ever since the first atomic explosion at Alamogordo. Alex was to confront these strangers at a diner where they had often been seen. "That's one of them," an informant told him. Alex took a seat at the counter a few stools down and eye contact was immediate. In his mind, he heard the man say: "Why have you come here? Why do you do this? You are just like one of us." All desire to communicate left him. "I got up from my seat," wrote Tanous, "and left the diner—to the intense disappointment of those who'd arranged the trip. But I could do nothing else."

The stranger radiated an energy that was familiar; Alex had felt it before—once at Stonehenge—and when he was introduced to Charles Hickson, a guest on the television program *To Tell the Truth*—Hickson was there to tell a national audience that he was taken aboard a UFO. The same energy had been encountered earlier when Betty Hill told Alex about her captors at the time she and her husband, Barney, had been abducted— "Her description," said Tanous, "closely resembled the man's I had seen in the diner." Had he ever been contacted by a flying saucer? This was a question frequently asked at his lectures: No, but he had seen a UFO once in Maine, and he was convinced that such things were products of intelligent beings.

Staunch Catholic, a man who devoted his life to research, healing, writing and lecturing, Dr. Alexander Tanous was an unforgettable presence: no one who ever met him came away without feelings of warmth and awe. His reputation as a gifted parapsychologist was worldwide, and many of his psychic demonstations were so incredible that he became both an Edgar Cayce and a Harry Houdini in the minds of those who witnessed his feats of absorbing light, OBE, communicating with spirits, projecting thoughts on a screen, and other ESP achievements.

Author of *Beyond Coincidence*, and *Understanding and Developing Your Child's Natural Psychic Abilities*, Dr. Tanous died on July 7, 1990. Shortly before his death, while hospitalized, and with the assistance of his brother, attorney Wakine Tanous Sr., Alex incorporated a trust dedicated to scientific research, an organization that fittingly carries his name. Literature from the Alex Tanous Foundation in Portland, Maine states: "At his bequest, his foundation will continue his work through research and our own creative powers which he helped us to develop. His family, friends, colleagues and now his Foundation are called upon to keep his spirit of love, friendship and continuous searching to improve the power within ourselves for all mankind."

THE HOUSE ON WASHINGTON STREET

The house on Washington Street in Bath, Maine with its three stories and a dozen or more rooms—constructed in the eighteen hundreds and probably designed for some sea captain or well-to-do merchant—had also functioned as a funeral home. A few years ago, these premises were rented sight unseen to a military family from another state. The husband and wife with two teenage daughters were to live there while their own home was being built.

It began gradually: faint creaking along the stairs, an unmistakable sigh behind a closed door, and from an empty room some soft utterance— perhaps someone moaning? These sounds were barely audible in the beginning, so low in tone and trivial enough for the family to blame their imaginations. Then there was a quivering spoon on the dining room table—this was just before a cloth napkin slipped to the floor. But the motion of inanimate objects became more irritating as cups and saucers rattled and dinner plates slid from their place settings. What had amused the occupants earlier now left them with feelings of uneasiness as they went about the business of living in a house with an unknown presence.

The military officer and his wife had asked the realtor to disable an elevator that once had been used to bring coffins from the attic to the ground-floor level; the couple didn't want their daughters playing with the conveyance as it looked unsafe. This was no problem, the rental agent assured them; he had the only key to the control box and promptly switched the mechanism off. All went well until one evening a week or two later: the family heard the grinding sound of machinery, and the empty elevator began going up and down floors with its door opening and closing.

At times, the spirit was less aggressive, but there seemed to be more activity when the mother was home alone. One day she was doing her washing and had carried the laundry basket to the top of the stairs to put away clothes. Suddenly, an interruption—probably the telephone—and on returning to complete her household task, she found the basket upside-down and clean clothes scattered about the hall.

Another incident occurred in the bathroom. She was cleaning the sink and in the mirror saw one of her daughters standing behind her. She spoke to the girl briefly without turning around, but when she left the bathroom the woman saw her daughter entering the house. "Where did you go?" the astonished mother asked. "I was just talking with you." And the girl replied: "That isn't possible. I've just come home." Weeks later, and after a number of troubling experiences, the woman began to suspect that the spirit was capable of making itself appear as a member of the family.

One night, when John, a boyfriend, took home his seventeen-year-old date, the girl appeared unsettled. Peeking through the mail slot, she returned to the car and in a frightened voice said: "I hope your parents won't mind, but I can't go home tonight—I'm so afraid. I just saw the rocking chair moving back and forth and no one is in the house."

Then the happenings became more violent. There was a deafening crash in the attic one evening—doors had been installed along the eaves in an area that was previously a repository for coffins, and one of these doors had been pushed aside with such force that hinges three inches long and an eighth-inch thick were ripped apart. The nervous family called the police, who soon determined that no one inside the house could have caused such damage. "These were steel hinges, not of the flimsy kind," said the boyfriend's father, "and they were shredded by superhuman strength."

"No person could have flattened the door that way," he continued, "and it was forced open from inside the storage area." This was the only time John's father went inside the house, and he recalled encountering a "cold spot" in the hallway. "I felt a sort of chill passing from my left side to my right."

   There would be another event that night to disturb the occupants. A large hallway clock had been hung on the wall out of reach; a timepiece that wasn't running. Suddenly, an hour after the crash in the attic, the clock began ticking and keeping perfect time. One would need a step-ladder to set the hour and minute hands precisely, and no one in the family had touched them.

   The police installed motion sensors in the hope that a human miscreant would be revealed, and when these devices failed to deliver, the family contacted an exorcist. Though he diligently visited every room in the house the paranormal activities kept escalating: books fell from shelves and pages fluttered between open covers; it reached a point where the family was afraid to leave knives on the dining room table. Near the end of their stay, the military officer slept with his dress saber close at hand. This decision was made after he felt the weight of someone on the mattress at the foot of their bed. Thinking it was one of their daughters, he turned on the light and no one was there.

   They began to wonder whether the spirit really meant to harm them. This Washington Street house wasn't the only place believed to shelter a restless presence. Several local residents reported hearing a piano coming alive late at night in the darkened Masonic hall just down the street. Could there be some connection? The family was now holding lengthy conversations about the impending move to their new home, and it seemed that after they talked about such changes the activities became more pronounced. Then one night husband and wife felt someone getting into bed with them. After hurriedly turning on the light and finding no one there, they felt even more threatened.

   John, who formerly dated the daughter, is now in the military. At the time these events took place he was so emotionally caught up with what was happening to the girl's family that his parents began to worry about him. Perhaps he needed counseling, they thought: it wasn't normal for an eighteen year old to bunk on the floor in the room where they were sleeping. John was fearful that he might bring the spirit home with him and involve them all.

   It finally became too much for the tenants; they decided to rent an-other place, and managed to find a small apartment—it was only a few weeks before the construction of their house was completed, but they couldn't stand the thought of additional nights on Washington Street. The ploy was successful; not once did the spirit manifest displeasure of their leave-taking, at the emergency shelter or the new home. The military officer and his family were now free to pursue normal lives.

The house has been vacant for months—it probably is becoming a realtor's nightmare with its many rooms and sprawling complexities of brick, wood, glass and mortar. There are people in Bath who believe the building is not habitable. Maybe another tenant unacquainted with the area will make the mistake of renting it and the strange incidents will be repeated. One easily can visualize that empty elevator coming alive again with its door opening and closing, and some rocking chair becoming increasingly nervous.

WITCHES AND THEIR WORLD

Witchcraft, a practice older than written records, found roots in a society based on agriculture. One of the important survival skills of early civilization was the knowledge of herbs and plants and how to grow and prepare them. A person learned and experienced in medicinal herbal lore was looked upon with respect. These pharmacists, often elderly women, were the midwives and doctors of their village or tribe. Soon, oils and minerals were added to their list of wonder drugs for healing and divining future events. In time, they became known as "witches"— from the old English verb "to wit," meaning to shape, turn or bend.

Early makers of magic could diagnose many ailments and prescribe medicines and rituals to heal their patients. These seers served as spiritual leaders, performed marriages, anointed the newborn, and counseled the dying in preparation for the next world. They were the first visionaries; prophets who quickly assumed central roles as they mesmerized their listeners with poetry in their voices. These were the ancient ways, the Old Religion at work, and these customs are still being reenacted by a minority to this day.

Primeval man believed that biological processes were spiritual and found divine meaning in every natural event. The great mystery of life was transformation: how things change, develop, die, and are reborn. The most obvious event was the transformation of the woman—her ability to conceive a new life, produce milk, and menstruate with the phases of the moon. Her centrality could not be ignored; early man soon recognized that both woman and nature shared motherhood. By closely identifying the woman with the earth, our ancestors assumed that the divine power behind creation was female. Some of the earliest works of art substantiate this belief: human figures depicted were fertility symbols, and these figurines have been found all across Africa and Europe.

It took much longer for the father's role in conception to be understood, and this is hardly surprising—a woman doesn't become pregnant
with every act of intercourse, and the connection between sexual rela-
tions and conception was only gradually perceived. Primitive man believed that life in the womb was a miracle performed by divine power,
perhaps placed by a spirit visitor, or (a more whimsical and imaginative
explanation) caused by the light of the moon.

How did this benign feminine magic become suspect? What brought
about the negative image of a witch—a picture repulsive enough to become so ingrained in our culture that the mention of such a person is
associated with evil? Scholars suggest that this condemnation rose from
the patriarchal revolution in the fourth century when the Church and the
Roman Empire joined forces. As Christianity gained acceptance, those
who disagreed were accused of being devil worshipers. Patriarchal prejudices, particularly against women, became institutionalized in Medieval Europe. St. Augustine, for all his benevolence, was quick to insist
that women did not have souls. "The history of civilization," observed
historian Otto Rank, "was the gradual masculinization of human civilization." The domination of one faith over another was only gradual: for
several centuries the Old Religion and Christianity coexisted. In 500
A.D. the Franks made it legal to practice magic, and in 785 a penalty of
death was imposed against anyone who burned a witch. Over the centuries, the Church became predominant—more imperious. In 1310,
conjuring, divination, and love potions were considered magic and
declared illegal. This was the beginning of the "Burning Times" when
victims were set afire at the stake for witchcraft and heresy—80 percent
of the people suffering this death were females.

"When a woman thinks alone, she thinks evil"—a male argument used
at the turn of the twentieth century when debates were raging to give
females voting rights. (This writer recalls a comment from a Maine
woman who was permanently scarred by such browbeating. "When
women got the right to vote at town meetings," she declared, "that's
when the country started going to hell.")

Throughout the Inquisition, clairvoyance was associated with the "evil
eye"—it was a terrifying concept for patriarchal authority. Witches were
forced to enter courtrooms backwards so they wouldn't have the opportunity of casting spells on the judges by "evil glances."

When a Christian missionary converted a person who embraced the
Old Religion, baptism in the new faith didn't wipe away earlier beliefs.
Conversions came about because it was too dangerous to practice witch-

craft openly. During the Burning Times many witches followed the Christian calendar of holy days but kept alive the old magic behind closed doors. In the privacy of the home there were herbs, knots, oils, bindings, candles, and sometimes the Christian converts ventured forth to hold magic circles in a wood beneath the moon.

Today, many Christians still enact spells once considered pagan: they hang horseshoes over doors to neutralize harmful energies, dry herbs and medicinal barks in kitchens for healing, and some bury scissors by entrances to discourage enemies. "Just an old superstition," is their reply to the curious, "but doing it makes me feel better."

In this country, the town of Salem, Massachusetts comes to mind when the execution of witches is mentioned. Twenty people were put to death in that event of hysteria, but this is only a fraction of the numbers who were burned at the stake, hanged, or crushed beneath heavy stones during those dangerous years. People from all walks of life were accused of practicing witchcraft, and this included a wealthy shipowner in Salem; a minister who had graduated from Harvard and possessed a sizeable estate in England; Captain John Alden, son of John and Priscilla of the Plymouth Colony; and even the wife of a Massachusetts governor. No one was safe when gossip and suspicion flourished.

Maine's early settlers used herbs, such as rosemary, sage, and pennyroyal, to protect themselves from witchery, and it was not uncommon for fennel and Saint-John's-wort to be hung over doorways to safeguard homes—particularly during Midsummer's Eve, a time thought to be popular for casting spells.

It took several decades after the Salem, Massachusetts trials for the witch craze to sweep through Maine, especially along the coast and in the western part of the state. Many old town records mention these dark sisters of the night. In addition to the 178 accused witches of the Salem hysteria, there were 147 witchcraft accusations and persecutions elsewhere in New England.

Later, people grew somewhat skeptical about the dangers of witchcraft. It became almost fashionable to believe that magic was only a hocus-pocus game played by a conjurer. Such thinking was part of the new era; a period when questions were being raised about medical practices and religion in general. In 1712, the last person was executed for witchcraft in England, though execution remained on the books until the twentieth century. There were occasional hangings for witchery on the European continent and in America, and people continued to harass innocent victims and cause bodily harm. In Hungary, as late as 1928, a court exonerated a family who had beaten an old woman to death. "She looked like a witch," said one family member when defending himself.

Among the 147 charged with practicing sorcery was Barbara Houndsworth of Belfast, Maine. The town fathers sentenced her to be hanged after a series of unfortunate events: a black plague struck cows pastured near her home, all the dog and cats were afflicted with distemper, the church mysteriously caught fire and burned, and several of Barbara's neighbors fell ill with an unknown disease. Mrs. Houndsworth was immediately blamed for these calamities, probably because she was the maker of aromatic potions and remedies. Some locals said she had murdered her only baby and poisoned her husband.

Barbara was manacled and led to the town square where she was sentenced to be executed. An angry onlooker hurled a stone at the condemned woman and the missile accidentally struck the town clerk in the forehead. He slumped to the ground, and in the ensuing commotion, Mrs. Houndsworth managed to break away from the mob. With her tormentors in pursuit, she ran toward the coastline. Unexpectedly, a gusty ocean wind and torrential rain forced the townspeople to give up their chase. When Barbara reached the path along the coast known as High Point, she slipped on the wet rocks and fell into a boiling sea.

The restless ghost of Barbara Houndsworth is sometimes seen walking along the rocky path at High Point—a thin manacled spirit wandering through flocks of circling seabirds, their cries mixing with her plaintive lament.

Logbooks and diaries of the late 18th century tell the sad story of John Merrill, the founder of Danville, Maine. His wife, Molly, was accused of practicing witchcraft. "Whenever Johnny did anything contrary to her," states the *Atlas and History of Androscoggin County, Maine,* "witch's trouble was sure to follow." Two accounts are noted to illustrate the range of Molly's wrath when she failed to get her own way.

Merrill sold a team of oxen to a neighbor without first asking Molly's permission. This transaction caused a row between husband and wife, and an angry Molly vowed revenge. The next morning, two dead oxen were found twisted on their backs with horns shoved into the ground. "My animals were killed by Molly the Witch," cried the irate farmer, and most people in Danville agreed.

Another neighbor, Samuel Talbox, borrowed a sled from John Merrill to haul grain that he had just purchased. Molly struck again when she learned that her husband hadn't charged the man a fee for use of the conveyance. She stood at a window and grimly watched the grain being loaded. When Talbox started to leave Merrill's dooryard, the sled tipped to its side, spilling both driver and cargo. The heavy sacks were reloaded, and when the horse was urged forward, grain and neighbor were upended again. Several more attempts were made with the same results. Finally, after a volley of oaths, a frustrated Talbox unhitched his horse and galloped home without the purchase.

Before Merrill succumbed to Molly's love spell and married her in 1773, he was far from being a star-crossed man. In general, the heavens had a tendency to favor him when Molly wasn't around. After the wedding, he purchased land in Maine, cleared portions of it for pasturing livestock, and built a log cabin. Molly resented having to stay with her parents while this wilderness claim was being settled. On his own, Merrill prospered and became a much-admired farmer and friend to other townsmen. In the diary of Andrew Robinson Giddinge, one of the first settlers of Androscoggin County, John Merrill is mentioned for "assisting in the building of roads and bridges, and the establishment of the first school at Danville Corner." It was nearly four years before Merrill sent word for Molly to join him.

From the start, Molly was judged to be a witch by settlers, and many of their misfortunes were attributed to her witchcraft. John Merrill struggled to keep his good standing in the Danville community, but most of his neighbors began to avoid him because of his wife. After the grain incident, Samuel Talbox barely nodded when the two men met, and once at a town meeting, Talbox refused to shake Merrill's hand.

Near the end of his life, Merrill was unable to pay his taxes and was forced to sell his holdings at a great loss. He and a bitter Molly left town with only a few possessions and moved to a small cabin in Minot, Maine.

Today, there is only a cellar hole to mark the plot where a witch and her long-suffering husband once lived. The logbooks and diaries fail to reveal what happened to the couple after the move from Danville, but records do indicate that Molly Merrill survived her husband by a number of years.

An eighteenth century witch, Hannah Stover, was buried in a Christian cemetery by the Old Meeting House in Harpswell Center. It is believed that several women bore her coffin through the woods to the burial ground. At the cemetery gate, they were confronted by an angry mob of fishermen who insisted that the body be consigned to Devil's Den, a cave on the shore of Harpswell Neck. But the men underestimated the womenfolk, one of whom, an old widow—she had been fed and sheltered by Stover at a time of famine—resisted by throwing herself on the coffin. This act animated the other female mourners, and the protestors dispersed to a nearby alehouse.

Residents of York Village have been encountering the spirit of Mary, "The Witch," since her death in 1774. Her grave in the Old York Cemetery is said to be haunted. Unlike most witches of that time, she soon gained the respect of her neighbors and was remembered for her kindliness. Mary's herbal prescriptions were in great demand, and she frequently was asked to exorcise evil demons from troubled houses. No one has ever been scared when having contact with her spirit. It is said that on one occasion her unseen presence pushed children on swings in a playground just across the road from the cemetery.

The wicked queen with the magical powers of being able to turn herself into a hideous old hag gave Walt Disney's film *Snow White and the Seven Dwarfs* a dramatic twist, but this did little to assure the frightened children squirming in the theater seats that it was only a pretend world flashing on the giant movie screen. Today's young viewers watching a television production are more savvy than their parents and grandparents—they have been repeatedly inoculated with massive boosters of media violence. They also have escaped some of the more potent prejudices and superstitions that colored attitudes and societal responses in the past.

Medieval practitioners of medicine were quick to condemn healers who offered alternative treatments; it soon became mandatory that only those who took formal courses of study could treat patients. What galled the medical community was the fact that many witches were good at healing: their remedies were painless and often more effective than traditional procedures of purging and leeching. Witches carried a bulging pouch of digestive aids, painkillers, and anti-inflammatory potions, and many of these herbal and natural wonders are found in today's pharmaceutical products.

Modern witches show flexibility when diagnosing and treating illnesses. One ancient method still in use is astrology: healers believe that this permits them to become familiar with the patient's susceptibility toward particular diseases. The witch also may read a person's aura to help with diagnosis—aura readers claim that diseased areas have a tendency to show dark discolorations. Pendulums sometimes are employed as diagnostic aids; they can be rings, crystals, necklaces dangling on a string and belonging to the person who is being healed.

When the general public considers untraditional doctoring, herbs come to mind—such plants are used, but not necessarily ingested: the power of a herbal prescription, according to witches, is compressed in the form of a talisman or sachet for someone to wear as the healer attempts to reach the source of the "disease" on psychic and cosmic levels. Other approaches include psychometry, Tarot cards, Ouija boards, and numerology. More controversial is the ritual performed by an entire coven during a distant-healing rite. The witch becomes a conductor or "lightning rod" for transmissions of "cosmic light." Supposedly, energy raised within the coven passes through the cosmos and into the patient.

Dolls have been used for centuries as vehicles of healing, and many people associate this practice with voodoo. In present-day witchcraft, dolls in the image of the unwell persons are believed to empower practitioners with healing energy. Cloth or parchment are materials frequently selected for the creation of makeshift models, and small dolls can be purchased at witch shops. A tag with the recipient's name is attached to the doll's back, or a photograph of the ailing person is pasted on the doll's face. A piece of clothing from the patient's closet—more effective if last worn when the subject was healthy—and stitched to the doll is believed to give beneficial results. Strands of hair, even fingernail clippings, are sometimes used. When the model is finished, an acupuncture or acupressure manual may provide helpful information for those who wish to locate healing points on the doll's body in order to cure specific ailments of the sufferer.

Since early times, humans have resorted to amulets as a protection from harm. We have no further to look than a charm bracelet dangling from a person's wrist. The horseshoe and rabbit's foot are popular amulets and have been for generations. When tearing down colonial houses for redevelopment here in Maine, the workmen frequently found horseshoes hidden in walls, probably placed there because owners were often accused of practicing witchcraft when such objects were displayed openly over entrances. Old railroad nails—the handmade variety—also were used to safeguard homes. Three of them driven into a window frame—one in each lower corner and the third nail in the middle of the top—formed a triangle for protection.

To illustrate the power of a talisman: In the late 1500s, a Dr. John Fian tried to make a talisman in order to draw a particular young lady to him. Foolishly, he asked one of the woman's relatives, a little boy, to collect some of her pubic hairs. The youngster told his mother what the doctor wanted, and to trick the amorous man of medicine she sent him some fur from a cow. Fian worked his magic, using what he assumed were the hairs from the object of his desires. Alas and behold—so the legend goes—a cow appeared at the doctor's door and followed him every-where he went.

There are many sects and traditions: some covens find inspiration from pre-Christian ethnic groups, such as Celtic or Norse; others are rooted in the liturgical writings of modern witch scholars, and some prefer to find within themselves the disciplinary guides for inspiration and direction.

Most Wiccan groups practice magic—the conducting of the natural but invisible forces which surround all living things. Many members spell the word "magick," to distinguish it from the kind used for entertainment. Wiccans employ chants, dance, hypnosis, and visualizations to focus and guide psychic energy for the purpose of aiding others and healing. Most groups keep a handwritten collection of lore known as a "Book of Shadows." Part of the religious education of a new practitioner consists of hand copying this work. New material will be added over the years, and access to the book is restricted to members.

Witches come from all walks of life, and it would be difficult to identify them in our midst. They raise families, have jobs, attend social functions, and barbecue steaks in backyards. Instead of every Sunday, covens often meet twice a month to worship together in a circle under the moon. There is no established form in the practice of witchcraft; one group may hold simple meditations while another gathering enacts elaborate ceremonies.

Always present in pagan celebrations are original earth-root songs, ballads and canticles to the deities—songs of magic and nature to ap-peal to those who seek a deep woods and tribal gathering. Some converts to Wiccan rituals explain that what persuaded them was their craving for observances and the need to induce "magic in their sterile lives."

The original Goddess is often referred to as the Great Moon Goddess, a female trinity of Maiden, Mother, and Crone. In artwork and scattered written accounts, her three faces are depicted as the three phases of the moon. Female witches align their making of magic with their own men-strual cycles. The crescent moon, virginal and vulnerable maiden, grows brighter and stronger each night and appears higher in the heavens as it achieves fullness. The full moon with its flooding of light is the mother Goddess swollen with new life. Witches everywhere call this phase a time of great power. The waning moon represents the crone, that point in life when her menstrual cycle is over. She now is an elder, no longer bleeds, and has acquired wisdom. Energies wane, the body shrinks, and she dies—the crone leaves the sky, just as the moon disappears for three dark nights.

Witches don't reserve their spells for certain days of the week or seasons of the year. For most in the craft, magic can take place whether they are awake or asleep—even dreams have power. But certain lunar phases can be more auspicious than others for casting spells. The waxing moon is the best time for initiation, growth, and enhancement; during the waning moon, spells are cast to banish evil, neutralize enemies, remove obstacles, and cure illnesses. Witches believe that the days just before the moon is fullest are the most powerful times to cast spells for fruition and completion.

Many women are drawn to pagan paths because mainstream religions preclude feminine divinity. The Wiccan concept of Mother of all Living, the Goddess, gives them a feeling of belonging and fulfilling their spiritual search. A nature-based religion also appeals to those who are concerned with the environment—individuals who want to change their lives and "get back to the Earth." In the past, men were known as warlocks, and the typical female practitioner was often seen as a crone stirring a pot of some vile-looking concoction over a flame. Women do predominate the Craft in the United States—men in England—and both males and females are called witches.

Wiccans prefer meeting outdoors, but climate or concern for personal safety usually forces them to conduct their ceremonies inside. Members gather in a circle, often nine feet in diameter; candles on the circumference are oriented to the four cardinal directions; an altar is at the center of the circle or by the northern candle; and rites begin with a casting of the circle for purification as the candles are lit. The central theme of each meeting may be to celebrate the new or full moon or a special festival. Included in the rituals are healing, divination, consecration of tools, and discussion of life-affirming and nature-based activities. After the major work of the meeting is completed, food (perhaps cake and wine) is consumed and the circle is banished.

The first books about modern witchcraft appeared during the 1950s when members of isolated groups and families established closer communications. Covens increased noticeably in the 1960s, and new policies were established. Pagan newsletters were exchanged, and by the late 1970s some witches daringly held seminars and opened their circles to individuals who professed interest. Memories of persecution, however, lingered in the minds of activists, and most semipublic meetings were set up with caution. By the 1980s, bookshelves were crowded with new titles on witchcraft, and witches' needs could be found in stores in most major cities. Today, local, national, and international newsletters abound, and there are countless Pagan and Wiccan websites.

A federal appeals court ruled in 1986 that Wicca was a legal religion. This meant that anyone practicing the belief was protected by the U.S. Constitution. Since the ruling, many followers have—as one text on witchcraft noted—"come out of the broom closet." The polling estimates vary, ranging from 100,000 to one million Wiccans in the United States.

Since the 1950s, with the publication of books by early twentieth century authors Robert Graves, Margaret Murray, and particularly Gerald B. Gardner, Wiccan membership increased here and in Europe—surpassing in numbers such established religious groups as Quakers, Unitarian-Universalists, and Buddhists. The Canadian census of 1991 recorded 5,530 neo-pagans, though this tabulation is probably inaccurate since many Wiccans were reluctant to reveal their beliefs to census takers in fear of future ostracism or physical harm.

An accepted way of working and celebrating within the circle is in the nude—weather permitting—as advocated by Gerald B. Gardner, one of the founders of modern witchcraft. The thought of naked men and women together in candlelight caused criticism and gossip among those who were convinced that such a Wiccan ritual was an excuse for a sexual orgy. Witches reply to this criticism by pointing out that attending a "skyclad" gathering helps erase social differences: to see your own and other people's nude bodies is a reminder that all humans are vulnerable and not permanent. Nudity, coven members reason, contributes to the theatrical side of ritual and sends a message to participants that this is a non-ordinary event.

Coven members believe that by chanting and dancing in their circle they meet the gods—archetypal forces that never die—and when drawing down the power of a god or goddess they acquire celestial energies of the moon, planets, and stars as their ordinary consciousness shifts and awareness becomes more god-centered.

Witches believe that human minds and hearts are capable of performing miracles through the use of natural psychic powers, and some do cast spells—largely based on the premise that what is sent out is returned to the sender threefold. Great care is taken when casting these magic formulas, and they are executed in a series of steps after appropriate training. These enchantments are somewhat like prayers: petitions to an external divinity. Wiccans believe that this deity resides in everything.

Witches don't turn the other cheek; they can't accept the premise that human beings are helpless and vulnerable. Suffering is never a kind of karmic punishment for evils done in past lives: they resist actively, and because of their endeavors to neutralize harmful energies they are often misunderstood and feared.

When witches place their hands or feet into a pool of water beneath the full moon, they are attempting to draw up its reflected power. Magic makers are convinced that they pull the moon's power into their bodies whenever they bathe in its light. Ancient rituals specified that potions be brewed in cauldrons under a full moon so the light of the Goddess could be stirred into the concoction. Even during cold Maine winters when covens meet before the fire in living rooms, members bring the moon's full shape into their presence by forming a circle.

In the seven dozen or so tribal societies that have survived, women are still the primary builders and keepers of fires—it is no coincidence that early ovens were constructed to resemble womblike mounds. Females were in charge of ceramics, pottery, and metallurgy, in addition to being appointed the gatherers of nuts, herbs, roots, and berries. With their knowledge of remedies, women were the first health-care workers—a role that hasn't diminished over the centuries: 95 percent of today's health care is provided by women.

Many covens participate in some form of community work or become politically active. They may lobby for social issues or join demonstrations. Environmental issues, animal rights, and the safety of nuclear power plants are leading concerns. Several Maine witches protested the Seabrook nuclear power plant in New Hampshire, and a number of coven members assisted beached whales on Cape Cod by helping them return to the sea.

One of the current Wiccan projects is to convince the publishers of encyclopedias and dictionaries to revise their definitions of witches and witchcraft. "Ugly old hags" and "pacts with the Devil" are expressions they want deleted. Witches would like the publishing world to declare that their craft is both art and science, and was practiced in some form or another in the past. Roots in pre-Christian European nature religions should be taken seriously instead of being ignored or equated with evil.

When witches set up altars, gather healing stones, prepare herbs, build fires, brew potions, and chant prayers, it is with the hope that these rituals are similar to those practiced by predecessors. Being in tune with wild things of nature and channeling energy from the sky and earth are direct routes to achieving the imagery and poetry of the past.

Today's witchcraft is not structured on a series of beliefs or precepts, but on the conviction that followers have within themselves the capacity to reach out and experience life. Covens are kept small—eight to fourteen members and frequently thirteen—so that within this group each individual may contribute more effectively to the efforts of the whole.

There are witches who prefer not to belong to a coven. Laurie Cabot, who is known as the "Official Witch of Salem" and author of several books on the craft, recalls meeting a solitary practitioner when spending several days on the Maine coast. There was a timid rap on her cabin door, and the caller was a woman named Janice, a witch in her early fifties who lived in a nearby fishing village and who had seen the black-robed visitor (Cabot's daily regalia) walking along the shore earlier that day. "Janice had been a Witch all her life," wrote Cabot, "using her magic primarily to help members of her family. She had never belonged to a coven. She came just to talk and share ideas about the Craft, and we ended up trading books and herbal teas."

"To begin with, we are aware of our own goodness and strength, and we are not afraid to admit it," wrote Valerie Voigt, widely-published author on pagan subjects and a practicing witch since the early 1970s. "We don't have a Devil to blame our mistakes on and we need no Savior to save us from a nonexistent Hell." Witches are not guilt-driven, claimed Voigt, and embrace their own powers to choose actions. "Indeed, we work to tune in to our own natures," declared Voigt, "balancing them with the other forces in the Universe, so that our choices may be worthy of us."

OUT-OF-BODY EXPERIENCES

Out-of-body experiences (OBEs) are not as extraordinary as one would think. Estimates indicate that five to ten percent of the world's population will have such an encounter during a lifetime, and this unusual trip can occur under a number of different circumstances—while resting, dreaming, sleeping, or reacting to medication.

Astral projection, an early description of the OBE, has been defined as the activity of our "Double," that "ethereal counterpart of the physical body, which it resembles and with which it normally coincides." Believed to be composed of some fluidic form of matter and invisible, this astral presence has in the past been described as the spiritual, mental, subtle, luminous or resurrected body—a phantom accompanying humans and sometimes thought to be the vehicle of the soul. Not so, materialists counter: it is merely a product of certain brain activities.

Dr. Hereward Carrington, one of the world's foremost psychic researchers, in his introduction to Sylvan Muldoon's 1929 study, *The Pro-*

jection of the Astral Body, pointed out two types of astral projections: the *spontaneous* and the *experimental*. "In the former, the individual undergoing the experience merely discovers himself 'projected' without knowing how or why; he finds himself outside his own physical body— which he can clearly see—but how he got there he does not know. In the latter, the experimenter makes a determined and voluntary effort to 'project'—and wakes up, to find himself there, or *en route*."

Muldoon contended that partial projection is quite commonplace. When one receives a physical blow or shock, there may be a temporary separation of the astral. For example, if a person is in an automobile and it suddenly stops, the phantom of the body may lunge forward for a moment leaving one with a feeling of sickness. Fainting, jerks before falling asleep, and a number of odd sensations may cause a partial separation of the double. Muldoon believed that the astral disengages slightly from the physical body during natural sleep in order to be replenished with "cosmic energy." In dreams of falling and flying, a person can experience some of the astral body's nocturnal travels. Even the breaking of a long-established habit can bring about a projection.

Celia Green of the Institute of Psychophysical Research found that 12% of cases of single OBEs came during sleep, 32% when the subject was unconscious, and 25% were associated with psychological stress, such as worry, overwork, or fear. Green was convinced that this experience could take place when people were standing, walking, lying down—in almost any position. Another researcher, J. C. Poynton, found that multiple OBEs happened to subjects who had one in childhood and learned to repeat the sensation. Poynton also discovered that single cases tended to occur mostly between the ages of 15 and 35.

Green reported that many people saw their own bodies and the rooms they traveled in as "realistic and solid"—though there was the appearance of normalcy, there were slight differences and everything seemed exaggerated. One unexplained feature of this OBE dimension was the lighting: objects seemed to have a glow of their own, and the surroundings were lit up with no visible source of light.

The second body moves differently than the one challenged by gravity. It isn't earthbound and can disregard objects. One doesn't need to open doors when leaving rooms—there are no barricades. Travellers can fly, roll, spin, slide, twist, bounce, bend, and stretch.

Voyagers often claim there is a cord which connects the physical body to the second body, a sort of communication link between the two— perhaps as a safeguard should any difficulties arise when one roams beyond the dimensions of muscles, bone and tendons. This cord is described as being silver in color, capable of extreme flexibility, and is often seen differently by various cultures. Descriptions include "a thin luminous ribbon, a smoky string, a kind of elastic string, a slender luminous cord" and "a thin ray of light or beam." Those who have tested this unusual leash agree that whatever the connector may be it is "infinitely long" and has great strength.

Robert A. Monroe, founder of the Monroe Institute, a center internationally known for its work on the effects of sound wave forms on human behavior, recalled his first of many OBEs in his book *Journeys Out of the Body*. Late one night Monroe was lying in bed with an arm draped over the side and his hand touching a rug. Idly, he began scratching the threads and suddenly realized that his fingers seemed to penetrate the material. "With mild curiosity," he wrote, "I pushed my hand down farther. My fingers went through the floor and there was the rough upper surface of the ceiling of the room below."

Monroe's journeys out of his body became so commonplace that one of his daughters in college reported that after she and her roommate had looked around the empty dorm room one night, the girl declared: "Daddy, if you're here, I think you better go now. We want to get undressed for bed." Actually, Monroe was physically two hundred miles away at the time.

There is an unusual type of OBE in which someone's apparition is seen at a destination before that person's actual arrival. This phantom is dressed in the same clothing that the individual is wearing en route, and the demeanor is identical. Sometimes, the specter answers a question but excuses itself and is gone by the time the real person appears. Mark Twain experienced this phenomenon one evening at a reception. He saw a female acquaintance on the other side of the crowded hall, and also spotted her at the banquet table. Twain learned later that the woman never attended the dinner. She was a passenger on a train heading toward the town where the function was being held when the apparition made its appearance.

As a laboratory experiment, Dr. Karlis Osis constructed an ingenious box in which the circuitry superimposes various images to give an apparently normal picture. But the subject has to stand in a particular position in front of the box in order to see the picture. Alex Tanous was asked to "project" himself and look into the box from the correct position. Tanous was able to see the picture immediately, which indicated that some part of him had left his body and was looking through the glass window into the box.

Illnesses, almost fatal, account for many of the once-in-a-lifetime OBEs. Often, after recovery, people radically alter their beliefs. "I know now that I will survive death," said a Saco woman who asked that her name not be mentioned. "To be conscious outside my body convinces me that I have an immortal soul. The thought of dying doesn't frighten me. Not at all!"

(When I was gathering material for my two books on the English novelist D. H. Lawrence, *Lawrence at Tregerthen* and *The Cornish Nightmare*, I completely overlooked an out-of-body experience that had been printed in several texts and collections of letters. This supernatural incident only got my attention years later when reading Sybille Bedford's biography, *Aldous Huxley*. Lawrence was near death, and when Huxley and his wife, Maria, came to Vence, France to see their dying friend, they found him "very weak and suffering much pain and feeling that he 'wasn't there— that he was two people at once.' He kept saying to Maria, 'Look at *him* there in the bed!' It was as though Lawrence were in a corner of the ceiling looking down on the body in the bed.")

Motorcyclists riding their machines at high speeds have been known to find themselves looking down at their own bodies while still driving safely along a blur of highway. More precarious situations have been reported by pilots of high-flying aircraft: they discovered themselves outside their planes struggling to get back at the controls.

First OBEs can be bewildering and packed with confusion. Robert Monroe recalled moving his hand along a wall and being surprised to find it smooth and unbroken by molding or wall ornaments. Suddenly, he realized that he was lying with his shoulder pressing against the surface. Monroe wondered if he had gone to sleep and had fallen out of bed. Gradually, it came to him that this wasn't the floor but the top of the room—he was floating and bouncing gently against the ceiling whenever he moved. Monroe rolled in the air and looked down. "There in the dim light below me," he wrote, "was the bed." Two figures were lying there: to the right was his wife, and beside her was someone else. What an unusual dream, he was thinking, and why should another person be sleeping beside his wife? "I looked more closely," he remembered, "and the shock was intense. I was the someone on the bed!" Had he died? Was this death? Desperate, like a diver, he swooped down at his body and dove in. "I then felt the bed and the covers." Monroe was alive!

A PAST-LIFE REGRESSION

(The Spiritualist minister from Florida who had held the table-tipping séance was scheduled to conduct the class in past-life regression. She had a presence that impressed her audience, but I wish there had been more privacy—twenty or so people scattered about a roomy chapel gave me the feeling that I needed more enclosure.

An introductory sheet was passed out before the program began. "If you can go back to a past life," I read, "you can go back to the source of what is happening to you now in this life." It seemed a formidable leap to me, though I had returned to the camp in hopes of discovering things about myself and gathering new material for this book. "What unfinished business do you bring from a previous life to this present life?" the sheet questioned. "How the hell do I know?" I heard myself responding. Memories could come through to me as images, thoughts, sounds and feelings, I was told. "Come with an open mind ready to relax and find how at least one past life may have influence on your present life."

It is estimated that 80 percent of the population can be hypnotized. This includes those who believe that they cannot be placed under such an influence against their will. A competent practitioner—I had read somewhere—is able to hypnotize an entire audience, even for the first time, and can do it within five to twenty seconds.

When told to close my eyes and relax, I found it difficult to allow the lids such a holiday. My left kneecap itched enough for me to sneak a quick scratch, and I felt a cough rooting in my throat. I was aware of slow deep breaths being dragged in and out of lungs as muscles tried to slouch in their length of arms and legs. Nothing is happening, I heard myself coaching my old self as a stiffness propped me in the chair. My mind hived a colony of fleeting thoughts, and I resisted the voice that trespassed from the chapel's pulpit.

"You are going deeper...deeper," I heard the soft voice lulling me, "deeper." And yes, I did feel a tingling in the palms of both hands as muscles slackened. An invisible shawl of warmth was being draped over thighs, and both legs were losing their restlessness. The eyelids were being glued shut and invisible cords bound my wrists to the arms of the chair. But these fetters were of my own making; I knew the shackles could be broken if I wanted to free myself. For a moment, a floating sensation swept through me. The voice now directed attention to the right arm: this was feeling lighter; the heaviness was leaving; the arm had a sort of strange buoyancy, as if submerged in drowning air.

"Deeper...deeper."

"You now will raise your right arm," the voice was telling me. This was said slowly and gently, though I sensed a firmness—probably because of the slight pause between words. There was no resistance on my part; it would have been unthinkable to hold back; more than anything, I *wanted* that arm held high. Around me in the chapel, I heard the rustle of right arms as pledges to heightened consciousness were given: my relaxed but ramrod timber of flesh became a buttress as I slumped further under a tent of warmth.

"You are going back...further...further," the intonation held me in its subtle grip as scenes from my life unwound in a hodgepodge of fleeting events: Maine, the years of living in Europe, Washington, San Francisco, Phoenix, marriage, my hotel career, college, the U.S. Army, grade school. Long-forgotten incidents flickered and mingled with more memorable souvenirs. "Back...back," the voice coaxed. "You are now eleven years old." The hallway of our house on Upper Main Street in Norridgewock, Maine was before me. I was carrying an armful of wood for the kitchen stove, and there was the smell of molasses cookies baking in the oven.

A moment from my first day at school tumbles from the snarl of events: the squeak of chalk and my teacher at the blackboard—I'm five. "Deeper, deeper," further back. The yellowing daylight of autumn can be seen in pulsating leaves, and I hear a commotion of pullets in the hen coop— I'm three. Further back, a dazzling pool of light, and a raw urgency as my new lungs inflate with aching air.

The voice is telling me to look at my feet. What kind of shoes am I wearing? Are they sandals or boots? I gaze into a timeless mist and find nothing there. The desire to see something, anything, stirs imagination. You mustn't pretend, I hear myself urging, just keep looking. But there are no square-toed boots with brass buckles, no rawhide laces tied in sturdy bows. Then I am looking down at knickers and long white stockings. Suddenly, I see an ornate wagon with a long whip stuffed into a fancy pouch resembling a scabbard, and pride ignites my grin as someone tells me: "That's some buggy, George Gable!" I don't like the person I am; my pomposity, vanity, and loudness—they sicken me.

There are no more stereoscopic glimpses of that other time and place as dual lenses prowl for solidity in the mist. George Gable, I hear myself saying; it is a plain and uninteresting name, and yet there is something familiar in its commonality. I seem to be wandering further into myself as the denominator of one name reaches up to complete this fraction. George, yes...George and Helen...that's it! Helen Gallagher, wife and mother...mother of Edward and William.

"I am going to count from one to ten," the voice is telling me from the pulpit, "and when the count is completed you will be back in the present time." But something isn't right: I feel no serenity; my subconscious seems to be playacting. Are names and dates being added to an illusive fabrication?

The leader conducting the past-life regression now asks each participant to share glimpses of that previous life. "Can you describe the shoes you were wearing?" Having us look down at our feet seemed a good idea to me should there be anything to be seen on the other side of that curtain; this was one way of fastening time and identifying environment—psychologist Helen Wambach, a life-before-birth researcher, had her subjects look at their dinner plates: were they consuming food placed on china or leaves? "What other things did you see? Who were you?" The responses were multifarious, and the views not always pleasant:

A man two rows over saw himself as an entertainer at a court in an Arabian-Nights setting. Then he was on a bier surrounded by lights—he had died.

A woman behind me saw moccasins. She was an Indian and felt herself betrayed by her friends.

Three rows behind me at my right, an elderly lady found herself in Italy. The year was 1839, and she remembered a sunbeam shining on her. She had learned to read and heard the words 'knowledge is within you.'

The woman in front of me was a man in a previous life. Black stockings, hairy legs, beard. There were barren rocks and sand. He had the sensation of anger being directed against him. Someone hit him on the head with a heavy piece of wood and he died.

The man in the front row was an academic living in the 17th century. He saw a countryside with windmills and guessed he was in Holland.

A woman behind him saw only bare feet, and the teenage girl beside her saw nothing.

Somewhere in a back row, I heard a woman say: "I was a man in that other life, and I had a servant called Jacobi Moore. He betrayed me. It had something to do with a stolen horse. I was locked up and starved to death."

"I was a man in that previous life," Stella told me on our way home. "I was wearing farmer's clothes and had a flat dark cap on my head. The ground I stood on was previously plowed ground, not freshly plowed. I remembered being very depressed and angry. A low dark wooden building was in front of me, and I stood looking at the ground." Stella had tears in her eyes as she came back from her regression; the bungled unhappy life of the farmer left her sad.

When asked to reveal impressions of my past life, my response to the group leader, and in the presence of everyone in the chapel, was embarrassingly candid—so much so that I began to distrust the validity of my statement almost immediately.

"In a previous life," I blurted, "my name was George Gable, and I had a wife called Helen Gallagher. There were two children, Edward and William. I lived in Kilkarney, Ireland around 1900 and died of pneumonia."

There were gasps of astonishment throughout the hall, and I felt myself sinking deeper into the puddle of my chair, as if I wanted to slump completely out of sight. Looking back on that outburst, I can't imagine what possessed me to reply with such precision. Why Ireland? Yes, I am of Irish descent, *look* and *feel* Irish, and I once lived six months in that country. But there are few Gables in that part of the world, and there is no dot on the atlas called Kilkarney. Further, why should pneumonia be the cause of Gable's death? Maybe I got muddled when regressing to my childhood—I did nearly die of pneumonia when I was four. And why on earth *Edward* and *William* as progeny? Later, Stella found that both these names frequently appeared in Gable genealogy.

It is possible that I was influenced by Morey Bernstein's *The Search for Bridey Murphy*, a book I enjoyed reading two or three times. Bernstein, a Colorado businessman and hypnotist, regressed Virginia Burns Tighe, housewife and mother of three children, in six tape-recorded interviews between November 1952 and August 1953, and the results were published in 1956.

Mrs. Tighe, who had never traveled abroad and spoke only English, described a life in Ireland. She was born in Cork in 1798, the daughter of a barrister named Duncan Murphy and his wife, Kathleen. Mrs. Tighe was Bridey Murphy in that life and had a brother named Duncan Blaine Murphy. Several attempts were made to disprove the sensational accounts of these six regressions, and some of the statements that Bridey made were refuted by researching skeptics, but were later shown to be correct after all.

Most revealing was the session centering on Bridey's last years in Belfast, Ireland. Mrs. Tighe's voice had a weary whine, and she spoke with an Irish accent—it was the brogue of a person living in a Belfast slum and coming from the mouth of a "typical American housewife" under regression in Colorado almost a century later.

If reincarnation is a reality, then there must be some lingering awareness, a retention of identity and knowledge, that connects one existence to another. Is it possible that when we give specifics of a past life, we may be attempting to fulfill a need to bring back something we have subconsciously hidden from ourselves? Some fragment of our psyche that needs to be integrated in order for us to achieve a kind of wholeness?

I had dozens of questions begging answers after this past-life regression. Here are a few: If we have lived other lives, how many—ten, two dozen, fifty? And what happens to us between incarnations? Are we kept waiting long before being reborn? Is life a battleground for the soul as it strives toward perfection? Is it possible in our attempt to remove the fear of dying we invent reincarnation? Just how many times on earth or other planets must we commit ourselves before achieving spiritual perfection? Do we return as male, female, Christian, Jew, Oriental? Do we choose our future parents, children, husbands and wives? Can we skip back in time to live our next life span? May we choose innate wisdom, physical beauty, talent and wealth? Are we born to die young and tragically? Have we married someone more than once in other lives? Was our present mate once our father, mother, sister or brother? Was I once a squirrel in York, Maine, a moose in Millinocket, or an insect in Island Falls? A plant or tree? Have I been or will I be born without hope of any kind? Who and where will I be in the year 2763?)

ENCOUNTERS AT HOME

The first documented sighting of a ghost in Maine was in 1799 at Machiasport. Abner Blaisdel and his family had begun to hear knocking noises in their seaside home the previous August, and on January 2nd, Abner and his daughter heard a woman's voice from the cellar declare that she was Captain George Butler's deceased spouse and her maiden name was Nelly Hooper.

David Hooper, Nelly's father, lived in a nearby township, and being acquainted, Abner sent word for the old gentleman to come and identify his daughter's voice. The curious but doubtful Hooper hobbled through six miles of snow to satisfy his skepticism. Why should the daughter, wondered Abner, haunt his premises and not her father's or husband's house?

The two men entered the cellar and a voice was soon heard. The questioning that followed was of a very personal nature, and involved such obscure details that only the dead daughter and live father could have known them. "I believe it was her voice," David Hooper later wrote. "She gave such clear and irresistible tokens of her being the spirit of my own daughter as gave me no less satisfaction than admiration and delight."

Abner's son, Paul, was the first to see Nelly's ghost—he was walking behind the Blaisdel house when he saw her "floating over the fields." Terrified, the young man rushed home to report the apparition to his father, and that evening a furious Nelly appeared to Paul and scolded him for not speaking to her.

It didn't take long for everyone in Machiasport and surrounding towns to know about Nelly Butler's ghost and many came to the Blaisdel home to hear or see her. Then, perhaps weary of crowds, she disappeared for several weeks. Her return to the cellar was described by one witness as "a bright light" and another noted that she "wore a shining white garment." A third observer described the glow of the apparition as having "a constant tremulous motion" until the form "became shapeless, expanded every way and then vanished in a moment." When Abner asked Nelly why she appeared in the cellar instead of the upstairs parlor where visitors could be more comfortably seated, she replied: "I do not want to frighten the children."

Before the year was up, more than a hundred people had heard or seen the ghost, and the local pastor, a Reverend Cummings, became perturbed—he did not believe in ghosts nor did he want his parishioners to take such nonsense seriously. Cummings was particularly upset with Nelly's comment: "Although my body is consumed and turned to dust, my soul is as much alive as before I left my body."

Abner Blaisdel was staging these events, Cummings concluded; this was the culprit creating a phony ghost; the man must be dealt with severely. In a fury, the minister stomped toward Abner's, but in a field on the way he experienced a revelation which changed his life: A woman, at first "no bigger than a toad," grew to normal height before his eyes. "I was filled with genuine fear," the Reverend admitted, "but my fear was connected with ineffable pleasure." Nelly said nothing as the light surrounding her faded and she disappeared.

From that day onward, Cummings spent his time preaching about the glories of life after death as experienced by Nelly Butler; he even wrote

a book about her, quoting her words of wisdom directed to those who
came to the cellar.

After the encounter with Reverend Cummings, Nelly was never seen
or heard from again, though it *was* reported that she made a surprise appearance in her husband's bedchamber one night and gave George Butler a terrible tongue-lashing for breaking a solemn vow: on her deathbed he had promised never to remarry.

In Newfield, a community west of Portland, there is a haunted residence known as the Old Straw House. This home was built in 1787 by
Gideon Straw, and it is the ghost of his daughter, Hannah, who keeps
reappearing. She died at the age of thirty, in March 1826. It had been a
cold winter, and when Gideon found that the cemetery ground was too
frozen for a grave to be dug, he buried his daughter under a flat tombstone
in the kitchen. Later occupants of the house tell of frequent encounters
with Hannah's apparition; these were sometimes accompanied by
poltergeist activity. During the 1960s her image appeared almost nightly
in a storeroom window near the kitchen.

In the small settlement of Dark Harbor by Muscongus Bay, the Stoner
House is a home that doesn't forget what happened once in its front parlor. No matter how often the carpet is replaced, the fabric lumps up in
the center of this room and bloodstains soon appear. It is a phenomenon
that has plagued families occupying these premises since 1900.

Salathiel Stoner met Amanda Carter while visiting friends in Falls
Church, Virginia, and after a brief courtship he brought his bride back to
Dark Harbor. Amanda immediately detested her husband's house: it was
too austere and poorly insulated for the severe winters. She begged him
to install a rug on the cold parlor floor, and he replied that wood flooring
was sufficient. After months of her nagging, Salathiel sailed to Bangor
and returned with a thick red-rose carpet. But as he was nailing it in
place, the wife told her husband that she hated the fabric's color as much
as she did him.

In fury, Salathiel Stoner raised his hammer and struck Amanda senseless. Instead of removing his wife from the parlor in order to complete
the project, he proceeded to nail down his purchase with Amanda underneath. She spent two days under the rug, often bleeding profusely,
before expiring. Mr. Stoner ignored the huge lump in the center of the
room, even when entertaining visitors. Finally the overpowering smell
from the parlor brought concerned town officials, and Salathiel was
committed to a Portland insane asylum.

In April 1948, Fred Kilgore, then in his eighties, left his house on Route

26 in Newry, Maine, and was never seen again. For more than eight years, his heirs were unable to sell the two-story house with an attic and barn. The property was attractive, but potential buyers were discouraged when they learned that Kilgore's ghost came with the place.

"He roams everywhere," said Karlene Bachelder, "but he's never done anything bad." She and her husband, Reginald, raised five children in the Kilgore house and occupied the premises for thirty-two years—until 1988 when they moved into a trailer next door. "The ghost is still there," Mrs. Bachelder assured Terry Karkos, a Lewiston *Sun Journal* reporter, in an October 2000 interview, "and I think he comes to our trailer and visits us once in a while."

Reginald Bachelder remembered being told by a neighbor that Kilgore had worked in the woods and had a blind horse. "Fred used to poke holes in his water pails," said Bachelder, "so he could tell which cows he had watered when he followed his trail back to the pump. He was quite a character!"

Kilgore, a kindly ghost with traces of mischief, was never actually seen by family members, but his presence was frequently felt. One night, a grinding machine in the shed began turning, and once the kitchen door slid from its hinges. At other times, windows would open and shut. "I had a cake on the refrigerator," said Karlene Bachelder, "and it fell off and landed right side up." She also recalled dishes in a drainer falling to the floor and not one dish breaking. "Everything unexplained that happened, we blamed it on Fred. My oldest daughter and oldest son's girlfriend thought he was buried in the cellar, and they were going to dig it up one time but didn't."

A woman who stayed in the house briefly, after the Bachelders moved into their trailer, claimed to have seen someone going up the attic stairs. Was this imagination? The lady was described as having "a nervous disposition," and she had been told that Fred Kilgore was still around.

"All the years that the children were growing up, Fred never bothered us any," said Karlene Bachelder, "and we accepted having a ghost. But he did bother my grandmother. She wouldn't sleep down there at the house—you couldn't get her to stay overnight. She could feel something was there."

Later, Kevin and Polly Slater bought the old Kilgore house, and the sled dogs they kept in the backyard would sometimes nervously whine. One day, while working in the woods, Kevin Slater found a large stone that bore a human likeness: there were two deep-set eye sockets, a bulbous nose, and the head was crowned with quartz hair. Slater gave his find to Reginald Bachelder who believes to this day that this rock is the petrified Fred Kilgore.

In Northport, on an unnamed one-lane road west of town, there is a charred heap of twisted metal and brick with a chimney still standing in the ruins. This is all that remains of the Cosgrove House which was destroyed by fire in December 1954. Two elderly baby-sitters and three Cosgrove boys, aged five, seven, and nine, perished in the flames. Nearby residents say they have heard the cries of these children coming from the rubble. In 1990, a family on vacation took a snapshot of the tall chimney in the ruins, and when they had the film developed, the photograph showed a large white building with two chimneys. Others with a curious bent have come with cameras and claim the same photographic results: a phantom mansion now known as "the house that wasn't there."

("My grandmother's house over in Richmond, Maine used to have a ghost," Jack Bates—not his real name—told this author at an Auburn Mall book signing. "They heard dishes rattling in the cupboard and saw red lights flashing. Then their dog ran under the piazza and started digging and digging. My grandfather came out and grabbed him and said: 'Hey, you get the hell out of there!' Gramp left and the dog went right back under the porch and started digging again. It happened three times, and the last time Gramp grabbed the animal's hind legs and hauled him out. That dog had part of a human jawbone in its mouth. So one of the hired men dug up the bones and put them in a bag. When Father came home it was decided that they would bury the remains down in the woods. Later, my father told the game warden and he was interested in seeing them. So they went to the woods but the bones were gone and the place hasn't been haunted since.")

Sam Kubic of Phillips, Maine was unable to explain why his newly-constructed house should have had a ghost. "It isn't haunted now," he asserted, "but it used to be." As soon as the Kubics moved in there were a number of unexplained happenings: windows opened and shut by themselves, sounds came from unoccupied rooms and the family felt a lurking presence. "One night we built a fire in the house," said Kubic, "and the next morning when we got up all the doors were wide open."

There had once been a haunted house on the vacant lot where Kubic built his home. "I remember it well," said an elderly resident, "and as a kid, I hated walking by that place." The spirit's stay in the new house was of short duration. "I don't know what caused all this," said Kubic. "It just happened and then suddenly stopped." Another Phillips resident thinks this haunting had something to do with a skull that was unearthed when backhoe work was being done. A veterinary student at the site thought that it was a child's skull.

In 1959, Mary Swain and her family bought a house on Highway 197 in Litchfield. On the day they moved in, the Swains suspected that this new home was haunted. Their Siamese cat behaved strangely, as if it sensed some presence, and the housepainters they hired were uneasy when doors and windows began opening and closing. Finally, Mary and a sister attempted to contact the ghost with a Ouija board. To their surprise, they discovered the spirit to be that of an Indian girl who had been dead for years and was trapped in an old maple tree on the property. The sisters called her Beatrice and learned that she had fallen in love with a white settler named Gordon. Tribal elders disapproved of this romance. They captured the man, and he was burned to death near the maple tree while a horrified Beatrice observed the execution. It is not known whether this unseen presence in the old maple is still trapped or just refuses to leave.

The Smith House on High Street in Wiscasset, a mansion of twenty-three rooms constructed in 1852, is haunted by the spirit of an elderly lady who is sometimes seen rocking by a window. In the deserted attic, an occasional rush of tiny feet can be heard and the laughter of children playing. The lady in the rocking chair is believed to be Lee Payson Smith, a descendent of former Maine Governor Samuel Smith.

Sheila Lizotte of Fort Kent lives in a house that her great-uncle built sixty years ago. It is a two-story structure, not unlike other homes in the area—on the outside. Inside, the decor is traditional with a scattering of personal objects signifying interests and lifestyle. It is a comfortable abode for Sheila and her two teenage sons, Daniel and Adam—that is, when doors and windows behave themselves and presences are not felt and seen.

Many families have occupied the premises over the years, and there is no telling what vibrations of sorrow and delight are contained behind the veneer of walls. A next-door neighbor spoke of "strange happenings" but wouldn't elaborate for fear of upsetting Sheila, and children of a former tenant said they had seen "little people" in the house. Phyllis B., the previous owner, was unable to make much-needed repairs on the building because of failing health—she had cancer and died in the house. Sheila Lizotte is convinced that one of the ghosts is this woman. "When I bought the place I was discouraged because everything was so run-down," she recalled. "Now, if I am having a hard time with repairs, I will ask Phyllis to help me because I know this would be something she would want done. And then I get a spurt of energy that doesn't stop."

Sheila Lizotte has seen cupboard doors close and heard "thumpings" on the floor upstairs, and there are never any logical explanations for these happenings. One day a plastic cup did a "complete flip-flop" and landed "right where it started"—there was no through breeze. "Didn't this startle you?" she was asked. "No," came the reply. "I am so used to these things."

Objects frequently get moved or come up missing in the Lizotte household. There have been two mysteries involving eggs. On one occasion Sheila counted five in the refrigerator and the next time she looked three were gone. Son Daniel spoke of an even more dramatic heist: "We had ten eggs and they all disappeared." There have been other incidents still unexplained. One evening their CD player was left on a bed, and the next morning it was found on the bureau. Then a double-paned window was broken from the inside, the glass shattering as if "a rock had hit it."

One night a trembling Daniel came to his mother's bedroom and told her he had seen something. The son had been sleeping on the couch downstairs and had watched "a yellow glowing light" coming down the stairs—an apparition about five feet high and it "looked like a boy." Two weeks later in a newspaper section featuring photographs of people from the past, Daniel spotted a familiar face. "That is the one I saw on the stairs," he said pointing. They were amazed to learn that the boy-ghost had grown up in the house, and later died in military service. A neighbor remembered the young man as being "a bit of an outcast" and the father was "rough" on him. "I guess," said Sheila, "he was coming back here because his childhood wasn't finished."

Adam, too, has had an encounter. One day he saw someone sitting at their picnic table, and as he approached the figure rose and vanished. When asked to describe the person, he told his mother it was a female wearing a cape and the hair was long and black. "It could have been Phyllis," Sheila Lizotte speculated. "I do know that she had long black hair."

The feeling that something is behind her occurs more frequently during the daytime when she is alone in the house. Even one of the house cats responds; though the hair on its back does not stand up, the animal is looking with interest at something behind her mistress. "The thumping is at night—it is just as if somebody has jumped off a bed upstairs, but when I go up to see what is happening there is nothing there."

More disconcerting is the urine in the flush upstairs. "Someone is using the toilet and not flushing it. This takes place when I'm alone in the house and the kids are visiting their dad in Madawaska. Unless my cats have learned how to use the toilet, there is no other explanation. Three times this has occurred."

"I have had experiences before coming to this house," replied Sheila Lizotte when asked if she might be susceptible to members of the spirit world. "When my husband's father was dying, I went into the living room, and the father would always sit in a certain seat—that was his place. I saw something sit down and there was smoke or mist and the figure disappeared." Moments later the ambulance people revived him, though he died soon after. "But you don't talk to some people about these things," Sheila concluded. "They will just look at you strangely."

THE NOTION OF VAMPIRES

The Turks dominated Hungary, Walachia, and Transylvania for more than four centuries and conquered Constantinople in 1453. During the early stages of this long conflict, the man who springs to the foreground when vampirism is mentioned, Vlad the Impaler, or Dracula, retaliated until his death in 1477.

Vlad Tepes, King of Walachia, enjoyed impaling his enemies on blunted stakes to prolong agony. It is believed that he executed more than one hundred thousand people in this manner during his lifetime. When Vlad was captured and imprisoned in Hungary for a time, considerate followers made sure that he had an ample supply of live rodents, birds and toads—creatures he could impale on tiny stakes. The king died in battle, or was assassinated by his own soldiers, and his head was taken to Constantinople and placed on display. In 1897, English author Bram Stoker immortalized Vlad as Count Dracula, no longer a sadistic monarch but a drinker of blood.

Bram Stoker's *Dracula* was published during the time when Sigmund Freud and Carl Jung were establishing the foundation of modern psychoanalysis. Before these theories were expounded in drawing rooms, most people accepted supernatural or romantic explanations for unusual behavior. Bizarre acts, once thought to be the work of evil spirits, are now diagnosed as symptoms of psychosis. Therapists and analysts have replaced exorcists and inquisitors.

In the Balkans during the late Middle Ages, vampires were suspected of infesting graveyards. Apparitions loomed, and there were reports of the dead returning at night to bite living victims, sit on their chests, and sometimes suffocate them. Between 1700 and 1740, there was an epidemic of vampire incidents in Central Europe—probably Transylvania—which within a decade had spread from Greece to Scandinavia. Many reports seemed too real to be dismissed as hysteria, and the sheer number of tales impressed scientists. This also generated apprehension and caused many a villager to keep a close watch on the nearby graveyard.

If burial rites were not followed properly, and something went wrong during the process of dying and crossing to that other side, the dead were believed to come back and cause trouble for the living—such superstitions fed the vampire legends of Slavic countries. Some scholars are convinced that this idea originated from ancient Greece while others argue that the vampire concept was brought to Europe by Gypsies from India. It became a tradition to give the departed a memorable "send-off" with flowers, singing, and ample refreshments for the mourners. The burial party made certain that the deceased was truly dead: carelessness could cause a vampire to return seeking vengeance.

When bubonic plague struck small Slavic communities in medieval Europe, vampires were blamed in a flurry of village gossip. Though there were no telltale fang marks, victims did complain of feeling weak before succumbing, and there were mysterious black bruises on their bodies. When a dog or a bull behaved strangely, superstition heightened: a vampire could appear in so many forms, including that of a werewolf, sorcerer, witch, ghost, or flesh-eating ghoul. In addition to sucking blood, these wicked presences could kill with the evil eye, scare one to death with noises, destroy property and livestock, and even drag babies and maidens into unopened graves.

Mortuary rites of certain cultures in Southwest Asia and Madagascar have been found to be similar to initiation rituals such as marriage, coming-of-age, and birth rites. The dead were looked upon as people who had attained a new level of society—they had joined the community of ancestors but had not lost their places among the living. This attitude toward death and burial is more common in tribal and village cultures where two stages of funerals are observed: In the first ritual, graves are dug, and the bodies buried; in the second, the remains are dug up, cleaned, and buried again. The dry hard state of a decomposed body indicates that the spiritual transition has been completed.

In Slavic lore, victims did not become vampires out of choice—there usually was some cause or condition, and most often it concerned an individual's birth, death or burial. If one had been born with a membrane (caul) over the head, a heavy head of hair, or a red birthmark, one might come back as a vampire; if the person died without being baptized, committed suicide, or expired after some ghoulish encounter, the unfortunate was a possible candidate; and if the body was buried without proper ceremony, consigned to earth at a crossroads, or if a cat jumped over the corpse before burial, the deceased also could expect a Draculean resurrection.

People wore pendants of garlic to discourage unwanted presences, and the planting of millet, hawthorn and sunflowers by entrances was a frequent defensive measure. The local priest said prayers, soldiers drove their swords into graves, and sometimes a white horse was led to the graveyard—if the animal refused to cross a burial plot, a vampire was surely there. Other remedies included the popular stake through the heart, the placing of nails, coins, fishnets, and flax seeds into coffins, and people born on Saturday were told to patrol crossroads and the nearby woods.

Intertwined with the history of vampires were other creatures of the night—evil beings that loomed in the imagination—for example, werewolves became popular characters in fiction thrillers during the nineteenth century. Many tribal healers were believed to possess shapeshifting capacities—these shamans during altered states of consciousness traveled on spiritual journeys and communicated with demons of other worlds.

Demonology was accepted as a serious study during the Middle Ages, and several volumes on paranormal subjects were written by priests. Among them was the infamous *Malleus Maleficarum* (Hammer of Witches) which was authored by two friars and sanctioned by Pope Innocent VIII in 1486. This book was used as a guide during the Inquisition to identify and execute witches. Vampires were not discussed in the *Malleus*, but there was information on the succubae and incubi—demons that seduced men and women in their sleep. The first study on vampirology, written by Leo Allatius, a cleric of the Greek Church, was circulated in 1645. Today, the best vampirologists are writers of fiction, and over the years they have established rules of behavior for their gruesome characters, though new ideas constantly are being introduced, and sometimes it is difficult to find congruity in these stories.

Vampires in fiction are "hot" literary commodities and this notoriety overshadows the fear provoked by such prowling presences two centuries earlier. As symbols, vampires are intriguingly complex, believable, yet bizarre. They are rooted in our superstition and can be easily fictionalized as the frightening and seductive living dead who wander about town in search of late-night suppers. Maine author Stephen King, the most successful spinner of horror tales in America, brought vampirism to the forefront in 1975 with his blockbuster *Salem's Lot*: A Maine town becomes a community of bloodsuckers, and perhaps the scariest thing of all in the book is the citizenry who have become vampires: these folks aren't much different from their former selves—they attend to their problems and needs in traditional ways as the place becomes a village of horror.

"Spook" shows on television quickly introduce young children to the behavior patterns of vampires, werewolves, ghosts, witches, and ghouls. Later, through comic books and computer games, these lessons become more sophisticated. In a survey administered to hundreds of teenagers across the country, 44 percent stated that they learned about vampires between the ages of 5 and 8. Another 40 percent in the polling said this knowledge came at the ages of 8 through 12.

A rational person will agree that the notion of vampires actually existing is a remnant from the Dark Ages. The objection to this view is that many early accounts of these creatures were presented with such authority that it sometimes was difficult to dismiss the reports as mere fantasy. Skeptics who write about vampires usually come to the conclusion that premature burials and sick individuals who "crave for blood" have given rise to the legend.

"Blood play" may be a rare activity in Maine, though support for the practice can be found on numerous websites and in the personal columns. Several major cities, including New York and San Francisco, have nightclubs that hold these rituals, and videos are available. Not all vampire lifestylers are players, but most subscribe to the magazines and films romanticizing the sport. The motivation seems deep-seated and satisfies desires for adventure and intimacy. In addition to cutting, many resort to body piercing and tatooing. One New York artist is doing well commercially with "the vamps"—he paints with his own blood.

The mysterious legends of vampires fascinate us, and we know so much about them from horror movies and stories. These toothy citizens have a way of making noticeable entrances in art and advertising, and we imagine them living by the same rules we all must follow—they are busy nightshift folks conforming to schedules. The one time they don't seem to fit in our social structure is when the writing and special effects in a film are bad and the acting deteriorates to the point of being hilarious. In fact, some of the worst movies ever made are vampire flicks.

People react and relate to vampires on all kinds of levels. Most enthusiasts are content to enjoy them in books and films and to accept them as frightening but imaginary characters. There are, however, those who feel they must identify with vampires on a more personal level, such as dressing up in costumes, mingling with other devotees of the night, or prowling the Internet for contacts. A November 2000 article in *The New York Times* stated that about 1,000 "lifestylists" (people who don their Dracula regalia and go out to nightclubs) were active in New York City. Folklorist Norine Dresser had prepared a questionnaire for 574 high school and college students asking whether they believed it possible that real vampires existed—astonishingly, 27 percent answered yes.

NEAR-DEATH EXPERIENCES

Although there are variations in near-death experiences—brought about by cultural, religious, and personality differences—there are common occurrences and recognizable patterns: the subject feels the "self" has left the body and is hovering overhead, and may later be able to describe who was present and what was happening. NDEers may hear a noise, enter a dark tunnel, meet other people—often deceased family members—and undergo intensely powerful emotions that range from bliss to terror. They may encounter a light which is described as golden or white, witness a rushed life review, have a sense of understanding all things, including the fabric of the universe, and finally be made aware there is a need to return to physical life.

The term "near-death experience" (NDE) was coined by Dr. Raymond A. Moody Jr. in his book *Life After Life*, 1975. But NDE incidents have been reported since the beginning of recorded history. In the New Testament, Paul describes one that he experienced (2 Cor. 12: 1-4), and Pope Gregory the Great in the sixth century had scribes compile a list of such happenings as proof of life beyond the grave. The phenomenon also can be found in Egyptian, Greek, Roman, and Near Eastern legends and myths.

Dr. Moody discovered the NDE to be more common than he had expected when beginning his research. "In any group of thirty," he stated, "I can find someone who has or knows someone who has had one." A recent Gallup poll revealed that there were an estimated 13 million adults in the United States who profess that they have had such experiences. If children and adults reluctant to admit NDEs were added to the count, the numbers probably would double.

Women seem to be more willing to speak of their near-death episodes than men. Dr. Kenneth Ring, considered to be the leading researcher in this field, found that 70 percent of the female experiencers readily shared what happened to them, but only 30 percent of the males were co-operative. Another polling by Ring was recorded in his book *Mindsight*. An investigation of near-death events among the blind revealed that 80 percent possessed sight during these episodes. Many of the subjects had been blind since birth, and it is difficult to determine exactly what they saw, though all of them experienced exceptional states of sensory awareness as to what sight might be.

Psychiatrist Elisabeth Kübler-Ross, in her book *On Death and Dying*, came to the conclusion that no person ever dies alone. She had heard thousands of stories from her patients suggesting that there was some form of life beyond, and in all these accounts of mystical experiences there was someone—a deceased relative, angel, or guardian made of light—who came to give comfort during the near-death episode. When her patients were resuscitated and interviewed, their descriptions of events were almost identical.

In the past, some scientists held to the theory that NDE is brought about by an increase of brain chemicals, which causes the subject to feel loved, see intense light, and to be greeted by deceased friends or family members. After consciousness is regained, the brain's chemical flood is remembered as a near-death episode. This assumption was successfully refuted when researchers collected hundreds of NDE accounts in which experiencers returned to life with information unavailable to them prior to the happening. A patient may be able to tell doctors what they were doing, what was going on in the hallway, or which anxious family members were in the waiting room.

Such revealments usually are ignored by members of the medical community; doctors often are reluctant to pass judgment on NDE—it is easier to dodge questions than to become involved in the age-old life after death controversy. Some physicians react vehemently by placing the phenomenon on the same low level as the once-published tabloid headline "I Dated Bigfoot."

English researcher Dr. Susan Blackmore, in the publication *Society for Psychical Research*, suggested that the tunnel and light adventures are due to brain cells firing "rapidly and randomly" through a deficiency of oxygen. In the same issue, however, it was noted that the tunnel effect also exists in some out-of-body experiences where there is no oxygen deprivation. Another theory attempts to explain NDE as a result of a specific chemical discharged by the brain in times of stress. This does not explain detailed life reviews that so many subjects remember upon returning to their bodies.

Studies have shown that the loss of oxygen to the brain can bring about a visual distortion, a narrowing of focus, which leads one to hallucinate a tunnel. Pilots having acceleration-induced unconsciousness—g-force reaction—undergo a similar oxygen deprivation and report many of the same characteristics found in a near-death episode. There can also be bright lights, and sometimes the sensation of being in beautiful places with family members or friends.

Not everyone has the same adventure. Some voyagers, especially children, can describe a deceased person they have met with facial details, mannerisms, clothing, all accurately noted. (My wife remembers meeting a deceased great-grandfather in a childhood dream—it may have been some form of out-of-body incident—and the next morning when she related the encounter, her grandmother was astounded by one detail: the old gentleman had reached up and tugged at the lobe of an ear. "That was a typical gesture of his!" she said, clapping her hands together in amazement.)

There is no consensus as to how near-death experiences can best be recognized and defined. Despite dramatizations and majority views, rarely will any near-death scenario have all the elements that are frequently mentioned—the tunnel event is present in less than a third of all occurrences, though the image of a tunnel does captivate experiencers, and some may fabricate such an episode to convince themselves and others that what happened to them was genuine.

The leading complaint voiced at a meeting of the International Association for Near-Death Studies was "My experience doesn't match the universal model." The classical synopsis is not necessarily followed. The unpleasant and sometimes hellish scenes, threatening presences, and feelings of distress afterwards may sometimes be minimized or excluded from reports. These encounters, though infrequent, are as much a part of the experience as the more peaceful happenings.

Many children who have returned from a near-death state describe God as a loving grandfather or father—the Supreme Being is seen as a male, never a female, and the younger the child, the more this distinction is made. Teenagers and adults are more likely to encounter Him as a sphere of all-loving light. When God is challenged to reveal His presence, there is often some burst of radiance "brighter than a million suns" and "more powerful than all the bombs on earth combined into a single blast."

Panoramic memory recall is the scientific label for the experience in which one's whole life flashes instantaneously through the mind near the moment of death. Many people would have questioned the reality of this fleeting vision twenty years ago, though the occurrence has been around long enough to be among our legends, myths, and superstitions. The majority of survivors reporting life reviews attest that this happened when they were on the verge of death, but panoramic memory recall also occurs among epileptics at the onset of seizures and with some who have ingested psychedelic substances.

These reviews can encompass an entire life, while sometimes only the highlights of a life are observed. Occasionally, images of the past are superimposed over present-life scenes during a crisis, and a visual montage is created. Reviews frequently appear after consciousness separates from the physical body. In many instances, that long dark tunnel must be traveled before the picture reel of a person's life is rolled back.

Mental activity accelerates during these visions, so swiftly that people are under the impression that time is slowing down: time seems to be expanding, and while this is happening, experiencers believe that they are intellectually capable of comprehending their entire lives in one panoramic moment. Flash-forwards are vivid, even though participants cannot make sense of these future events; they might believe that they have accurately perceived a future mate, children yet to be born, and where they are destined to live.

One researcher was struck by cultural differentia—in Africa, NDEers see tall buildings and shiny cities instead of a bright light; Christians may see Jesus Christ, and Buddhists may encounter Buddha. In the you-become-what-you-believe world, advocates insist that anything can happen. Those who hope for heaven will get there, and those who expect hell will find it. People who are quick to say "when you're dead, you're dead" may end up in a void.

Noted NDE researcher Dr. Michael Sabom was confronted at one of his lectures. An irate cardiologist, who had been a doctor for thirty years and had brought hundreds of people back from the brink of death, declared: "I've been in the middle of this stuff for years, and I've never talked to a patient who had one of these near-death experiences." Before Sabom could reply, a man behind the cardiologist rose and said: "I'm one of the people you saved, and I'll tell you right now, you're the last person I would ever tell about my near-death experience."

"A large number of people claimed transformations that were paranormal," wrote Dr. Melvin Morse after interviewing hundreds of subjects, many of whom had a much higher intelligence after such episodes. A snowplow operator in upstate New York found himself "writing a string of numbers and symbols within a year of his experience." The man had no idea why he was writing them or what they meant. "When he showed these musings to a college professor," stated Morse, "he found that he was writing the equations of Max Planck, a physicist who contributed much of what we know today about atomic theory."

Personality changes occur and there are frequent lifestyle alterations when people resume their lives. Some return to school and become counselors or teachers; others do volunteer work at hospitals and nursing homes. One noticeable transformation is that most NDEers become kinder and more loving individuals, and these conversions usually last a lifetime.

Morse also found that everyone who had an NDE as a child had little or no fear of death, even if the experience happened decades earlier. "It was like I had a new life," one ten-year-old girl told Morse. "I'm not afraid so much of dying because I know more about it now."

It is not unusual for a child having a near-death experience to be met on the other side by a being who has the role of a stern but loving parent. This figure may encourage, praise, and offer reassurance when preparing the young person for his or her destiny. These loving-parent types are found most often in near-death cases from the Orient, and especially with Native Americans.

Occasionally, child experiencers are met by future siblings. One young girl, who "choked to death" but was later revived, spoke of her "little brother" as standing by with a smile while assuring her that she would be fine. The mother was amused when the daughter told her this—a doctor had said another child was impossible. Seven years later, the mother gave birth to a male child who grew to exactly fit the description of the boy her daughter had met during the episode.

Adult experiencers believe that their near-death adventure gave them another look at life—for many a second chance—but the reaction displayed by children is different. The phenomenon appears to have "rewired" their nervous systems. Some researchers conclude that these experiences by young people come at a time when the brain's circuitry is still being developed.

It is commonplace for children to go to extreme lengths to be like others after a near-death episode—to banish from their minds anything that sets them apart—but in their adult years to suddenly have a total recall of the experience or to learn unexpectedly that the event once happened to them. One middle-aged woman, after reading a book on the subject, realized that she exhibited the aftereffects of the phenomenon. "Why should this be happening to me?" she asked her mother. "I never had any close brush with death." The mother replied: "Have you forgotten that high fever you had when you were five and we rushed you to the hospital. The doctor said you nearly died, and when the fever broke you started talking about an angel who came and took you to a city filled with bright lights and how much love you felt. We nearly lost you that night, and I'm surprised that you've forgotten the incident. I haven't."

The record for the number of near-death experiences by an individual is an astonishing 23. This person had severe physical handicaps early in life and was not expected to live. Looking back on the long ordeal, the man admitted to a researcher that he never would have survived his countless surgeries and health setbacks without the healing strength he gained from each episode. There are noticeable benefits for most people who encounter this phenomenon. Very young children with only one incident are six times more likely to forget it than adults. For many young experiencers the memory fades completely, though they may display the full aftereffects.

Personal issues arise after an NDE, and many of them seem unrelated to the event. The participant's psyche undergoes a thorough scrubbing, and the residue of psychological blocks is washed away, though such a process often takes years. This may account for the unusually high divorce rate long after the occurrence—most researchers estimate the separation of married couples to be more than 75 percent.

In response to a 1992 questionnaire inquiring how close to physical death they were when their episode occurred, 23 percent of the subjects claimed that the phenomenon came during actual clinical death, 40 percent acknowledged that it was experienced at the time of trauma or serious illness, and 37 percent stated that it happened in a setting that was not life-threatening. It made little difference whether the participants were close to death or never in danger—their reports had the same structures.

Researchers are unable to explain why one person experiences a near-death episode and another doesn't, though they have discovered a few conditions that appear to have some bearing on who may undergo such an event: The fewer drugs in the person's system, the better, as these impede the phenomenon and can lead to hallucinations; people who are at critical points in their lives, depressed, and with little self-confidence are prime candidates—those who lead happy lives centered around service to others seldom report such a happening; and the closer one is to physical death, as opposed to being in a coma, the more likely a near-death experience.

Pamela Coupe, formerly of Bangor, Maine and now living in Connecticut, had an NDE in 1978 which changed her life. "I was on my way to success," she e-mailed this writer. "I didn't care whose toes I stepped on to get to the top—dictation 140 wpm, typing 100 plus wpm—I was good at my job, young, and I got a kick out of hurting feelings."

One evening she came home from work with a chill and fever. She went to bed with several blankets over her and suddenly everything went black. "I could hear a loud rasping noise, and I came out in this beautiful field—it was gorgeous and such a sunshiny day and the colors were so vivid. I was just sitting on the ground (still cold and shivering) but far across this field—I could look a hundred miles—was a wonderful carousel with several beautiful ladies holding parasols. They were dressed in light summer pastel-colored clothing. One of the ladies got off the carousel and came across the field to me. She took my hand and immediately I stopped shivering. I felt wonderful! Although no words were spoken, she slowly shook her head 'no.' I screamed not to be sent back—I felt so great. Then I heard again the loud rasping noise, saw the blackness, and the next thing I knew I was in the hospital. I had a 105 fever with double pneumonia."

The years have changed Pamela Coupe. Her main interest in life now is helping those who are terminally ill, and she has become a certified hospice worker. Pamela also has done extensive research in near-death experiences. "I didn't know I had an NDE until 7 years ago when I first heard of them," she wrote. "I'm where I really want to be now. I enjoy what I'm doing, and my patients give me so much love."

Gary Baril of Poland, Maine had a near-death episode when he was twelve. The incident occurred in Lewiston during a tonsillectomy. Gary suddenly found himself in a corner of the surgery looking down while several concerned adults surrounded his inert form. "There was a long, long tunnel," said Baril, "and a bright, bright light." Did he meet anyone at the end of that tunnel? "Yes, I had a conversation with someone, but I can't remember the person. I do recall being told 'it isn't time yet,' and then I was back in my body."

A Winthrop resident found reassurance and exhilaration in her near-death experience. "The last time I had a heart attack and fell on the floor," she recalled, "I died. I saw the three members of the rescue team working on me, and they were having difficulty with the oxygen while we were on our way to the hospital in the heavy afternoon traffic. I remember thinking: Maybe they should be told why the equipment isn't working. Suddenly I realized it wasn't necessary to let them know—I felt so light, and everything became so perfect: I was everywhere and nowhere. Then things started getting gold. It was such a beautiful gold," she said in a broken voice with the beginning of tears. "You can't imagine the colors and how wonderful it was! I didn't want to go back. Now, I know everything will be all right. I'm no longer afraid."

James Turner (not his real name) of Rumford, Maine was badly injured in an automobile accident. While waiting for the ambulance, he recalled looking down and seeing himself lying by the roadside with several people hovering around him. "I knew I was dying," said Turner, "but I felt totally at peace. After a tunnel of darkness, there was a golden kind of light, brighter than the sun, though it didn't hurt my eyes. I wanted so much to go into that light, but somebody—it felt like my grandfather who died when I was nine years old—communicated to me: 'It isn't time. You must go back and finish what you have to do in life.' The next thing I knew, I was being slammed into my body with all that pain. It was just awful to be back."

Thousands of near-death events have been scrutinized, and studies reveal common elements. Some travellers report skipping through a pasture or finding themselves in a lush garden. Others behold cities sparkling like gems in radiant sunlight, and find it is possible to ride a light beam through the universe. The more studious may enter huge libraries or find themselves in grandiose galleries and archives. Many talk with deceased loved ones, play with former pets, and the more religious visitors to this realm may encounter Jesus or Buddha, angels, and beings of light. The last words of inventor Thomas Edison were reported to be "It is very beautiful over there."

Some physicians believe that the drugs they give their patients can cause near-death aberrations, yet researchers in the field have shown in studies that drugs actually depress or nullify the phenomenon. Medical mistakes, resulting in people nearly dying, sometimes occur. This happened frequently during the early to mid 1900s when doctors used too much ether for tonsillectomies, which led to many near-death incidents experienced by children.

Near-death events usually last from 5 to 20 minutes, though it is not uncommon to find clinically dead experiencers who revive 30 minutes to an hour later. A few individuals have been known to "awaken" in morgues 12 to 16 hours after the episode began. Such occurrences are looked upon with disbelief by the medical community since the brain can be permanently damaged in three to five minutes without sufficient oxygen. People who defy such odds suffer no ill effects and return more alert and creative than they were before it happened.

There are a surprising number of avoidable funerals in the world today. Many countries still have a scarcity of doctors, are without medical equipment, and there sometimes are religious restrictions preventing proper care. Even in developed nations, grotesque headlines appear: As recently as 1992, a London newspaper carried the gruesome story of a 71-year-old man who had choked on a chicken bone, was pronounced dead of a coronary, and after the funeral he was placed inside a wooden coffin. Grave diggers heard knocking from inside the box and found the man alive. It took the former deceased several weeks to cancel his death certificate and reinstate himself with acceptable identification papers.

A curious historical footnote—or story—can be added: The woman who was to be General Robert E. Lee's mother was pronounced dead after an undiagnosed illness, was given a funeral, and without embalmment was interred in the family vault. A relative who arrived too late to attend the ceremony requested to be shown the body. When he looked at her, he saw her chest move. After regaining consciousness, Mrs. Lee severely scolded her relatives and the local barber, who had acted as a medical consultant, for their carelessness. Three years later, she gave birth to the general who would command the Confederate Army during the Civil War.

Dr. Sam Parnia, a British scientist at the California Institute of Technology (Caltech), in a June 29, 2001 Reuters' dispatch, reported finding evidence that consciousness continues after the brain stops functioning and a patient is clinically dead. This research intensifies the long debate over whether there is life after death and if there is such a thing as the human soul.

In the early 1900s, a Dr. McDougall and five physicians at a Massachusetts hospital had been in pursuit of just such "soul evidence" when they constructed a large and very delicate set of scales. On one platform they placed counterweights and on the other a dying patient. At the moment the heart stopped beating this scale balancing condition was broken, and a pointer indicated a weight loss from the now dead patient's body. "The amount of weight loss which we encountered," wrote McDougall, "in tests conducted over a six-year period varied between one-half to one ounce."

Parnia's study involved 63 heart attack patients who were declared dead but later revived. When interviewed a few days after their brush with death, 56 of the subjects had no recollection of the time they were unconscious and seven reported having memories. Four of the subjects recall moving about, reasoning, and communicating with others after doctors were convinced that their brains were no longer functioning. Some patients spoke of feeling intense joy; others were aware of time accelerating as their senses sharpened and they no longer felt need of their bodies. Bright lights were seen as they entered another realm and met with dead relatives. One person, who no longer embraced his Catholic faith and declared himself a pagan, reported encountering some mystical being. None of the patients had low oxygen levels. "Here you have a severe insult to the brain," observed Parnia, "but perfect memory.

Since the initial experiment, Parnia and his colleagues have found more than 3,500 people with lucid memories who were thought to have been dead. One patient was a 2½-year-old boy who had a heart seizure. His parents contacted Parnia after their son had left the hospital. The child had drawn them a picture of himself looking down at his body. When the little boy was asked why there was a balloon stuck to him in the drawing, he answered: "When you die you see a bright light and there is a string." (cord) Six months after this near-death experience, the child kept drawing the same scene.

If you, the reader of this book, have had a near-death experience, there are things to be weighed carefully: To share this happening with others could well mean ridicule or scorn, perhaps even being called a fake or suspected of trying to pose as a prophet; to integrate the event into your day-to-day routine may mean having to relearn and redefine your life; and should you choose to reject the episode by pretending that it never occurred, your own sense of honesty and integrity might be challenged. Rejection would be practical and sensible, you tell yourself, at least one's lifestyle will be preserved; on the other hand, you hear yourself contradicting, acceptance will mean having the satisfaction of remaining true to oneself—you are caught in the middle.

MEDIUMS AND THEIR WORLD

Most people think of deceased loved ones when the idea of contacting spirits is brought up. A 1991 study, conducted by the International Social Survey Program, found that 40 percent of those responding to its questionnaire stated that they had experienced contact with the dead—some felt a presence nearby, while others heard or saw the loved ones. A theory gleaned from this poll suggests that people overwhelmed by grief have scattered energies and a lower ego boundary, thus creating a more inviting environment for spirits. The poll also revealed a variety of contacts. Some experienced frequent visitations, which often help survivors to shed feelings of guilt and to resume their lives.

E. B. Tylor, the founder of modern anthropology, in his 1871 book, *Primitive Culture*, published his theories on the beliefs of tribal societies concerning the dead. Although some of Tylor's ideas have been dismissed, much of what he found confirmed that early man believed in some sort of survival after death, and the possibility for the living to contact the departed. Tylor noted two types of spirits: those that were once human, and those that come into being in various ways, independent of humans. Every society, he found, had a class of people capable of communicating with the deceased—the beginning of mediumship: these shamans cured the sick and acted as intermediaries between the worlds of the living and the dead.

Among the most famous mediums of the nineteenth century was D. D. Home. His remarkable abilities and reputation for integrity helped to popularize the Spiritualist movement. Home's demonstrations were phenomenal: he could levitate his body, order an invisible spirit to play an accordion, and on several occasions he made hands appear in the air and commanded a spirit to pour water into a glass. "Do be careful," he would warn, "that pitcher may be heavy." Then water could be seen filling the glass and not one drop was spilled.

Rosemary Brown, a British medium, has astonished the musical world in recent decades with new compositions, which she claims were dictated to her by the spirits of dead composers. Brown insists that Franz Liszt was her first spirit visitor when she was seven years old. The Hungarian pianist and composer explained that he was going to work with her. Other musical giants who supposedly gave dictation were Beethoven, Chopin, Bach, Debussy, and Rachmaninoff. Both skeptics and experts agree that several of these dictated pieces are typical of compositions produced by these composers.

Experiments are now being conducted to confirm the theory that when many minds focus on a single topic, they can generate a measurable effect—this group-mental-focus idea has been employed for years by mediums in conducting séances and past-life regressions. Measurements vary according to location, focus, and the number of people involved. Scientists are surprised by the evidence: something does occur when several individuals concentrate simultaneously on the same event.

In 1973, a documented séance in Toronto involved a character called Philip, and his appearance did somewhat increase skepticism as to the existence of a spirit world. Eight people in a circle decided to create an imaginary personality. They were surprisingly successful, and Philip immediately began communicating with the group while the experimenters and their invention were closely monitored to ensure the integrity of the research. There were a number of theories as to what made a completely nonexistent character appear, though the majority of theorists agreed that Philip had to be a product of a collective unconscious mind—the eight people had somehow created the character through a type of group concentration.

Spiritualism upholds the doctrine that the dead survive as personalities and can communicate with the living through mediums. Another belief is that mediums can cure diseases with the aid of spirit guides—spirits serving as special assistants. It is further accepted that counseling over a wide range of practical and personal affairs is possible for mediums when they draw upon their insight and knowledge of that other world.

The earlier practitioners operated independently as mediums, but in 1893 several of them formed the National Spiritualist Association. A complete manual was compiled to furnish appropriate forms of worship with responses and prayers not unlike those in Christian churches.

Today, the three largest Spiritualist bodies in America are the International General Assembly of Spiritualists numbering about 160,000 members; the National Spiritual Alliance of the USA with some 3,000 followers; and the National Spiritual Association of Churches with an estimated 9,000 members. Here in Maine, there are several churches that hold medium fairs, readings, and message and healing circles. There has been, however, a decline in activities since the 1893 formation, broken only by an upsurge of interest during World War I. The "Golden Age" of the great mediums was roughly from the 1880s to the end of the first decade of the 20th Century.

In Sir Osbert Sitwell's autobiography, *Great Morning*, the English author describes how he, with several brother officers, had requested readings by a celebrated London palmist shortly before World War I. "I don't understand it," said the palmist after studying their hands. "It's the same thing again! The line of life stops short and I can read nothing." Then came the outbreak of war, and a generation of men died in battle.

Over the years, a number of societies have been formed to visit haunts and to communicate with spirits. An early ghost hunter and founder of the New England Spiritual Society was Sir Arthur Conan Doyle, the author who created Sherlock Holmes. On a visit to Boston, several years before he developed an interest in ghosts, Doyle had declared: "If there is an afterlife, and I doubt it, I'll cross that bridge when I come to it." Doyle's son was killed in World War I, and on a return visit to America the British writer attended a séance conducted by Boston medium Minnie Meserve Soule. She was able to bring his son back for him to see. "Every spirit in the flesh passes over to the next world, with no change whatsoever," said the surprised and converted Doyle.

One of the curiosities of mediumship is the "control." This alleged spirit from the dead acts as a medium's link to the netherworld. The unseen assistant takes over for extended periods during altered states of consciousness and communicates through the medium by using vocal cords or providing mental impressions. In rare instances, controls have spoken in voices independent of the clairvoyant, but normally they do not intrude or disrupt—controls are not the equivalent of discarnate beings who communicate in the process known as channeling. Today, most mediums find the word "control" outdated and prefer terms such as "spirit helper" and "spirit friend." Their primary function is to provide evidential messages—facts a medium is unlikely to know.

Channeling, a form of mediumship, became popular in the United States during the 1970s when the writings of Seth, speaking through Jane Roberts, became best-selling books. A number of researchers propose that the channeler does not communicate directly with an entity but draws material unconsciously and takes on an entity's personality. Doubtlessly a percentage of all channeling is fraudulent, though most practitioners are convinced that they are in contact with an outside presence. There are psychologists who believe that this form of mediumship is pathological in origin and symptomatic of multiple personality. It should be noted that most channelers are average people who find in this form of communication a source of happiness and fulfillment.

Distinctions should be made when identifying a channeler, medium, and a psychic. No two of these practitioners get their information in exactly the same way. Some may see spiritual manifestations, but most depend on other sensations, such as sensing a presence, feeling an emotion, hearing voices, or even tasting and smelling something unusual. Channelers are appropriately named—they actually channel the spirit so that the spirit's voice and words come through; mediums are those who act as "go-betweens" for the living and the dead; and psychics are individuals who present a heightened awareness of things that many of us miss in our day-to-day lives.

There are two types of mediums: physical and mental. Today, there are few convincing physical practitioners, but during the early nineteen hundreds they flourished by their incredible performances: they made trumpets blare, amazed their audiences with ectoplasmic extravaganzas, and sailed grand pianos and heavy Victorian tables across rooms. These feats were allegedly accomplished by generating power from the sitters; witnesses to the events found themselves "drained" and "too weak to rise from chairs." One sitter at a spirit session conducted by well-known medium Mme. d'Esperance subsequently died—she had contributed too much power for one of Madame's materializations. Mrs. Leonore E. Piper, a titan of mental mediums in an age of physical ones, exhibited only one manifestation: she could extract the scent from flowers and cause them to wilt in a very short time.

Early spiritualist mediums employed direct voice communication by having a trumpet act as a condenser of psychic energy and amplifier of the spirit's voice. The musical instrument would levitate and float about the room where the séance was being held. An "artificial larynx" was a common description of its purpose when the horn was introduced in the 1850s. Without such a voice box, a medium had to construct an alternative larynx through the exuding of ectoplasm. Researchers of psychic phenomena often suspected mediums of speaking through trumpets themselves or using ventriloquism. Many fraudulent séances were exposed, but some exhibitions were impressive enough to avoid criticism.

Unconscious muscular movement, *automatism*, is sometimes attributed to supernatural guidance. This can occur in virtually any activity, especially in the fields of creative endeavors, such as writing, drawing, acting, playing musical instruments, singing, dancing, and composing. In automatic painting, for example, an individual having no training in art suddenly is obsessed with the desire to paint in a distinctive style. The amateur's hand feels guided by a spirit—some unseen being is pushing and pulling the brush as paint reveals itself on canvas. In some instances, the style is that of a well-known deceased artist.

Various forms of automatic writing can be traced back to ancient times. Spiritualism made this activity popular as a means of communicating with the dead. It was a shortcut replacement of the much slower methods of spelling out messages, such as the counting of letters through rappings at séances. This writing, done in a dissociated state of consciousness, can easily be attributed to discarnate beings. Practitioners are convinced these spirits manipulate the writing tools in order to communicate; the automatic writer claims to have no knowledge of what is being written, and frequently the handwriting is markedly different. Some critics, however, suggest that the messages come from the subconscious mind or through extrasensory perception and have no direct channel to the spirit world.

It is impossible to prove the authenticity of entities who claim to come from other dimensions and who now wish to express themselves by "automatic writing" while the human subject is in an entranced or sleep state. Many who hold the pen or face a keyboard could never consciously create such outpourings; the work is often highly complicated, profound, and well organized. Some unexplained force is at work in the spontaneous rush of words.

This knowledge has to come from somewhere. Thorough tests and backtracking into the lives of these intermediaries prove that they had no access to the material they wrote about. Is it possible, through imagination and unconscious inspiration, that one can induce a flow of logical wordage? Could such creativity be unleashed by some force of self-hypnosis? ("I've written reams of the stuff," an automatic writer told this author, "and I still do it whenever I feel called." *Feel* called, I thought, then no voice was *heard* demanding a session: perhaps the command was an impulse, all too subtle to comprehend, as if the sitter were under the influence of a secondary personality—his or her own, but not recognizable.)

Early psychologists encouraged automatic writing as a therapeutic aid for patients suffering from mental disorders—it was one way for the unconscious mind to express feelings and thoughts that could not be verbalized. Demonologists cautioned that such usage could do immense harm to a vulnerable person: demons who masqueraded as the dead could possess the helpless writer.

By the mid 1800s, table tipping had become popular. Such parlor games were fashionable with rich and poor alike. People were eager to join hands in a circle at séances for chats with Grandpa William and Aunt Agnes who had been dead for decades. Pantries and hallways were alive with the rapping and rattling sounds of spirits. Later, through the 1870s into the 1890s, automatic writing and trance voice mediumship were in vogue.

Another favorite parlor game is the Ouija board (a trademark name joining the French *oui* and German *ja*, both meaning yes.) The Greek philosopher and mathematician Pythagoras held frequent séances using a mystic table, similar to a Ouija, which moved on wheels and glided toward signs, as early as 540 B.C. Boards today are less cumbersome; they usually are simple cardboard affairs with the alphabet in large-type capitals, numbers from 0 to 9, and a "yes" and "no." Sometimes a "maybe" and "don't know" are in the kit.

A word of warning is issued by experts to beginners: This is not a "kindergarten toy" and should never be used carelessly. Don't ask it for answers involving materialistic concerns, and limit the yes and no questions. Make the board talk; let it say what must be said. If an objectionable personality shows up and is too brazen, demand the visitation of someone else. Above all, don't take every message literally—much of the material received is disjointed nonsense, especially when novices are participating. Orderly grammatical syntax is an impossibility since there are no punctuation marks and lowercase letters: compressed messages must be separated by vertical slash marks to be understood.

There are two opposing views for a Ouija board worker—there is little room for an in-between—either the messages produced are from the subconscious minds of the experimenters or external influences are present, namely those of purported discarnate personalities.

Ouija boards are said to enable spirits to communicate freely without having to work through the mind of a medium. Critics of the board agree that Ouija's spelled-out messages come from a part of the operator's mind that dodges rational thought and will sometimes attract lower-level presences—perhaps tricksters rising from the fun-loving landscape of imagination. No matter how innocent and engaging these strangers seem, we are warned that they may not have our best interest at heart. If one must play the game, board users are advised, always insist on knowing the identity of the spirit before getting involved.

In *Conversations With Seth: The Story of Jane Roberts's ESP Class*, Susan M. Watkins reports that the idea of communicating with spirits through table tipping was at first vehemently rejected. "It just smacked too much of all the stuff I wanted to avoid," Roberts exclaimed. But after witnessing a demonstration, Jane reluctantly decided to try it in her ESP class.

The usual preparations took place with the seating arrangement, selection of the furnishing—a small scallop-edged table—and a few introductory remarks. In this instance, the orders were slightly irreverent and couched with humor: "Spirits," said Roberts, "move this table! Spirits move this goddamn table!" And to everyone's astonishment, the object began dancing around the room while hands and fingers slid over the surface.

When the table refused to cooperate, Roberts asked Seth, the nonphysical energy personality who spoke through her in trances, to join the group. "Seth," she pleaded, "will you please make this goddamned table move!" Immediately, the object galloped about the room with class members in pursuit. When Jane Roberts called her husband Robert Butts from his painting studio where he was working at the time, she shouted: "Go table! Go get Robbie!" And without hesitating, the furnishing skidded across the room and pinned Butts against the wall.

Stories of individuals who can move objects, levitate tables, and even float themselves in the air by willpower alone are as old as the languages telling the tales. What is startling to some skeptics is that these accounts are more than just fanciful legends. The study of psychic phenomena has gained the support of researchers in such fields as biology, psychology, physics, and even anthropology. Serious attention is now given to a host of unusual occurrences, including mind over matter, ESP, and out-of-body experiences.

In the heyday of crystal balls and traveling mediums, one of the more curious spirit performances seen in Maine involved ectoplasm. This was a substance that resembled cotton wool, paste or dough and emanated from the mouth or other bodily orifices. A Canadian medium, who billed herself as Mary M., was known for the human faces that sometimes appeared on the ectoplasm that she extruded—these ectoplasmic portraits usually were of deceased notables who were easily recognizable.

Extrusions of ectoplasm often appeared milky white in color, had the smell of ozone, and seemed warm to the touch. The substance had weight and would wax and wane from the medium's orifices—it also could pour from the eyes, nipples or navel. Ectoplasm sometimes would form as a cloud, even in thin-rod shapes and wide membranes resembling nets. If exposed to light, the substance would disintegrate or snap back violently, occasionally injuring the medium or a nearby sitter.

As with more ethereal events, the physical manifestation appeared best in an atmosphere of faith; when greeted with skepticism, ectoplasm quickly lost its light, airy, sticky, and smoky presence. Some samples were found to be nothing more than strips of muslin, egg white, and mixtures of soap or gelatin, but analysis of other samplings yielded few clues. The magician Harry Houdini once observed that he couldn't understand why "the Almighty would allow the production of such disgusting substances from a human body."

Theories about this substance abounded when the practice was all the rage. Some witnesses believed that spirits formed themselves from the medium's body or soul, and others felt the source was a combination of the two. Spectators at séances were strictly forbidden to touch the material; handling the ectoplasm would cause the medium bodily harm or even death. Those who did sneak a touch claimed that it felt very much like cloth. One performer, who finally declared himself a fraud, admitted that his ectoplasm of choice was chiffon. This fabric was easy to manipulate and when treated with a phosphorescent substance gave a ghostly appearance in a partly-darkened room. Chiffon could be crumbled into capsule packages and hidden in the medium's orifices, or even swallowed and regurgitated.

Does the following description fit you?

"You are basically a serious person, but with a fine sense of humor. A loner by temperament, you nevertheless have a talent for working with others. You prefer people whose intellects equal yours, but you are never unkind to inferiors. You are very sensitive but tend to maintain a stiff upper lip in difficult times. You sometimes feel insecure, but you mask it so well that friends see you as confident and outgoing. You are me-ticulous—a perfectionist—though an overabundance of details bores you. You crave adventure but are never irresponsible. You have a complex nature and wide-ranging interests, coupled with a great ability to focus all your energies on a single task."

You are probably nodding affirmatively, because most people have an upbeat image of themselves—they don't want to admit to being humor-less, shallow, boring, frivolous, ignorant or insensitive. It's the kind of reading one might expect from some fraudulent psychic in a rundown backwater off a turnpike, or over the telephone at an exorbitant fee per minute. Such exploiters make insightful statements, such as "You han-dle stress by becoming angry at others"—this could apply to anyone. Another method of gaining credibility is by repeating information that a client may have unconsciously alluded to earlier. According to a survey published in the February 1998 issue of *Harper's Magazine*, 70.2 per-cent of phone-psychic users belong to minorities and 48.3 percent live in poverty.

Fortune-tellers who pitch their tents at county fairs and carnivals are often given the same societal berth as sideshow contortionists and barkers. Many crystal gazers and palmists do act in a fraudulent manner, but this doesn't mean they lack psychic ability. Some are convinced that spirit voices are being heard. It is the environment, the noisy world of the midway, that forces them to become performers. One first has to sucker the rube behind the tent flap, and this can only be done by executing showmanship.

"Your mother is here," one so-called medium told her client.

"No," replied the sitter, "my mother is living."

"Then your grandmother is here."

"No, my grandmother is living."

"Well, then," said the spirit communicator, "your great-grandmother is here, and damn it, she's dead!"

It takes little sleight of hand to trick a person beset with grief over the loss of a loved one. A dishonest medium can get enough information on the departed through generalized comments and fishing expeditions for names to deceive the client into thinking that certain messages are coming from the spirit world. A clever use of props, such as noises, lights, or the touch of an unseen hand may further the deception.

Mediums may sincerely believe that they are directly in touch with the spirits of the departed when in reality they could be in contact with the minds of the sitters. It is an assertion that is as difficult to prove as to disprove. Some show perceptive abilities, such as telepathy, clairvoyance, and sometimes precognition, but many are self-deluded performers. About five percent of them, however, possess powers that transcend the physical and have produced phenomena that have profoundly impressed investigators and scientists on every continent.

One of the most active skeptics of the paranormal is James Randi. Trained as a magician and escape artist, he has embarked on a crusade to prove that pseudoscience and supernatural claims are hoaxes. Randi has pursued psychic spoon benders, faith healers, mediums, and has been "a thorn in the sides" of all who, as he states in his literature, tried "to pull the wool over the public's eyes in the name of the supernatural." In some instances, he has taught people how to commit fraudulent acts in order to fool scientists. His best-known caper occurred in 1979 when he taught two teenagers how to fake psychokinetic powers, and then sent them to McDonnell Laboratory at Washington University to demonstrate their skills. The teenagers' feats were publicized by a researcher until Randi exposed his stunt to an amused public.

Randi argues that all psychic demonstrations are trickery, and he has flamboyantly offered one million dollars to anyone who can prove psychic abilities. The ground rules and standards to be followed are, naturally, on Randi's turf. Such antics and calls to expose paranormal practices are not new: scientists in the past were known to invite "magicians" to witness psychic experiments in order to rule out fraud.

Perhaps the world's most determined skeptic, prior to Randi's appearance, was Houdini. He always made it clear that his own feats were based on sleight of hand, and he took pleasure in exposing fellow magicians who boasted superior powers. When the Spiritualist movement became popular, Houdini was active in discrediting mediums. Later in life, though still skeptical of all things mystical, he promised his wife that if he died before she did, he would communicate with her in a séance, if at all possible—he never did.

Some early researchers reacted negatively when asked to assess the authenticity of mediumship. Professor Lombroso, a leading Italian investigator, felt that there was an affinity between such practices and hysteria. Not to be outdone, Professor Richet, another skeptical researcher, claimed that it was "a morbid state" and that mediums were "more or less neuropathic, liable to headaches, insomnia, and dyspepsia." But most modern authorities agree that mediumship is not pathological: psychic awareness doesn't detract in any way from so-called normal activities. "I am a more successful gardener than I used to be," remarked trance medium Gladys Osborne Leonard in her book *My Life In Two Worlds*. "My health and nerves are under better control, therefore they are more to be relied upon than they ever were before I developed what many people think of as an abnormal or extraordinary power."

Mediumship seems to appear early in life and spontaneously. Some feel that the gift is "catching." Many who have sat with persuasive mental and physical mediums soon discover themselves to be capable of displaying powers. Nationality seems to make little difference in the possessing of such abilities, but the percentage of female spiritual workers is much higher than males. Kate Fox, one of the Fox Sisters of Hydesville, New York, who produced a series of spirit rapping in 1848 and gave impetus to the Spiritualist movement, felt that mediumship could be inherited. Her five-month-old son got recurrent spirit raps on the railing of his metal crib and at this time began automatic writing. There were other cases in which the talent manifested itself early. One infant was said to have levitated a table weighing 100 pounds, and another could allegedly do automatic writing at the age of nine days.

Mediums may indeed be the go-betweens for different dimensions, rather than fortune-tellers geared to prophesy. (Somewhere I read that "the keynote of a séance is first, to give proof of the continuity of life, and secondly, to give guidance and spiritual guidance." I concluded that those interested in attending such a meeting should never go hoping to find answers to mundane questions, such as, Must I close the deal now? or, Will I marry poor Horace or fun-loving Percy? I'm told that a person's receptivity, attitude and open-mindedness contribute much to the success of a séance—the medium, spirit and sitter must all work together.)

WOODLAND APPARITIONS AND CRIES

As a child in Bowdoinham, David Hall saw a giant white deer, a creature from Indian legends and still roaming the woods in that part of Maine. Many hunters have fired at this animal, and much to their astonishment the deer disappears the moment triggers are pulled. "Maine is rich with paranormal activity," said Hall. "Because of its Colonial and Native American heritage, there is much to explore."

For example, the Penobscot Indians believe that their reservation is haunted by an evil white man who married an Indian woman in the 1890s. He treated his wife cruelly and tried to intimidate the tribe in an effort to rule the area. His apparition appears on the forested island at the center of the reservation.

There is an Indian legend that involves Mount Katahdin, known as "Greatest Mountain." Tribal members profess that Maine's highest peak—5,268 feet—is haunted by Pamola (Pomoola), a strange apparition having the head of a bull moose, the body of a human, and the wings of an eagle. This vengeful storm spirit makes sure that mere mortals daring to invade the area are never seen again.

Another in Indian lore is the *bhut* or *bhuta*. This evil presence may be detected by his lack of a shadow or the nasal twang in his speech—it is frequently the ghost of a man who has died by execution, accident, or suicide. As this spirit never rests on the earth, it can be avoided by lying on the ground. Another kind of *bhut* is the man killed during a hunt; a ghost that roams with a pack of spectral dogs, has a poisonous saliva, and the mere sight of it usually causes one to die of fright. Those strong enough to survive such an encounter are rewarded with treasures.

Hall admits that he had few personal encounters with the paranormal while growing up, but there were "rumors," such as the spirit that "still lives" in an old church near Lisbon Falls, and he has friends who saw ghosts in a colonial-era cemetery in Portland.

Years ago, David Hall's sister saw a "gremlin-like creature" on the Meadow Road in Topsham. "My cousin was with her," recalled Hall, "and both were quite shaken. The description reminded me of a hobgoblin or such. They were quite serious with their story, and my sister still mentions it."

Scott Desjardins of Soldier Pond, Maine remembers a story his father told him, and years later Scott talked with several people who were able to give him additional details.

It was in the fall of 1926 that a hunter named Allen and three companions went on a hunting trip near Quimby at St. Froid Lake in Aroostook County. The men separated in the morning and planned to meet at the lake for supper that night.

After a day of hunting, the three companions arrived at the campsite on time but Allen failed to show up. When their evening meal was over, they worriedly began to search the woods surrounding the lake but there was no trace of the missing friend and their shouts went unanswered.

The hunt for Allen was intensified the following day with no results. That night the three drove to Eagle Lake, a larger town where volunteers could be enlisted. A long line of searchers fanned the woods for miles, and after three days the crew decided that Allen would never be found.

The next fall another party of hunters were sitting around their bonfire at a campsite near St. Froid Lake. Stories were being swapped and a jug was making the rounds as the night hovered with a myriad of stars. Suddenly, one of the party looked puzzled as he cocked his head. "What is that?" he asked the others. Laughter stopped and they all listened; in the distance came a plaintive cry. "Someone is lost," said a hunter as the men rose and gathered their flashlights. They heard the cry several more times as they advanced through tangles of brush but the calls could not be pinpointed; they seemed to shift with the wind and finally there was silence.

Allen's body was never found, but outdoorsmen frequently have heard a cry in the distance while sitting around their campfires. "That *is* his voice," affirmed one of the three companions who had searched for Allen that night. "There's no mistaking it."

To further substantiate what has become a local legend, there is a campsite in Quimby at St. Froid Lake called *Lost Cry of the Hunter Campground*. "I never heard him calling," admitted Scott Desjardins, "but some people claim they hear it, even to this day."

AT A GIVEN MOMENT AND PLACE

Astrology is acknowledged as man's first science, and probably the earliest laboratories were Sumerian temples where changes in the skies were observed and calculations made to confirm and improve the human predicament on earth. The magi of Mesopotamia were studying the stars as they looked for omens in the weather and made predictions of the future from the livers and intestines of animals. For these ancient practitioners, there were no accidents: everything in the universe was connected and established.

These initial astronomers determined that the sun went through various constellations at different seasons of the year and people born at the same time of that year shared certain characteristics. Students of astrology soon learn that these constellations are not directly overhead as their diagrammed zodiacs indicate. Over the centuries, because of the earth's wobble and shift in space, the points of reference have taken up new positions, but the names are still used by Western astrologers.

In ancient times, astronomy and astrology could not be separated. Later, the astrologer was obliged to be an understudy to an astronomer; in fact, the horoscope forecaster wasn't permitted to exercise this calling on his own. In the absence of available tables and documentation, it was necessary to observe the state of the heavens firsthand at the very moment of a birth to achieve accuracy. Modern astrologers rarely look at the sky; they simply consult manuals and record the computations found in them.

During the Middle Ages, and until late in the seventeenth century, astrologers were employed by royalty, rich merchants, and individuals of influence to produce an exact abstract of the heavens at the precise instant of birth as a future guide for the newborn child. These charts of nativity included character, morals, state of health, the maladies with which the subject would be afflicted, and every meaningful event, happy or unhappy. The date of a person's death would be disclosed, and elaborations included, especially for violent endings. In some parts of the world where marriages are arranged, astrologers still are consulted to determine whether the bride and groom are compatible—often, a second and third chart is prepared before parents give their approval.

One of the most faithful defenders of astrology was the Italian mathematician Jerome Cardan, 1501-1576. His demise caused controversy among intellectuals during the sixteenth and seventeenth centuries. Having determined the exact date of his death in his horoscope, Cardan starved himself at the age of seventy-five in order to fulfill the horoscope and avoid discrediting astrology.

Early astrologers divided life into different categories and named these areas houses: they are the places where one is revealed by what one does. Each house represents the space above and below the horizon of a birth chart—half the sky is visible, and half of it is hidden. For the purpose of orientation, imagine yourself standing at the top of the world, facing south, and it is the moment of your birth. A horizontal line drawn through the center of this globe will designate the horizon—east is on the left, west on the right. Above the horizon are the six houses of your development in the larger world, which include areas such as social concern, relationships, career, goals, and your unconscious; below the horizon are the six houses of your *personal* development, which include areas such as responsibilities, health, home, possessions, knowledge, and personality. An astrologer must determine the location of the planets at the time, date, and place of a birth in order to accomplish the necessary calculations. Each planet represents different energies and parts of an individual, and each area manifests those energies in a variety of ways. It is the combination of all this information that establishes a person's birth chart.

Sun, Moon, Mercury, Venus, and Mars are the personal planets: Sun has energies of self, life spirit, creativity, willpower; Moon's energies include emotions, memories, instincts; Mercury has mental activity, intelligence, communication; Venus represents love, harmony, social graces, art, possessions, resources; and Mars has physical forces, boldness, action, anger, courage, ego.

Jupiter and Saturn are the social planets: Jupiter claims energies of abundance, luck, wisdom, exploration, growth; and Saturn governs self-discipline, perseverance, limitations, responsibilities.

Uranus, Neptune, and Pluto are the transpersonal planets: Uranus deals with the sudden or unexpected, radical changes, liberation, authenticity; Neptune has spirituality, idealism, intuition, clairvoyance; and Pluto represents power, rebirth, destruction, regeneration.

Many newspaper readers admit that after checking the headlines, obituaries, and weather forecast, they read their horoscope for the day. Even disbelievers occasionally cast a wary eye on what unpleasantness or possible ruination is in store for them. Uncertainty is a lucrative business—one has only to get quotes for an astrological reading on telephone hot lines to confirm this—and many of these so-called professionals have little knowledge of astrology. They simply get their client's birth information and consult one of the innumerable manuals on the subject in order to prepare charts and answer questions.

Predictions of rain and periods of drought in *The Old Farmer's Almanac* were taken very seriously by Maine tillers of the soil during the nineteen thirties and forties. The waxing and waning phases of the moon ordained a number of green-thumb rules, and leading the list was the exhortation to plant annuals that were harvested above ground during a waxing moon, and to plant biennial and perennial bulbs during a waning moon. Cabbages, broccoli, cauliflowers, celery, endive, lettuce, parsley, and spinach gave a better yield if planted during a new moon; beets, carrots, potatoes, radishes, and turnips were full moon vegetables; and pity the foolhardy seeder who labored during the moon's last quarter—this was the phase best for weeding, killing bugs, and turning the sod.

All liquids are affected by the moon, from ocean tides to fluids in living creatures. As a species, we have an inclination to retain more water during the full moon, and this causes an increase of pressure in the skull, sometimes resulting in uncharacteristic behavior known as "Full Moon Madness." Some doctors in emergency rooms and surgeries report that hemorrhaging is more likely during this quarter of the month. Humans "feel" the pull of the moon, and this lunar high marks an emotionally and intellectually favorable period for the launching of challenging projects. The best dowsers have an awareness of astrology as they sense the magnetic influences of the planets. Down the length of the dowsing rod—or is it up?—with all the intensity of a ley line, mysterious forces are interpreted as messages.

If the moment of birth influences one's life and character, then what is this exact moment? Is it when the mother's cervix has dilated sufficiently, when the baby's head appears, is it achieved at the first breath (the majority choice), the first howl, or the severing of the umbilical cord? And does induced labor or cesarean procedures interfere with the fate of the infant? Some followers of astrology dodge these questions by declaring that everything is so soundly organized and inspired that a person's birth is a predestined event.

Most readers are familiar with Sun sign forecasts in the horoscope section of their daily newspaper, but only a few are aware that all twelve signs of the zodiac are involved in this simple recap. Based on date, place, and time of birth, along with the positions of planets and signs in the twelve houses, a full portrait of a person is presented. Astrologists can find themselves in a technical quagmire as they go about the process of explaining how the various energies behave and where these forces unfold on a birth chart.

It seems incredible that man should take seriously a theory based on the erroneous notion that there are only seven planets, including the sun and moon. There is, however, a simple explanation for continued confidence in this faulty cornerstone: defying all logic, astrology *does* work. Somehow, bodies in the solar system exert various energies on one another, and all living things are influenced by this interaction. Ley hunters find nothing strange in this arrangement; for them, the earth is a magnet, and so are the planets. It is immaterial how many constellations are in the circling whirl: what influences living things are the forces themselves.

That an outdated and illogical chart can frequently measure with bewildering accuracy the best and the worst of an individual is a supernatural wonder. No one has the same birth data—there are as many combinations as a DNA. Despite these odds, one's own sign and the degree of the zodiac that rises above the eastern horizon at any moment can reveal an astonishing dossier.

The psychoanalysis pioneer Carl Jung called astrology a symbolic system that seemed to work by way of synchronicity. What takes place overhead, he ventured, is merely a reflection of what is happening below. Celestial bodies don't influence people to respond in certain ways; they are like barometers, or indicators of the same energies occurring here on earth.

Astrologers must have a specific point in space and a precise point in time to define an astrological chart, and that point is you. "We are born at a given moment, in a given place," declared Jung, "and like vintage years of wine, we have the qualities of the year and of the season in which we are born."

THE LOUP-GAROU

Stories of a half man, half beast living in the woods of Eastern Canada and Maine have circulated for generations. In French and French-Canadian folklore, the loup-garou (loup garoux) or werewolf is an entity resembling Bigfoot. When it is seen by a woodsman in the solitary surroundings of remote logging country, the witness of that encounter is never completely forthcoming. The storyteller wants to share his experience, but not at the expense of jeopardizing himself—something may happen if he says too much.

The wolf has a threatening presence with its howling, that glow of yellow eyes in the dark, its nocturnal stalking, and those predatory raids on sheep. Man soon learned to cringe at the wolf image—surely this was a creature of demonic identity. During the Middle Ages, witches were accused of metamorphosing as wolves, and in obeisance to the wishes of their master, the Devil himself, they prowled the European countryside killing and devouring defenseless peasants and careless travelers on lonesome byways.

"Did I see an animal?" asked a witness when recalling her 1998 encounter in Bucksport. "I'm not sure. I may have been walking in some sort of energy field and not realizing that I was in it. I know it sounds far-fetched, but I had the feeling that this was some traveler from another dimension." When asked if she had returned to the field where she saw the visitor, the beholder replied: "Something in me doesn't want to do that right now. Several months ago, I did drive down that road near where it happened. I just wanted to sense what kind of terrain was there." The creature she saw briefly had fur and stood upright; after several moments of mutual scrutiny, the woman was left with the impression that here was a "kind and gentle" entity. "I was led there for a reason," she concluded with conviction, "and I have embraced him (it) into my being."

The idea of an energy field in place for travelers from another dimension is a science-fiction straying for most people, though there are a few who remain steadfast in defending this position. "I know such a place where that sort of energetics happens," said a believer. "There's an area near Houlton, right on the Interstate—I can't pinpoint it on the map but I've experienced it twice. You can feel exactly where that corridor of energy begins and ends."

There have been several sightings by motorists of a Bigfoot entity in the Leeds/Turner area of Maine, and there is one reported incident of an apelike animal that was seen lying by the roadside. When the couple backed up their vehicle for a closer look, the creature had disappeared. Several people out walking late at night have had feelings of being followed, and one person was "chased." Those who encounter these hairy strangers are not sure what they are seeing: could they be loups-garous or victims of lycanthropy?—sufferers who are under the delusion that they have become wolves.

"I'm convinced that some of the Bigfoot sightings in Maine are the Loup Garoux," stated David Masse. "Two years ago, while living in the woods near Bridgton, I heard a heavy panting behind me. It was a sound that reminded me of a wild boar snorting—a noise louder than what a horse makes. It terrified the crap out of me!" The incident caused him to have recurring nightmares, and he was ravaged by uncertainties. "Demons took over my sleep," claimed Masse. "No human being should ever be put through the terror and misery I experienced."

Christopher Gardner, a student of anthropology at the University of Maine-Orono and an investigator of the paranormal with an office in Bangor, contributed an article in the July 2001 issue of *The Maine Eagle Magazine* with this conclusion: "I think that the Loup Garoux sightings in Maine are of Bigfoot/Ape type creatures....We live in a world of many mysteries and wonders, so who knows what will be discovered next. For now, the mystery continues."

PHANTOM ENCOUNTERS

Researchers rarely agree when asked whether apparitions have intelligence and personalities; they also differ when it is suggested that ghosts are psychic remnants of past events. Every culture has superstitions concerning spirits. (I overheard Uncle Ed Stevens tell my mother—he may have been unloading one of his exaggerations—that ghosts cannot cross running water and as a consequence "you rarely find a haunted house on the bank of a river or brook.") In European folklore, one is cautioned never to touch a ghost. Other slanted notions are that ghosts only appear at night, have noticeable smells, and are caused by excessive electrical charges in the atmosphere. Contrary to popular belief, most specters are not seen in graveyards, but in homes, public buildings and deserted structures. In more than a century of intensive scientific inquiry, no one has any definitive answers about ghosts and their natures.

A person may have a vision of an apparition from the past, or perceive some nonphysical form in a place reported to be haunted. There is, however, a disparity of experiences: one person may encounter a phantom while another (often a nonbeliever) sees nothing. In most publicized cases of hauntings, some of the testimony comes from individuals who declare they experienced nothing unusual. When there are several witnesses, researchers speculate that one person may perceive an apparition and telepathically communicate it to the others.

When a child has an imaginary friend, the little one is called cute, but when an adult has one, he or she is called crazy. Carl Jung, a renowned expert on mental health, held regular conversations with an imaginary friend throughout his adult life. In some individuals, this kind of communication with unseen beings goes beyond imagination into the realm of the spirit world. Mediums, and people who claim to have guardian angels, display this ability, and how can we as bystanders preemptively declare that these invisible beings don't exist?

Child behaviorists and alien abduction specialists have in recent years concentrated on children's experiences during the time when the temporal lobes in the brain mature. Scientist regard these lobes as the seat of imagination and creativity. Most young people between the ages of three to five years exhibit some paranormal activities such as flying dreams, disembodied voices, out-of-body episodes, and heightened intuitions: their imaginative playtime becomes rehearsal, a way of preparing themselves for future demands. This is the same age span in which most of the childhood cases of extraterrestrial abductions, alien sightings, and near-death states are documented.

If a ghost does nothing unusual—like disappearing into a wall or slipping under the sash of a window—the witness may never realize that something extraordinary has happened. The following two questions beg themselves: How many spirits have we seen without realizing it? and, Do ghosts appear when we are not there to see them?

There are ghosts that call out the names of the living, and whenever this happens, the person being addressed is advised to remain silent. This warning is rooted in the superstition that the ghosts are trying to attract attention and lure their victims to disaster. According to lore, they are disembodied female voices. "Sirens," they have been called, and probably this superstition had its genesis in Greek mythology: Odysseus outwitted the Sirens by having his men plug their ears with wax before sailing past these enticers; he, desirous of hearing their song, had himself tied to his ship's mast.

Electronic voice phenomenon (EVP), the receiving of voices on audiotapes by means of no known physical source, is controversial, though some EVP researchers are convinced that they have recorded the voices of the dead, extraterrestrials, and spirit beings. Skeptics contend that the scratchy voices come from radio, citizens band and television transmissions—EVP sounds are faint and difficult to understand.

The possibility of such communications was announced in the October 1920 issue of *Scientific American* by none other than Thomas Alva Edison. It was his belief that such a machine could be built. Spirits could be captured on film, Edison insisted, so why couldn't they be reached electronically? The inventor had begun work on such a device, but it wasn't completed at the time of his death in 1931.

Experiments were conducted in 1936 with a record cutter and player, and the results yielded what sounded like male and female voices, whistles and rapping sounds. In 1959, Swedish opera singer, Friedrich Jurgenson, taped birdcalls and when playing the recording he heard a male voice discussing nocturnal birdsongs. At first, Jurgenson thought it was radio interference, but from a cacophony of static someone could be heard giving the opera singer information and instructions on how to hear more voices. This sensational playback caused a flurry of messages from EVP enthusiasts around the world.

Because of reduced broadcast interference, several experimentalists claim that recordings are more effective if done at night, and sensitive microphones, amplifiers, and high-quality tapes are employed. Many researchers, in their quest to prove survival after death, prefer to ask questions and leave a tape running to seize answers that are inaudible during taping, but audible in playbacks.

When the dead are visually perceived, they are sometimes seen as foggy-looking apparitions, or similar to projections from a motion picture camera. The majority of witnesses, however, report that these specters look absolutely real and lively: they seem younger and give the appearance of having been cured of any illness or injury that caused their death. The words "glow" and "shine" are often used to describe the strange lights that seem to accompany them.

There have been untold numbers of supernatural manifestations of the Virgin Mary, and several Maine residents—all with religious convictions—claim to have experienced paranormal phenomena, such as heavenly music, singing, and luminous presences. Only a few of the many sightings worldwide since 1531 have been deemed authentic by the Catholic Church. In most cases, a lady appears and identifies herself as Mary. She urges people to pray more and to lead devout lives; the apparition also asks for the construction of shrines and churches. Miraculous healings often are reported after such events, and many of the sightings are witnessed by small children. The Church's position is that these religious apparitions are not ghosts; they are believed to be mystical phenomena permitted by God.

The authenticated sightings are *Guadalupe, Mexico*, 1531, when Mary appeared five times to Juan Diego, a middle-aged Aztec convert to Catholicism; *Lourdes, France*, 1858, when 14-year-old Bernadette Soubirous saw "a girl in white, no taller than I, who greeted me with a little bow of her head"—the Lady spoke in the Lourdes dialect, and on the last encounter after a fortnight of appearances, the apparition identified herself, saying, "I am the Immaculate Conception"; *Fatima, Portugal*, 1917, when Mary appeared to three children and was seen by tens of thousands of spectators on six other occasions; *Zeitoun, Egypt*, 1968, and lasting about 14 months in more than 70 appearances where "a woman dressed in dazzling white stood on the top of the central dome of the church in the late night hours"; and in *Medjugorje, Bosnia-Herzegovina*, 1981, when six young people saw apparitions of Mary.

Phantom images witnessed by hundreds defy common sense, yet one such event during the Battle of Gettysburg caused Secretary of War Edwin Stanton to hold an official investigation—an inquiry that ended in confusion. The incident occurred as the 20th Maine Division approached the battleground and the troop commanders found themselves disoriented. Suddenly, a figure on horseback appeared. This phantom—wearing a tricornered hat—was immediately recognized as General George Washington as he took over and led the soldiers in the capture of Little Round Top. Colonel Joshua Chamberlain, who led the Maine division, told a newspaper correspondent after the battle: "We know not what mystic power may be possessed by those who are now bivouacking with the dead. I only know the effect, but I dare not explain or deny the cause. Who shall say that Washington was not among the number of those who aided the country that he founded?"

For the thousands of staunch followers who believe that the rock-and-roll musician Elvis Presley is still alive, it may be comforting to learn that the pianist Liberace was seen by hundreds of witnesses in the village of Fyffe, Alabama on February 19, 1989. A 12-foot-tall vision of the popular showman along with his oversized piano descended from a banana-shaped spacecraft. Liberace, dressed in ermine elegance, played several popular tunes on his glowing instrument before fading away into the normalcy of an Alabama countryside. This phenomenon of absurdity remains unsolved, and can only be explained as a case of group hysteria or some unknown short-circuiting of reality.

A ghostly apparition may only be an image trapped in a particular place—a mirage with no purposeful intention. A group of tourists traveling in Death Valley saw an old passenger train being pulled by an engine known as an "iron maiden." The engine's funnel was billowing smoke as the cars rattled along nonexistent tracks. Somehow, in a mysterious time warp, the image of a real train of long ago had become visible. Can images of the past be seen or heard when configurations of energy recur in the exact location where they were first imprinted? It has been reported that General George S. Patton sometimes could hear the sounds of muskets being fired when he walked in the vicinity of an old battleground.

There are few drivers on the highway who haven't had the frightening experience of seeing a vehicle *suddenly* approach them— "that car just came out of nowhere" is a statement frequently repeated. Ghostly automobiles, usually traveling at high speed, are a widespread type of haunting. Windshield, bumper, and grill appear to be real as they flash into view, and often there seems to be no one behind the wheel— "going too fast to catch anything" the orderly mind reasons as rear window, trunk, and back bumper disappear. Occasionally, fatalities occur: drivers swerve to avoid collisions and smash into utility poles or plunge down embankments. Some phantom vehicles are associated with sites where tragic accidents or murders have taken place, often said to be haunted. Then there are the sharp curves and lonely stretches of highway that have no histories of violence, but the same speeding automobiles are seen crowding the centerlines and dissolving in blurs of motion.

One popular ghost legend—with countless variations and frequently told here in Maine—depicts the appearance of a young female standing by the side of a lonely road. It is a stormy cold night, and the woman looks bedraggled from the wind and rain as she frantically waves to a passing motorist. The driver, usually a man alone, stops and asks if he can help. Her white dress is torn and smudged, there seem to be severe bruises on her arms, and she is shivering. The beautiful young woman in distress is going to the same town, and she tells the driver the name of the street and number. The shy hitchhiker, obviously exhausted, accepts his offer to take her home. He tells her to get into the backseat and gives her his coat against the chill. The woman may reveal her name but not the circumstances that left her alone on that deserted Maine road at such a late hour. When the motorist reaches the address she has given him, he stops the car, turns around, and is astonished to find that she has vanished. The passenger may have left behind some personal object—perhaps a pin, purse or scarf—and the cushion of the seat is wet. The driver goes to the house, rings the bell, and an elderly couple opens the door. He explains what has happened and is told that the young woman is their daughter who was killed in an accident on that lonely road some years back and this night is the anniversary of her death.

Ghosts are not talkative. They usually move in silence and seem unaware of—or disinterested in—their witnesses. Many people have reported hearing phantom footsteps in their homes, but there are few instances when ghosts have been seen and footsteps heard simultaneously. When an apparition does speak, it is difficult to engage it in any lengthy conversation.

Many communications from spirit beings suggest some sort of telepathic conversion into language; a theory bolstered by cases in which foreign ghosts converse easily with people who speak only English. Then there are ghostly disembodied voices, and these may be hallucinatory in nature, though on rare occasions they have been recorded. Voices from the past are heard unexpectedly: one Maine author claims that her dead father telephoned his congratulations when she published her first book.

Telephone conversations with the dead are not seriously regarded by parapsychologists, though numerous devices have been invented by researchers in hopes of capturing ghostly voices. Recipients of such exchanges are often spouses, parents, children, siblings, or other persons who had close emotional ties with the departed. Most communications are said to be initiated by the deceased in order to impart messages, such as a warning of impending danger or illness, a request that the living carry out some particular task, or a farewell not given in life.

People who admit receiving a phone call from the spirit world report that the voice sounds the same, and pet names and familiar words of endearment are exchanged. The telephone rings normally, though there may be a noticeable increase of static or line noise when one picks up the receiver. Often, the voice of the dead grows faint as the conversation continues, and those who claim to have received several calls from the other side believe that the line reception is better when one is in a passive state of mind. If the recipient knows that the telephoner has died, the shock of hearing from the departed may cause the conversation to be brief; if the dead caller is thought to be alive, a long talk up to a half hour may take place. People who claim to have experienced this phenomenon report that most of these calls were placed person-to-person, long-distance with the assistance of a mysterious operator. When the telephone company is asked to check their records to verify the connection, they are unable to do so.

THE WAY OF TAROT

The roots of Tarot date back to antiquity; it was seen as a way of talking to God. When one shuffles a Tarot deck and views its pictures, feelings, worldly issues, a sense of destiny, and future events can be spread out before one in storytelling tradition. In the beginning, such celestial communications were rights reserved for royalty—any serf caught using Tarot faced the punishment of death. It wasn't until the invention of Gutenberg's printing press that decks became widely accessible.

Designed to represent a history of human drama and consciousness, these Tarot pictures are symbols that express our past, present, and destiny. The 78 cards in the deck depict every element of life, lesson to be learned, and condition one should know. How they are read depends on the individual who has them in hand; the cards may appear to fore-tell the future and seal a person's fate, but they have no powers of inev-itability—the deck can only reveal possibilities, not certainties.

A Tarot deck has 22 Major and 56 Minor Arcana cards. (Arcana is defined as "mysterious knowledge, language, or information accessible only by the initiate.") Its purpose is to describe everyday issues and events, and to remind one that everything is interconnected, has synchronicity, and no event can be described as mere coincidence: many can use the symbols of the Tarot in their search of personal answers to Big Questions.

There are recommended guidelines for a person who is about to have a reading: one should relax and be receptive to the unexpected; there is less chance of information being blocked if the sitter has confidence in the reader. Before the cards are shuffled, it is advisable to concentrate on what one wants to know foremost. The big picture must come first and details later.

The Major Arcana cards of the Tarot deck are visual metaphors for the human experience. They represent life's journey toward enlightenment and depict situations of major significance. Users think of them as sign-posts at the crossroads: they may show where one presently is on life's journey, what is known, and what must be learned.

The Minor Arcana cards, known as Wands, Cups, Swords, and Pentacles, symbolize everyday events and the things that are within control. They are suits representing the four areas of life—material, emotional, conflict, and enterprise—these cards, as a whole, signify what may happen.

Tarot decks come in many varieties, and users often select the one that fits a lifestyle or individual taste; for example, popular decks have the descriptive inducement of such names as *Angel, Native American, Zolar's Astrological, Witches, Cat People,* and *Aquarian.* Tarot, the experts assure us, is an "instinctual art," and its many meanings are found intuitively—the cards present endless possibilities.

Shuffling the cards is one of the most important aspects of a Tarot reading, and the seeker should be the one to shuffle the deck. This gives the reader a more accurate sense of the sitter. The division of the cards into three stacks by the seeker is recommended. According to "ancient wisdom," this separating is considered to be an act of blessing the deck.

Many reach out to the Tarot experience in hope of finding a new direction. Perhaps some pattern from the cards can give one hints of unwelcome influences or provide glimpses of greater potentials. A good reading occurs when a person comes away feeling that certain known truths have been validated, and there is an awareness of future conditions and available avenues.

THE HOUSE IN MOUNT VERNON

"This house is very definitely haunted," declared David Caldwell when interviewed at his home in Mount Vernon, Maine. Built in 1742, and for many years the residence of Noah Greeley, a Revolutionary War veteran, the sprawling structure was once part of a hundred acre farm by scenic Parker Pond.

One particular chamber in the old colonial has had more paranormal happenings than any of the other dozen or more rooms—the Caldwells call this "the guest room" or "the ghost room," depending on the sensitivity of the person occupying it. David's sister, Kyle, has never forgotten an incident that occurred there when she was a child: the little girl looked up from her bed and saw "fairies and lights" dancing in a circle.

Years later, when Kyle was a student in college and visiting her grandmother, Helen Caldwell Cushman, there was another encounter in the same chamber. "Helen was out and Kyle was alone in the house," recalled David's wife, Rhonda, "and she had the light on because she was reading in bed. Her eyes were tired so she just laid back for a moment and looked toward the ceiling." Again, there was a ring of festivity; this time "tiny women singing and dancing in the air, and it was for a few short minutes this happened." The incident proved too much for Kyle. "She hasn't stayed a night alone in the house ever since," said Rhonda Caldwell.

There may be another reason for not wishing to be an overnight guest: it is the abundance of unexplained happenings. Personal belongings continue to come up missing and are retrieved eventually in some unlikely place in another room, turned-off lights are found burning, and there is a rocking chair that nervously returns to its original location after having been moved. This furnishing, to the Caldwell's dismay, somehow "seems to make a wet spot on the ceiling or the floor below it."

Old houses with a history have a language of their own, and the colonial structure that David Caldwell's great-grandparents named "Greentrees" is no exception: there is a cacophony of mysterious complaints as the creaking timbers shift on their pedestal of ancient granite. Sometimes, there is the threat of intruders. On several occasions, there have been the sounds of adult footsteps in the hallway while the only adults on the premises were sitting quietly in their living room.

Helen Caldwell Cushman made Greentrees her permanent home in 1927, shortly after her marriage to novelist Erskine Caldwell—his two best-known novels, *Tobacco Road* and *God's Little Acre,* were written while he was living in the Mount Vernon house. Helen and her first husband enjoyed talking about presences that lurked in deserted bedrooms, and Raymond Skolfield of Hallowell, an impressionable teenager at the time, remembered a weekend visit.

"There were stories about the house," said Skolfield, "stories told in the evening as we sat by the big table in the large living room. They said the building had once been an inn on the old Post Road and how the room we were staying in had been a barroom tavern where lumberjacks gathered to drink and carouse. Many fights took place there, I was told. Then they said that skeletons of some of the victims had been found sealed up in the walls. How slaves fleeing to Canada were hidden. Caldwell informed me that there might be dungeons. I was made to feel I was in a real haunted house.

"Afterwards, I was given a small room upstairs with a small iron bed to sleep in—I slept with a kerosene light on. They had told me that two ghosts walked through the old inn at night. Then there were these laughing loons on the small lake that was part of their property—those birds were so spooky and noisy!"

Over the years, Helen Caldwell Cushman became comfortable with the ethereal inhabitants of her home, and she had a number of ghost tales in her repertoire when masquerading as "The Green Witch" in storytelling appearances at local schools.

One of the two or three spirit occupants in the house became a favorite of Helen's, and she named him "Henchie." David Caldwell spoke of his grandmother's confidence in this ghost's ability to locate missing items. "I do remember if you lost something in this house—and this place swallows things because it's so huge—Helen would have me call on Henchie to find it for me." To the young David, it all seemed so astonishing, and looking back on those miracles, he wondered if his grandmother "would go find the things for me and make them available for me to bump into them."

The Caldwells' daughter, Molly, had a late-night adventure when she was three years old. "It was three in the morning when she woke up," said Rhonda Caldwell, "and pitch-black out. You couldn't even see any light coming through the windows at all, so you couldn't see any shadows in the bedroom." To calm the child, the mother brought Molly into their bed, but a few minutes later the parents heard a small voice say, "Who's that Mom?" And Rhonda asked, "Where?" "Right there!" replied Molly, obviously frightened. The child insisted that someone was in the room with them, though nothing could be seen.

David Caldwell thinks his daughter saw the ghost of Gertrude. Years earlier, his grandmother had described this apparition as a young woman in her late teens or early twenties. The details of her death have become smudged by the years, but the Caldwells believe that Gertrude died in the house.

On two occasions, in the same room, Rhonda and David smelled a perfume—a scent impossible to identify. It seemed to linger, aimlessly hovering, as they inquisitively stalked its invisible presence.

"I guess," said Caldwell, "all I can report is that sometimes, especially when alone, it's unexplainable, but I move quickly through the upstairs hallway. Sometimes, it's with the hair on my neck a little bit bristled—I get the feeling that someone, or something is there."

PETER HURKOS

Pieter Cornelis van der Hurk was born on May 21, 1911 in the small industrial town of Dordrecht, Holland. It was no ordinary birth: Peter entered the world with a filmy membrane wrapped around his head—"born with a veil," a sign that here was someone who had capabilities of seeing into the future. This "fleece" around the head was no stroke of fortune. Hurkos was blind for the first six months of his life, and much of his childhood was spent in dark places; he grew up morose and brooding. His brother Nico remembered: "Yes, yes, Peter was a very strange boy. He saw things which we couldn't see."

Hurkos was a poor student at school, and his lessons ended abruptly when he hurled an inkwell at a teacher. He ran away from home and went to sea as a cook's assistant—Peter was only fourteen at the time, but he looked years older. On one of his home leaves, a beautiful Dutch girl, Bea van der Berg, smiled at him, and they were married in 1937. Two years later, he gave up being a sailor and went to work for his father as a housepainter.

On July 10, 1941, Peter was helping his father paint a four-story apartment building in The Hague. His father was painting the interior and he the outside, starting at the roof and working down. Witnesses who saw him fall from the fourth level agreed that if Peter hadn't landed on his shoulder, he would have been killed instantly.

He lay unconscious for four days, and doctors believed there was no hope of recovery. When he did regain consciousness, he had lost his memory for many things, including faces, names, and dates. At first, he could recognize his family only by the sounds of their voices.

Then it happened: the gift or curse. "Bea, what are you doing here?" he cried angrily when he heard her voice. "Where's Benny?"

His wife had left their son with a neighbor, and when she tried to explain her reasons for doing so, he lashed out at her.

"You belong at home with Benny. You shouldn't be here in the hospital. You're not a good mother. You go now and get Benny. Quick! Now! Oh, God!" he screamed. "The whole room is burning with Benny!"

Peter's timing was off. The fire happened five days later and firemen broke down a door and rescued his son.

Hurkos astonished his parents when he came home from the hospital. "My father said, 'Look at him. He is not the same. Peter gets religious!' Because I buy a secondhand Bible for two guilders in the market. And my mother thought I was crazy, and my father laughed at me because I sit all the time studying the Bible. I wanted to find the key to what is wrong with me."

Hurkos acquired his powers unexpectedly and later in life; some are born with the ability to perform incredible feats: five-year-old Benjamin Blyth was a calculation prodigy. "What time is it?" he asked his father. "Half past four," the parent replied. A minute went by and the child said, "In that case I have been alive..." and named the number of seconds since his birth: about 158 million. The father got out a sheet of paper and began multiplying. "No," he told his son, "you were wrong by 172,800 seconds." "No I wasn't," said the child. "You forgot the two leap years."

In March 1978, a Russian woman, Yuliya Vorobyeva, 37, was pronounced dead after receiving a 380-volt electric shock. Two days later in the morgue, a passing attendant noticed that she was alive. After several days in a hospital, Yuliya was sent home but was unable to sleep much for the next six months. Then one night after sinking into a deep sleep the woman awoke and discovered that she had paranormal powers— they were as startling as those displayed by Peter Hurkos. A Russian newspaper reporter interviewed her, and Yuliya Vorobyeva looked at his stomach and told him what he had had for lunch. Within seconds of meeting a doctor, she informed him that one of his ears was weaker than the other, and the same was true of his eyes.

During the Nazi occupation of Holland, most able-bodied men were arrested and sent to labor camps. Hurkos escaped en route, returned home and worked for the Dutch underground. When asked what he did during the war, his reply was short. "Blow up," he said—he dynamited bridges and railroad tracks and tunnels to prevent the shipment of food to Germany. (Hurkos was decorated as a war hero by Queen Juliana of the Netherlands, and there is a statue commemorating him and seven other Dutch underground workers in the Center Square in Rotterdam.) Risking his life didn't matter, he told a friend, because in the back of his mind there was the hope that he would be killed and all his "head trouble" would be over. His gift was never much help to him personally, he admitted. "I cannot even find my own shoes."

"Well, you can say it is God's gift," Hurkos told a friend, "but that is not all the answer. There are many things we do not know yet. I remember the time I was falling and I didn't want to die. Then everything was black. And when I woke up I had no mind of my own. And then I got my gift. I was in somebody else's mind, and I was scared because I didn't know what was happening. My father and mother said it's not the same Peter anymore. You can ask my father, I swear it. He will tell you the real son Peter died and I came back with two minds."

After the war, Hurkos took a part-time job in a coffee shop and began giving "readings." He and Bea drifted apart, and Peter spent the next five years working with police investigators in Paris. His accuracy in solving cases earned him respect throughout Europe, and he became more in demand as a public performer. His success would have been sensational if he had had better control of this gift: he was inclined to blurt out whatever he saw—this included details of disasters, deaths, and extramarital affairs.

When Hurkos was working in the coffee shop, a customer asked him to help locate a missing document. He told her to look *behind* her husband's file cabinet, not *in* it, as both had done when searching the files. "You will find it caught at the back between two drawers," he told her. And so it was, as the woman later discovered.

"I appreciate your assistance," she said reaching for her purse to pay him.

Before she could open the bag, he held her arm.

"Madame, please, you need your money," said Peter. "But if you don't mind, I would like the chocolate which you have next to the money."

Hurkos worked for a short time as a psychic consultant to a doctor in Paris who was developing a new polio serum. Though Peter had no medical background, his performance as a researcher was remarkable enough for him to be featured in *Paris Match* magazine. Dr. Henry K. (Andrija) Puharich read the article and was so impressed that he invited Peter to come for six months of experiments at the Round Table Foundation laboratory in Glen Cove, Maine.

Should he leave Europe now, Hurkos agonized, just at a time when he was earning substantial fees from private readings? Six months was a long time in a person's life, and he was on a yearly retainer with several industrial firms. It also would mean going to a country where he didn't know the language and leaving his family and friends. But Peter was driven: he needed answers and wanted a better understanding of the faculty that often seemed an affliction.

Billed in Europe as "the man with the radar brain," he was subject to blinding headaches and physical strains. His was a volatile temperament; Herkos was easily hurt and unable to control his mood swings. Instead of pursuing a career as a performing psychic on European circuits, Peter decided to travel to America and offer himself as a guinea pig. Perhaps this was his one chance of finding out what was wrong with his head.

Dr. Puharich's decision to have Peter for six months of testing was financed by department store magnate Henry Belk who had read about Peter's work in Europe. Belk revealed his reason for wanting Hurkos in America: "I got to thinking we could use someone like him to help us operate our new stores in Miami and Atlanta—we had trouble with shoplifting and dishonesty among employees. So I put Puharich and Hurkos together on a farm to experiment on Hurkos. It cost me fifty thousand dollars."

Belk was soon disenchanted with Peter; his business predictions were not encouraging enough for the tycoon's high expectations. But it was a family tragedy that caused a painful rift between the two men.

In June of 1957, Belk's ten-year-old daughter disappeared from his home in North Carolina. When police were unable to find her, Belk telephoned Hurkos for help. Peter thought for a while, drew a blank, and promised to call back.

"Then, soon as I hung up the phone," recalled Hurkos, "I saw a clear picture that his daughter was drowned by the boathouse, in six-foot-deep water. I don't know how to tell him this, but I call him back and I tell him she is drowned, and that is too much for him."

Belk went to the edge of the river and found the girl's body in the exact location and position that Peter said it would be. "If he could see ahead," declared an angry Belk, "why couldn't he have told me what was going to happen in time to save my child?"

"So he fired me," said Hurkos, and with bitterness showing, asked: "If my gift brings me the picture after, why can't it bring it sooner so I could save his daughter? Why? Why? I'm sorry, but I can tell only what I see."

In the Glen Cove, Maine research laboratories some of the most re-markable records were scored in psychic readings that dealt with dis-eases. "I would stake my professional reputation on Peter Hurkos," said Andrija Puharich near the end of his time as director of the center. "I have screened two hundred persons for extrasensory perception in the last twelve years. I have found only six who could be considered to have genuine ESP—and of these Peter's abilities were the greatest." In experiments, observed Dr. Puharich, Hurkos obtained the best evidence on record for telepathic interaction between two minds. "He seemed able sometimes to pierce the past, present, and future by means of something more than simple telepathy."

Peter's fellow workers at the Round Table Foundation found him loud and rambunctious. He was in his late forties, a huge man, six foot three, and usually in good humor and radiating vitality. He was often clumsy, and always ungainly in his sprawling way of abusing chairs—his laugh-ter was contagious. Hurkos loved to tell jokes, and his favorites were, as one laboratory assistant observed, "downright dirty."

Hurkos had no difficulty in describing what was inside an envelope, and when handed a watch, ring, or some trinket, he could, while being blindfolded, reveal detailed information about the person to whom the object belonged—he had a remarkable 90 percent score in psychom-etry. Most intriguing for Puharich was Peter's ability, after two photo-graphs were rubbed together, to look at one and describe the other. Could it be that some form of energy was being conveyed from one print to another?

Dr. Puharich's investigations of psychic phenomena went beyond the traditional procedure of using ESP cards. He made a study of Peter's brain cell functions during tests and gave him certain mushrooms that produce various stages of hallucination. The first day in the research laboratory was a frightening experience for Hurkos—there were so many cables and machines jumbled together. Puharich's Faraday cage terrified him. This enclosure was lined with copper to prevent electromagnetic waves from passing through the walls—even a radio broadcast would be cut off when the door was closed. The purpose of the booth was to isolate a psychic from interference or help from outside sources.

The six months with Hurkos stretched into two and a half years, and laboratory and field material about Peter was collected and analyzed for nearly a decade after the team of experimenters broke up. It took Puharich several weeks to get accustomed to Peter's blustery way of displaying his psychometric abilities—there was no denying the evidence of skill: four times out of five, when researchers handed Hurkos concealed objects (safety pin, button, butterfly, even a blank sheet of paper) Peter had only to touch the sealed envelope to identify the contents.

Guests at the Glen Cove laboratory often found the occupants unusual and the atmosphere bizarre. In a collection of Aldous Huxley's letters, there is a description of his vist.

"I spent some days, earlier this month, at Glen Cove, in the strange household assembled by Puharich—Gladys Davenport and Mrs. Puharich, behaving to one another in a conspicuously friendly way; Eleanor Bond, doing telepathic guessing remarkably well, but not producing anything of interest or value in the mediumistic sitting she gave me; Harry, the Dutch sculptor, who goes into trances in the Faraday Cage and produces automatic scripts in Egyptian hieroglyphics; Narodny, the cockroach man, who is preparing experiments to test the effects of human telepathy on insects. It was all very lively and amusing—and I really think promising; for whatever may be said against Puharich, he is certainly very intelligent, extremely well read and highly enterprising. His aim is to reproduce by modern pharmacological, electronic and physical methods the conditions used by the Shamans for getting into a state of traveling clairvoyance. At Glen Cove they now have found eight specimens of the *amanita muscaria*. This is very remarkable as the literature of the mycological society of New England records only one previous instance of the discovery of an amanita in Maine. The effects, when a piece as big as a pin's head, is rubbed for a few seconds into the skin of the scalp, are quite alarmingly powerful, and it will obviously take a lot of very cautious experimentation to determine the right psi-enhancing dose of the mushroom."

Puharich kept a journal, and in it he noted encounters that Hurkos claimed to have had with extraterrestrials while at the laboratory in Glen Cove. Peter was quite "perturbed for a while and kept talking about 'flying sausages' as he called UFOs." This was from August to November 1957 when a number of sightings had been reported in the Camden, Maine area.

"One day near the end of September," wrote Puharich, "Peter came to me and said: 'Andrija, you know that my powers are my powers. I don't believe in spirits or ghosts, and I always thought that flying saucers were baloney. But believe me, Andrija, I swear on my baby's eyes, I have been awakened many nights by beings from flying saucers. Last night again, I went down to the rocks by the ocean, and at about four in the morning, all of a sudden there appeared a flying saucer over the water about 100 meters away. It was about 15 meters across and shaped like a lens. It was all transparent. I could see through it like through glass. But it glowed all kinds of changing colors. I will draw exactly what I saw.'

"Peter then quickly made a sketch of a biconvex object and its interior. He was quite emphatic that the power plant was in the center of the craft.

" 'As this saucer hovered over the water,' Peter continued, 'it lit up everything around it, including the spot where I sat on the rock. Then suddenly there were two beings standing near me. They were small, and looked very old with young bodies. They wore tight fitting outfits that looked like leather motorcycle suits. They just looked at me. No word was spoken. But I felt that they were telling me things, and I understood it. I don't remember anything that was told me. Suddenly they were in the saucer that had come close by. Then there was fire and smoke, and the saucer went away silently. You have to believe me, Andrija, that's what I saw. I didn't want to tell you, but it's driving me crazy.'

"I didn't know what to say. I could not believe it, but neither could I deny it.

"Peter said that the rocks were probably blackened where the saucer had taken off. We went to the spot at low tide, but there was no evidence of a burn on the rocks."

Andrija Puharich was born in 1918 and received his medical degree from Northwestern University in 1947. During the Korean War he served in the Medical Corps and did research in chemical warfare. From 1948 to 1958, Puharich was Director of Research for the Round Table Foundation. In his laboratory, he developed a hearing aid called the "tooth radio," a device that could be implanted inside a person's tooth. After several years of study on neurophysiological problems, he determined that a certain mushroom, *amanita muscaria*, found in Maine and Massachusetts, would stimulate latent extrasensory perception in human beings. His two most popular books, influenced by the Glen Cove years of experimentation, were *The Sacred Mushroom* and *Beyond Telepathy*. The arrival of Peter Hurkos at the laboratory in 1956 produced extraordinary results in furthering the scope of ESP studies.

Puharich left Glen Cove, Maine and moved his laboratory to Carmel, California in 1958 where he continued his research and served as a consultant to universities and industrial corporations. From 1963 to 1968, he led a number of medical research expeditions to Brazil for the purpose of studying the healer Arigo. Known as the "Surgeon of the Rusty Knife," Arigo worked at lightning speed, performing operations in less than a minute and treating an average of 300 patients a day. In his biography of this Brazilian healer, John G. Fuller wrote: "He could cut through flesh with an unclean kitchen- or pocket-knife and there would be no pain, no hemostasis—the tying off of blood vessels—and no need for stitches. It is a *fact* that he could stop the flow of blood with a sharp verbal command. It is a *fact* that there would be no ensuing infection, even though no antisepsis was used." Arigo died in a 1971 automobile accident at the age of 49.

Andrija Puharich's book, *Uri: A Journal of the Mystery of Uri Geller*, published in 1974, though a straightforward narrative of his three-year investigation of the Israeli psychic, left readers bewildered and confused. Not long after their first meeting in 1971, according to Puharich, both men were contacted by "Spectra," a voice they believed to represent an extraterrestrial intelligence called "Hoova." If so, this would make Geller and Dr. Puharich the first individuals in modern history to have had extended contact with non-earthly beings. "Hoova" is quoted at length in the book on the source of Uri's psychic powers. The young Israeli and Andrija began their collaboration with warmth but parted with a mutual chill. "The moment I saw Andrija," wrote Geller, "I knew by instinct that I could work with him. He didn't look like my picture of a scientist, but more like a hippie Einstein."

During the 1970s, Puharich distanced himself from the establishment with psychic experiments conducted at his complex in Ossining, New York called the "Turkey Farm." Andrija assembled twenty young people from the ages of nine to the late teens and trained them to receive messages from aliens. The youngsters were known as "Gellerlings" or "Space Kids." Puharich asserted that they were able to materialize objects huge as trees, and that six of them arrived at his complex by teleportation. The Turkey Farm was destroyed by fire in 1978, and the suspect in the arson was a Space Kid who insisted that aliens were harassing him. Puharich implicated the CIA and later claimed that he had been the target of four assassination attempts by this organization. Andrija Puharich died in 1995 after tumbling down a flight of stairs— "pushed" was how one defender of the doctor's name described the fall.

Hurkos never consciously practiced healing, though many people who knew him felt the power was there. One woman recalled his prediction that her daughter would walk again after five doctors had said otherwise, and Peter revealed the exact date when the girl would take those first steps.

Once he shook hands with a woman he had never seen before and said abruptly: "You have arthritis."

"Yes," she replied. "Since I was twenty-four."

Hurkos asked her to write something, anything, on a piece of paper. She did and he rubbed his fingers across the writing.

"Your mother is ill," he told her. "She is having trouble in this area." Peter drew his hands down to his pelvic area.

The amazed woman admitted that her mother had fractured her hip and was now convalescing.

Peter upset a lady at a party.

"You have two little children, haven't you?"

"Yes," she replied.

"You would have had three, but you lost one last August. It was a miscarriage. And then you became pregnant again right away."

The hostess of the party found her guest cowering alone in the kitchen shortly after Peter's impromptu reading.

"Even my husband didn't know about my miscarriage," said the dazed and trembling woman. "How could *he* know?"

Peter Hurkos never asserted that he was a healer, but on one occasion he exhibited miraculous healing powers on himself. When Henry Belk, though no longer a sponsor, friend, or believer told the story, there was awe in his voice. The incident happened on the evening of May 17, 1958 in Belk's New York apartment when a group of associates were having a party. While mingling with the other guests, Hurkos tripped over something and fell. He twisted his leg so badly that, according to Belk, "One of the bones broke clear out of his skin, and there was blood all over the place." Peter cried out in pain as several men lifted him onto a bed. He bowed his head as though in prayer, "and before our very eyes, the bone went back into place and the torn skin healed and became smooth. I was there," said Belk. "I actually saw the bone stick out and go in."

When asked if he had used self-hypnosis in healing himself, Hurkos didn't know. "Concentration, that's all," he said. "I'm thinking, 'What am I gonna do now? I don't want to be in a hospital.' I think it's what you call mind over matter."

Peter's reputation as a psychic detective spread nationally, and he soon became a regular crime consultant. Most of his investigations ended in success, though he was ridiculed for his efforts in the highly publicized Carroll Jackson murder case in Virginia.

"Oh, I picked the wrong man," said Hurkos nonchalantly. "I found the right house, the one the murderer lived in, but he had moved, and now his friend, the trashman, lived there. He was a friend of the piano player. I was not sure which one did it, and I picked the trashman. Anyway, I found the right house."

Hurkos never claimed total accuracy; he averaged about 87 percent. Those who knew him alleged that he sometimes drew a complete blank. He once was given a box containing jewelry of a teenager who had been murdered in Chicago. The grieving father wanted Hurkos to find the murderer. "I'm sorry," he said after inspecting the contents of the box. "I don't see anything. I don't feel anything. Nothing. I don't know why. But I can't tell you what I don't see."

His reputation soared when police asked him to help solve the Tate-LaBianca murders which were headlined in newspapers during the late 1960s. "The man behind all this," said Peter after a cursory inspection of the victims' possessions, "has a beard and is called Charlie." It was indeed Charles Manson.

Peter was lured to Hollywood in the spring of 1960 when he was asked to tell of his experiences as a psychic for *One Step Beyond*, a television special. Too soon, he became an odd sort of guru for stars, and some regarded him as an "entertaining spook" who prostituted his skills for shallow purposes. He was asked to calm film idols when an emotional crisis arose, and many insisted that he advise them whenever a new film role was offered. Once, his assignment was finding a star's lost cat.

Actor Marlon Brando asked Hurkos to tell him the contents of two sealed boxes. Peter held the first box for a moment and said: "I see a fire or an explosion on the sea. You have here a golden spike, a nail from a ship." Then he picked up the second box. "In this package you have a letter, and I'm sorry to tell you, sir, but the spelling is lousy." Peter was right in both cases. The first box concealed a golden spike from the ship *HMS Bounty* and the second contained a letter with several misspellings.

A number of members in the scientific community had expressed disappointment that Hurkos did not submit himself to more long-range testing after leaving the Glen Cove laboratory. For Peter, finances were always a concern: he was willing to give his time for experiments, provided that someone paid the bills while he was being researched. Couldn't he have benefited himself and mankind more as a healer, instead of becoming a popular sidekick for Hollywood stars? Yet his crime work was more an act of charity; he rarely charged fees when helping the police as a psychic sleuth.

"These cases make me sick," he complained shortly before his death in 1988. "They are too hard on me and take too much out of me. I am a human being too, even if I do have the gift. I feel things, same as you or anybody. And how you think I like it when they bring me clothing with blood, or part of a leg from a dead person? No, I don't like working on cases. Sometimes they make me sick to my stomach."

"I know it sounds funny, but yes, yes, I am happy that I cannot know about myself," said Hurkos when looking back on his peculiar journey through life. "You get this gift and it will make you nuts. If I didn't have this gift, I would be the most happy man in the world."

POLTERGEIST

The poltergeist has aged with mankind, though it wasn't until the late nineteenth century that it began to be closely scrutinized. Before this, people interpreted such paranormal activities in terms of religious beliefs—most happenings were diagnosed as being the work of demons. During the 1960s, when scientists began to study poltergeist incidents, there were only 375 cases reported around the world. Gradually, people started to doubt the presence of witches and goblins; now onlookers were trying to find out what caused these disturbances. Instead of the wearers of the cloth, investigators from the scientific community were usually the first to be summoned.

Translated from the German, *poltergeist* means "noisy ghost," though it is not always a harmless loud phantom. It can be a relentless stalker and vicious attacker with a malevolence equaling its destructiveness. Whenever the poltergeist pounces, all hell breaks loose, but fortunately most incidents are short-lived and often focused on only one member of a family.

The behavior of this noisy presence is like that of a child or immature person when frustrated: things get thrown, walls are pounded, people in the household annoyed. But those who believe that the childish energy is merely a projection of an adolescent could be underestimating its powers. There may be different types, which we classify under one heading because of similar characteristics.

Psychic researcher Guy Playfair describes the poltergeist phenomenon as a "football of energy." When people become tense, they exude a nervousness—the kind of energy many teenagers have during puberty. Playfair believes that most poltergeists are spirits: "Along come a couple of spirits and they do what any group of schoolboys would do—they begin to kick this football around, smashing windows and generally creating havoc. Then they get tired and leave it. In fact the football often explodes and turns into a puddle of water."

There does seem to be a pattern when a poltergeist erupts in a home. Objects will move about or break by themselves during a typical disturbance, and these events usually occur for only a few weeks or months. The poltergeist centers on a specific family member—often a child, an adolescent around the age of puberty, and sometimes a mentally disturbed young person or adult. There can be considerable property damage during such outbreaks, but seldom do the occupants suffer bodily injuries.

We know so little about the phenomenon—its nature is mysterious—and we are baffled by the energy of the projections. Where does the force come from, and what intelligence directs it? There is no reason to assume that all manifestations are alike. If considered as types, the first seems devoid of sophisticated intelligence and the behavior rather childish. Type two is more complex and violent, showing more levels of external will, such as teleportation, bodily levitation, personal attacks, fire setting, and the movement of heavy objects. Type two poltergeists do accomplish acts beyond the physical capabilities of the agents.

Though there are several differences between poltergeist activity and haunted houses, there is a tendency to confuse the two. The presence of a ghost in a dwelling is usually a prolonged affair and totally independent of the observers: ghosts inhabit a place; poltergeists infest people. A specter rarely hurls crockery and stones or sets fires—it prefers to let one see apparitions or hear footsteps.

The Eastwind Restaurant on Main Street in Wiscasset, once a boarding house built in 1800 by Charles and Lydia Dana, sheltered a poltergeist that had been known to upset teapots, unlatch doors, move chairs, and slap people on their backsides. This mischievous presence was thought to be unladylike Lydia, known locally as Mother Dana.

Also in Wiscasset, the Marine Antique Shop at 14 High Street was once a dining room, and during this time employees and customers encountered a poltergeist that moved tables, chairs, and dinnerware. There were fewer incidents when the business featured antiques, as if the spirit felt more comfortable with older furnishings.

Jennifer Maguire was at one time a supervisor in a group home in Wiscasset. There were several residents, along with two mentally challenged children and six staff members. "The things that occurred," Maguire told this writer in an e-mail communication, "were odd noises coming up from the basement through the heating vents in the floor, LOUD banging noises inside and outside the house late at night, a desk chair on wheels rolling across a wood floor (more than once), the sound of a car pulling into the driveway but when you look outside there is no car (happened almost daily), smoke detectors on an electrical system going off for no reason, motion detectors not working, water being turned off, and doors without locks would continually get stuck when I would try to get out of a room or the house."

Two months after Maguire was hired there was a staff layoff and the two children were moved to another home. This didn't lessen what could well be described as possible poltergeist happenings. "One of the children," wrote Jennifer, "spoke of a friend named 'Ace,' and the child would talk into thin air as if looking at something only she could see."

One evening Maguire had a medium give personal readings for herself and several friends, including the new supervisor of the group home. When asked to explain the occurrences, the medium felt a female presence and the name she got was "Grace." This "made sense" to Jennifer since "the child had trouble speaking clearly" and the names being so much alike.

"I was also told by more than one of my female staff members (none of the males believed in paranormal activity) that everything was extremely intensified once I came to work there. But just within the last few weeks," Maguire concluded, "I heard a few stories of objects being moved. I guess Grace is still gracing the rooms of the house with her presence."

Many witnesses have described how object-throwing incidents are sometimes accompanied by detonation-like pops. The sound of glass breaking or furniture moving about in unoccupied rooms is a common occurrence. During one vigil in a haunted house, a researcher heard what sounded as if all the dishes in the cupboard were being broken, but upon entering the kitchen he found everything in order. Such performances are typical of the poltergeist.

On Saturday nights, the sizzle and smell of fried onions and pork chops coming from an unlit stove in the kitchen marked the beginning of the hauntings for one Waldo County couple. They later learned that this was the favorite dish of a woman who had died in the old colonial they were renting. Then came the noisy slamming of a door—this disruption was particularly irritating since the sound came from a wall next to their bed. An old house plan of the building, found in a storage shed, revealed that an entrance to the bedroom had been in this location before renovations. The new tenants also learned that their noisy ghost was known locally as Aunt Angie, a woman who befriended all the stray animals around, but who showed little tenderness for her husband, Uncle Ned. In this house the sound of crockery smashing was not just the whimsicality of a poltergeist—Aunt Angie hurled plates at poor Ned when she was displeased.

Some poltergeists seem to possess a sense of humor and enjoy the tricks they play on their victims. In 1974, an English housewife complained to a reporter: "It's nerve-racking living here. I have to keep my purse and pills on me. If I don't, the poltergeist hides them!" Her husband's complaint was more embarrassing. "He loves to have fun with my underwear. He throws them downstairs, and if I don't pick them up he creates chaos in the kitchen. Once I had a bath and asked my wife to get my pants but she couldn't find them. The next morning I was astonished to see them hanging on a branch at the top of a tree at the back of the house."

Frank Podmore, one of the leading researchers in the late 1800s, found that in most cases investigated, a teenager lived in the infested home, and usually that young person was a girl. Female poltergeist agents no longer outnumber the males—since the 1960s more boys than girls have been reported. It also should be noted that a great number of these agents are children who are living away from their natural parents.

The following phenomena are the most commonly reported manifestations of the poltergeist: *raps and blows*—loud sounds emanating from the walls, more like detonations than knocks; *stone-throwing* where rocks will bombard an outside wall or fall on the roof of a house, and there have even been recorded cases of stones being thrown inside a house; *movement of objects* which may make odd zigzag movements or slide slowly as if being carried; *fire-lighting* incidents, when objects myste-riously break into flames several times a day; *teleportation*, as house-hold objects disappear—even out of locked containers; and *biting* cases involving family members who suffer lacerations and bite marks during a poltergeist infestation.

In his book, *After Death—What?*, Cesare Lombroso, a researcher of poltergeist phenomena, remembers being asked to investigate a res-taurant where such paranormal activities were alarmingly on the rise. As Lombroso stood in the cellar, empty bottles began spinning on the floor and shattered against a table. A half dozen more rose from the shelves and smashed on the floor at his feet. As he and the proprietor went back upstairs, they heard another bottle explode behind them. Lombroso glanced at a waiter, an unusually tall youngster of thirteen. His height suggested that the boy's body was being overpowered with growth hormones, including those that intensified sexual awareness. Reluctantly, Lombroso suggested to the proprietor that the young man be dismissed, and the poltergeist disturbance ceased immediately.

Patients suffering from paranoia and some forms of hysteria often complain that their minds are being terrorized by outside entities. In what is known as poltergeist-possession syndrome, victims hear raps or explosions, suffer convulsions, shout obscenities, exhibit a hatred for religious objects, and sometimes predict future events. In some cases, bodies levitate, beds shake, and sufferers speak languages they never previously studied.

A news item in the April 7, 1947 issue of *Time* magazine illustrates the persistence of an arsonous poltergeist: "In Woodstock, Vermont a fire broke out in the basement of the Wendell Walker home on Sunday; the staircase caught fire on Monday; an upstairs partition blazed on Tues-day; the jittery Walkers moved out on Wednesday; the house burned down on Thursday."

While rarely mentioned in accounts of today's poltergeists, animal ap-paritions were often reported during the seventeenth and eighteenth centuries. Sometimes gargoylish in appearance, they were often de-scribed as small, and notably of the cat family. Witches were said to possess "familiars"—supernatural creatures to carry out the sorcerer's evil wishes. The witch with her cat was an easy companion for the pol-tergeist, accommodating popular cultural beliefs of the times.

This "noisy ghost" prefers to disappear when outside observers are brought on the scene, though there is a tendency to follow its primary victim—the one central to the disturbance. On rare occasions, poltergeists have been known to infest neighboring houses when its agent moves.

Sexual energy as it increases at puberty has a definite connection with psychical phenomena. (This author recalls an incident at an Augusta, Maine drugstore. The woman in front of me wasn't certain if the bathroom lightbulbs she had purchased would fit a standard-sized socket. The female teenager at the cashier's counter opened the package and pulled out one to examine it. As she held the bulb by its stem, much to everyone's surprise, it glowed a full 100 watts of power for a long moment before fizzling. Such cases are quite common with adolescents, I read afterwards, but this electrical demonstration still astonishes me.)

English medium William Stainton Moses connected sexual energy with mediumship in certain adolescents, but considered this a sensitivity they lose after puberty. The blossoming forces of sexual potency occurring in the body may, instead of being channeled normally, be externalized by the body itself.

Poltergeist cases are among the most frequent of paranormal incidents—there are hundreds of thousands of them going on all over the world as you read these words, and probably one is occurring within a dozen miles of where you are now. This is not an extraordinary event, considering our sizeable adolescent population.

The notion that a poltergeist is a manifestation of repressed sexual energies gained in popularity among researchers during the 1930s, though evidence of this had been exhibited in the 1878 Esther Cox case which took place in Nova Scotia. It all began when the twenty-two-year-old Esther escaped during an attempted rape by her boyfriend. He fled the area to avoid arrest, and Esther became disturbed and depressed. One night she woke to find her bedclothes flying about the room, her pillow inflated, and she herself began to swell like a balloon. A loud explosion followed as her body "deflated." She watched as an invisible hand scratched on the wall above her head the penciled warning, "Esther, you are mine to kill." The young woman was threatened for several weeks: fires started spontaneously and metal objects stuck to her flesh as if she were a magnet. Esther was jailed for arson when a nearby barn broke into flames. Unable to prove her guilt, the authorities released her, and shortly after she returned home the manifestations suddenly ceased.

D. Scott Rogo, in his book *The Poltergeist Experience*, points out the phenomenon's independence: "In other words, once the poltergeist is unleashed it is no longer dependent on the unconscious, which engendered it. It can take on a consciousness, will, direction, motivation, and intelligence of its own. This is why it may or may not show independent intelligence."

Perhaps some split-off portion of the victim's mind commands the poltergeist. This splinter of the mind could carry a will of its own. All the agent's guilt, hate, repression and aggression may construct an artificial personality capable of performing independently.

The poltergeist is extremely sensitive to the attitudes and beliefs of those who witness its disturbances. Call it a demon, and this entity readily assumes the role. People soon see how quick it is to change strategies. If this "noisy ghost" is allowed to become more powerful, it will expand its repertoire of irritations and leave witnesses to think that they are dealing with an actual disembodied entity who is directing a full-scale attack.

MYSTERIOUS FLAMES AND FORCES

Phosphorescent lights have been observed flickering in the skies and along marshes at night all over Maine, and usually these oddities are identified as northern lights or marsh gas. If the bizarre glows cannot be explained, they are consigned to some rubbish bin of information as electrical discharges or atmospheric disturbances. But what about crimson, white, and blue flares observed outdoors and *indoors*? In folklore, numerous accounts exist of such occurrences; corpse lights, they are called, fetch candles, jack-o'-lanterns, and corpse candles. Some people claim they have seen these lights hug the ground, float in the air, hover along the roof of the doomed person inside, and appear over the chest of a cadaver.

There have been hundreds of reliable reports of ball lightning, some witnessed by scientists, but this phenomenon has been slow in gaining scientific acceptance. These mysterious balls of energy come in various sizes, from an inch to six feet in diameter, and have been described as yellow, red, bluish-white, purple and green as they hiss and buzz about and sometimes leave behind the smell of sulfur. They can travel rapidly into a stiff wind and somehow enter houses when all the doors and windows are closed.

Smaller balls of lightning, usually less destructive than the larger ones, seem to be driven by a conscious force as they explore the interior of homes. What compels these enigmatic forces to prowl buildings is unclear, though they may be attracted to electrical appliances or even the electricity in humans. Ball lightning also has been known to pursue and enter aircraft in flight—somehow slipping past the sealed exterior of a plane without causing damage. (An uncle and aunt of mine—they lived on a farm that had nearly a dozen lightning antennae on the house, barn, and outbuildings—recalled seeing a yellowish ball the size of a grapefruit "leap" from a wall telephone, whirl slowly in flight across the length of their living room and "shrink through" the keyhole of the front door. Immediately after this performance, there was a deafening crash of thunder and a burning smell which was "sharp and mustardy.")

Ignis fatuus—the name for a wide variety of spectral lights whose alleged purpose is to play tricks on travelers at night, or in some instances to herald death—literally means "foolish fire" and is so named because anyone who follows such a light is foolish. These glows appear as bluish or yellow globes, and float through the dark countryside. There are various legends explaining this phenomenon—perhaps the most popular one is that the ghost of a sinner whose soul cannot rest has been doomed to prowl the earth forever.

Here in Maine, the Penobscot Indians call it "fire demon" or "fire creature"; an omen of death is this spirit who spins his lighted fingertips in a wheel to skim the milk at dairies during the night. Among the explanations given for these "death candles" are electrical and magnetic phenomena, marsh gas, and forms of unknown "earth energy."

In 1972, scientist Max Toth at a conference on Kirlian photography, discussed such natural curiosities as "fireballs" and Saint Elmo's Fire—the latter is defined as "a flaming phenomenon sometimes seen in stormy weather at prominent points on an airplane or ship and on land that is of the nature of a brush discharge of electricity." Many human beings become living storage batteries, Dr. Toth observed, and cited two examples: a girl in Missouri whose electrical charge was powerful enough to knock a man senseless, and a boy who was virtually a walking magnet and could dangle heavy steel rods from his fingertips. These were cases in which the normal human electrical charge had increased radically. It seemed likely to Toth that such conditions could explain the hundreds of incidents of spontaneous combustion, in which people suddenly incinerate themselves in fireless rooms. Under certain circumstances humans may produce a powerful and destructive electrical storm.

In the January 14, 1943 issue of the *Ellsworth American*, the mysterious death of Allen M. Small of Deer Isle, Maine was noted. Mr. Small was found on the floor of his home, his body and clothing burned, but the floor and carpet "only slightly scorched." Investigators were unable to explain why there was so little structural damage to the house. Small's pipe was on a shelf, and all the lids were in place on the stove. "It must have happened all of a sudden," observed one fire official at the scene. "Like an explosion of some kind."

Humans are believed to have traces of magnetic materials that function similarly to those found in homing pigeons. Since the earth is surrounded by a magnetic field, certain frequencies may affect us. It has been ascertained that a greater number of traffic and industrial accidents occur when the earth measures a higher level of geomagnetic energy. Probably, in subtle ways, we are influenced by these forces.

While scientists were exploring the geomagnetic effects brought about by the cycles of the sun and moon, Andrija Puharich, in a 1965 experiment, showed that telepathy peaked during the full-moon phase, was relatively high during a new moon, and registered very low during the half-moon phase. Scientists found that geomagnetic forces decreased during the full moon, which may authenticate Puharich's cycles of the moon hypotheses.

Studies in Kirlian photography reveal that a plant recently pruned will continue to include in its aura the missing leaves and limbs. Scientists have yet to determine just why such vibratory manifestations remain after appendages are removed, though there is some evidence that the more intense the energy—physical and emotional—the greater impact the aura will have on the field surrounding the missing parts. It should be noted that Kirlian photography shows that the aura around the hands of healers intensifies during a healing session.

The power of willed concentration can be demonstrated in the parlor trick of four people attempting to lift a seated person from a chair by using their index fingers alone. The procedure is simple, and even an enormous individual can be a candidate for this experiment. The four weight lifters begin by placing an index finger under the subject's knees and arms to show that such a feat is an impossibility. The heavy person in the chair doesn't budge. Then the four place their hands on the top of the candidate's head "in a pile." They concentrate on the task ahead, remove their hands, place index fingers under knees and arms, and try once more. Immediately, the subject is airborne for several seconds. During a televised demonstration in which the sitter was a man of considerable girth, one of the lifters was the seated person's little daughter.

Some physicists believe that it is the accumulation of willpower from this brief period of simultaneous concentration that contributes to the experiment. Others assert that the same results are achieved when four people lay their hands *separately* on a subject's head. Whatever the explanation, it is likely that the sudden concerted effort produces a super-charged supply of strength.

A similarly surprising performance is interpreted by dowsers as "being dependent on the earth's forces." An arm is raised parallel to the body and a witness to this experiment is asked to pull the arm down. This request is accomplished easily. Then the demonstrator begins shaking his arm to remove muscular tension: the hand first until it rotates loose-ly on the wrist, then the forearm, and finally the whole arm. Again, the witness is asked to begin pulling, and this time the arm seems to be made of iron—even with two hands tugging at the raised wrist. When asked how such a feat was accomplished, the demonstrator replied: "As I stretched my arm...I tried to imagine the earth forces moving up the soles of my feet, and out along my arm, like a ray of light. This gave me my rigidity."

It is ill-advised to draw a sharp line between orthodox science and theories that seem on the surface to be more imaginative than credible— consider the sudden disappearance of dinosaurs. In 1957, science writer Jacques Bergier told a French television audience that the extinction of these creatures was caused by the explosion of a star close to our solar system. Bergier's idea caused a furor among scientists; "the fantasy of a crank," they proclaimed before going about the soothing business of turning their backs to such thinking.

Later, in 1975, an American geologist, Walter Alvarez, took a chunk of clay from an Italian hillside, a half-inch layer of which represented the period when dinosaurs made their massive exit. Analysis showed that the clay contained a high proportion of the rare element iridium, an element that usually sinks to the middle of the planet but is scattered on surfaces after eruptions. Further testing revealed an absence of a certain radioactive platinum, which would have been present after the explo-sion of a star. The only explanation now was that the earth had been struck by a giant meteorite which produced a greenhouse effect and raised the temperature by several degrees, thus bringing about the extinction of many creatures, including dinosaurs.

Perhaps Jacques Bergier's "supernova" theory should have been given more attention by the scientific community, but the science writer couldn't resist decorating this unsolved mystery of prehistory further by suggesting that the explosion was the handiwork of advanced terrestrials who wanted to exterminate the dinosaurs, thus giving intelligent mammals an opportunity to flourish on our planet.

Humans are newcomers and our sciences are still primitive toys as we strive to establish a firmer footing on our uncertain territory. A time line for comprehending how long we have been part of the earth, a planet 4.6 billion years old, can be scaled down to 46 years. By this ratio, humans have been around for four hours, and the Industrial Revolution began about sixty seconds ago.

ANIMAL COMMUNICATION

Psychic Eugene Marais, in his book *The Soul of the White Ant*, called instinct "inherited memory." Just as we humans have in our subconscious selves capacities that predate our civilizations, so do animals and other life-forms possess instincts which we know little about that go back to the dawn of their existence.

"I was just thinking about you," says a surprised Harry. "It's been more than twenty years and there you are!" And Tom, in order to keep this unexpected meeting from sounding too weird, replies, "What a coincidence!" Such telepathic experiences occur frequently. Or perhaps the telephone rings and the person getting the call knows who is on the line before picking up the receiver. A bit of Early Man lingers; we still have that invisible wiring used before the refinement of grunts.

This sensitivity, however, is more obvious in other species. At a 1976 conference on the subject of abnormal behavior before earthquakes, scientists noted that humans were slow in sensing impending disasters— many creatures react well in advance of the first earth tremors: snakes leave their dens, chickens roost in trees, dogs rush madly about, and cats find sanctuary in the woods. In China, several thousand volunteers studied the behavior of animals before seismological disturbances and were able to predict eleven earthquakes in a five-year period. A Chinese radio broadcast stated: "The Tibetan yak lay sprawling on the ground. The panda was holding his head screaming, and the swan got up from the water and lay down on the ground." Before the 1960 Agadir earthquake in Morocco, which killed 15,000 people, stray animals were seen fleeing the port city.

A number of people claim they have had interaction when approaching insects as intelligent beings—such meetings usually occur when humans attempt to persuade flies, cockroaches, bees or ants to find another area for their habitat or food supply. Animal communicator Penelope Smith recalls a fly that kept landing on her hand while she was outdoors meditating. After several attempts to shoo the pest away, she brought the perched fly up close and began talking to it. Her mental picture of stroking the insect's back and the softness of her voice lulled the creature, and it allowed itself to be touched. Then the fly flew away, according to Smith, and quickly returned. The game was repeated five times, and she was struck by how incredible it was to feel a fuzzy back. (Mrs. Plante, an Augusta, Maine woman, recalls a strange experience: two flies followed her about the house for many days until they died.) "In fact," wrote Smith in her book *Animal Talk*, "if you get inside a colony of social insects, like bees and ants, you'll find they are more like humans than most other animals, amazingly so."

Smith, a leading pioneer of interspecies telepathic communications, discovered in 1971 that animals could be helped through emotional traumas by the same counseling techniques used to relieve humans. "I believe there will come a day when all species are reunited in close connection and cooperation," she predicted. Smith explained that many people have difficulty in "accepting the spiritual aspect of animals because they have established notions that animals are objects or less than human." When this happens, insensitivity or cruelty follows.

(I recall Irwin Barnum—not his real name—a mean-spirited woodsman who competed in many of the horse-pulling events at county fairs in Central Maine during the nineteen forties. His team of horses could pull several slabs of granite on a drag—well enough to qualify for top prizes, though Barnum's pair often came in second. When his animals strained and failed to tug the drag forward an additional few inches, the man took his displeasure out on them by using a whip with such force that it brought trickles of blood down their lathery flanks. Though there were no witnesses, Barnum's death seemed no accident to most people around the county: his horses bolted while hauling logs, and a toppled sledge crushed him.)

No two from any species are identical as they defend their territories, hunt for food, breed, and raise their young, though there is the unifying urge for group interaction: it can be observed over a disturbed anthill and when a flock of birds or swarm of insects shifts direction. Often disregarded is the ability some creatures have in expressing themselves orally. (Six or more owls surrounded our rural home in the foothills of Maine late one night and held a lengthy discussion—perhaps over the best way of devouring a colony of moles that resided near our bird feeders. There was no hoo-hooing. My wife and I lost count after hearing over two dozen distinctly different calls—not just owl gutturals but a language sweetened with phrases.)

When a friend suggested to Anita Curtis that she write a book on how to communicate with animals, the author turned to her Arabian horse, Porcia, for advice. The mare had been a "force" in a previous book called *Animal Wisdom—Communications With Animals*. "No problem," said Porcia telepathically. "Humans must learn to hear us, and you must help." Later, when Curtis was undecided as to how she should set up a table of contents to avoid offending any of the creatures by listing others first, the quadruped again came to the rescue: "Alphabetical," was the mare's reply. "We will be fine with that."

Curtis realized that most people would laugh at the notion that the Porcias of this world have a knowledge of our language beyond the few sounds recognized when we give commands or show fondness—surely horses can't handle the concept that "dog" follows "cat" in the order of our letters and "Zebra" comes last: the general reaction to Curtis's claim is that creatures have their own ways, not human attributes given to them by fanciful communicators.

"You need an imagination to be able to do this work," admits Curtis, for if a person is unable to visualize there is little chance of success. It is also important to talk "with as many animals as possible." Her technique in sending and receiving messages is in the form of pictures: she allows them to enter the mind after breathing exercises and meditation. Negative thoughts must be replaced with forceful energy as auras blend. ("Don't run in the road" should be presented as "Stay on the grass.") In her instruction manual, *How To Hear the Animals*, there are various meditations to help span the interspecific bridge, such as on being a bird of prey, dog, horse, fish, small bird, cat, and even one on being a snake. These meditations allow the communicator "to become an animal and understand what it is to live in that body."

(When photographing a small herd of Toggenburg and Nubian goats in the state of Oregon for my animal behavior book, *One Day With a Goat Herd*, I became aware of the intricate circuitry of sixteen animals as they interrelated telepathically. I visited their enclosure twice a week for more than two months, and during these two- and three-hour sessions I got to know them individually and as a group.

They were restive at first and not always willing photographic subjects. It wasn't my presence that made them uneasy, but the whine of the camera lens bringing them into focus. Only Wish, a Toggenburg doe and herd leader, found the courage to come forward and sniff at the fussy black box. A half hour went by before we all settled down: I, mingling, as they went back to their workaday world of browsing and keeping their order of dominance. At first, the goats appeared scattered, as if they were no longer in need of their queen, Wish, or dependent on physical proximity. But this was an illusion. The sound of a dog barking from the bed of a passing truck brought them closer; they became a herd once more—a unit alert and ready to defend their ground and *me*. The group moved outward from the protected center only when the sound of the barking dog faded.

The most memorable encounter that my wife and I had with animals occurred one morning on a back road in Franklin County. The incident was recorded in my book *Maine Mining Adventures*, and is one which I feel bears repeating. Stella and I were out walking when two yearling moose appeared in the road no more than sixty feet away. We stopped and waited to see what they would do. One was shy but the other was obviously curious. What kind of creatures are these? the lead moose seemed to be asking as it stared at us. We exchanged an awed glance and hung by the side of the road almost breathless. The moose in front moved toward us curiously and the shy one followed. Forty feet away they stopped. The braver one was now cocking its head and we could see the brown liquid fire of eyes. They stepped closer, slowly now, the one in front consumed with curiosity. Twenty feet. Ten feet away they paused. Somehow, all four of us had crossed that awkward chasm that exists between wild animal and human. The skittish one stood still while the other edged closer. Six feet away it towered over us, the massive shoulders motionless and those eyes burning with a need for understanding. Slowly, I reached out and pulled a clump of grass from the roadside and offered it—a symbolic gesture. As we stared at each other, I realized that the moose understood my act as an offering to signify we were no threat. "Let us move along," I whispered. We edged up the road, and the two moose began following us no more than four feet behind. Then a pulp truck broke the miracle of that morning with its roar and approaching cloud of dust. The two fled into the brush and were gone. Stella and I knew, if given the chance, before that day was over we could have stroked them; we all could have had the benefit of being friends.)

Welsh researcher Henry Blake, author of *Talking With Horses*, studied this animal's ability to communicate through ESP for more than twenty years, and out of 120 experiments in thought transference he tabulated 81 cases as successful. Blake was convinced that horses could receive and transmit thoughts over considerable distances among themselves and with other animals and humans.

Geese, goats, seals, rats, and even Toby—a pig that amazed Londoners by correctly indicating numbers thought of by audiences—have stimulated the imagination of the public. Such exhibitions are magnificent theater and people warm to the sideshow idea of animals succeeding in word games and arithmetic puzzles. But when such stunts are found to be fraudulent, a backlash occurs. "Of course horses can't talk," scoffed a disbeliever when Lady Wonder, "the educated mind reading horse," was under a full-scale psychic investigation.

Lady Wonder and her owner, Claudia Fonda, never traveled the carnival circuit. The horse was stabled near Richmond, Virginia and stood poised behind an alphabet of metal cards triggered with spring mechanisms—a sort of giant typewriter. Lady Wonder had only to peck answers to questions by nudging the keys with her nose. For more than twenty-five years, at the admission price of adults $1.00 and children 50¢, she made headlines by predicting winners in sporting events, the outcome of elections, and often the results of horse races—though her guesses were not infallible it was a remarkable performance.

In 1927, Joseph Banks Rhine tested Lady Wonder. At first, he was astonished by the horse's gifts, but when subjecting the animal to tests similar to those conducted on humans he was convinced that the clever quadruped was responding to signals from Mrs. Fonda. Other tests conducted, one by magician Milbourne Christopher, confirmed Dr. Rhine's suspicions. But the doors of the stable remained open; Lady Wonder continued to nose her keyboard as she predicted newspaper headlines. Even the most ferocious debunkers of animal communication were silenced by this horse's ability to comprehend subtle physical clues from Claudia Fonda.

Since before recorded history, man and his horse have been companions, and a definite psychic link was soon established. "I believe that animals have been talking to human beings ever since we were all made and put into this world," wrote Barbara Woodhouse, author of *Talking to Animals*, "and I feel that, as animals are so much quicker in picking up our thoughts and words than we are in picking up theirs, they must have a very poor opinion of the intelligence of the human race." Farmers have done less communicating since the invention of the automobile and tractor, but any equestrian who stables a horse soon learns that here is a creature with individuality—this animal can be intractable with timid riders and docile when a human approaches with confidence.

(There once was a rural remedy for correcting behavioral problems—all one had to do was notify the horse-whisperer. These technicians were popular in farming communities throughout Great Britain, and though the practice was used less frequently in America, this writer recalls Arthur Hooper, a blacksmith who shoed horses from Bingham to Smithfield, Maine, performing such magic.

My Uncle Leon Witham's workhorse, Elizabeth, was a difficult animal—she twisted whiffletrees and was frequently willful. The mare was being particularly ornery one day when Arthur was shoeing her.

"She seldom listens," my uncle commented.

"Bitchy, perhaps, but she looks like a good enough nag to me," replied Arthur moving off to sizzle a thick squirt of chewing tobacco into the forge.

"All hell sometimes breaks loose when we hitch her up with old Chub." This was the other workhorse on the farm—sturdy, good-natured, and totally dependable.

"Elizabeth isn't all bad when she's by herself on the horse rake," Uncle Leon went on, "but she isn't much when haying or spreading manure."

"Probably just nerves," said Arthur. "It's not unusual."

"What she needs is a good dose of swaps!"

"You don't want to trade in an animal like that, Leon," said Hooper. "Why don't you let me talk some sense into her?"

"What do you mean?"

"Just a little something my father picked up years ago from a logger who worked for the paper company."

My uncle nodded. I think he probably knew what Arthur Hooper had in mind—there had been talk around town about the hocus-pocus science of horse-whispering.

The blacksmith circled Elizabeth, his short legs unwinding, and when he paused close to the mare's right ear, Hooper emitted a wheezing sound that immediately captured her attention. Elizabeth slumped forward noticeably, ears erect as she became more receptive to Arthur's lecture. After a minute or more of guidance, Hooper backed off and fumbled in his coat pocket for more plug tobacco.

"She won't be perfection," he declared, "but I think you'll see improvement."

Uncle Leon never could make up his mind whether Arthur Hooper had done any good. At times, he thought so, and there were days when my uncle felt that better results would have been realized if the blacksmith had shouted.)

Most people who have pets are swept into the role of communicator without being aware of it: teaching the young dog to beg or to balance a treat on its nose in order to be rewarded requires patience and un-structured verbal skills—it isn't easy for an animal to master the rig-marole of obedience in surroundings crowded with distractions.

Studies have proved that dogs can read the minds of humans and often react before thoughts have been formulated. Jason, a boxer, was asleep in an armchair when the master of the house decided to conduct a simple telepathic experiment. He asked his daughter to call the dog silently at a certain time from another room. Immediately, when the silent command was given, Jason woke, jumped from his resting place, and ran to the girl.

("Oh scared!" We would say to our much-loved dog, Ezra, and as we pretended to cringe in fear, our behavior prompted the beginnings of a snarl. I recall a summer job of assessing property for the town I lived in—usually during daylight hours when home owners were away and watchdogs were hitched outside. On several occasions I was intimidated by growls and the showing of teeth, but Mel, the assessor with me, ap-proached these sentries calmly, confidently, and with the unmistakable message that he was "top dog"—there wasn't one unpleasant incident.)

Bill Schul, in his book *The Psychic Power of Animals*, comments on how differently pets react to death: "Some animals seem to be unaware of its approach, while some make preparations for the event; for ex-ample, certain dogs and cats search for places to be alone at the time of death, knowing that it is imminent." (Our dog, Spock, was a notoriously poor passenger in an automobile—just the sight of our vehicle triggered motion sickness—but on the heartbreaking last journey to the veterinar-ian, Spock was totally alert: every moving object on the twenty-mile trip was greedily taken in—motion sickness was forgotten; these were last long looks.)

Are we the only species privileged with an afterlife? The Society for Psychical Research has been recording ghostly animals for more than a hundred years. Typical of the incidents described in their archives is a report from a mother and daughter. The two were having their midday meal when they saw a white Angora cat under their table. The animal marched out, went to the door, and halfway down a passage, turned, stared at the two women then "dissolved away."

Spiritualists readily accept an afterlife for family pets, and there are numerous accounts of dogs greeting their masters and mistresses with joyous barks at séances. "Do animals have souls?" was the question raised in a recent survey, and a third of those polled were reluctant to admit the possibility. One finds no reference to animal survival in the scriptures of

Western religions; only the ultimate destiny of humans has been considered, despite the fact that a number of leading religious thinkers have displayed flexibility when confronted with such unorthodox views.

Living creatures share a closeness. Dolphins, those remarkable small-toothed whales with comical snouts, enjoy playing with people, especially children, and have imitated human whistling. John C. Lilly, a scientist who has studied dolphins for more than two decades, observed: "I have heard most distinctly the following words and phrases 'copied' in an extremely high-pitched and brief fashion: 'Three-two-three,' 'Tee ar Pee' (the letters TRP had just been given) and a host of others, less clear but verging so closely on humanlike rhythm, enunciation and phonetic quality as to be eerie."

"When my cat, Peaches, and I first moved to the country," wrote Penelope Smith, "she used to present mice or birds at the foot of my bed in the morning." It was a gift for the mistress and the cat's way of validating its ability as a huntress. (Our cat, Blither, made a similar gesture. My family and I spent one summer camping in the woods; we slept in one tent and had another canvas set up as a storage area for cooking utensils and food supplies. Blither, free to roam the woods, killed a large snowshoe rabbit and dragged the animal into our makeshift pantry—this was her contribution as breadwinner.)

The homing instinct of cats, called "psi-trailing," was the subject of an experiment conducted in 1940 and the results were published in a number of scientific journals. Cats were let loose in unfamiliar surroundings and followed by teams of observers. There were fields and intersections to cross, hedges and fences to squeeze through, and unexpected detours. Not one of the animals was disoriented; they all made their way homeward without hesitation.

Cats have a definite precognition of events. This sensitivity often has helped their owners to extricate themselves from disastrous situations. A German psychiatrist, Ute Pleimes, in one university study, described over 800 incidents in which pets have warned their masters and mistresses of impending catastrophes, and a large proportion of these sentries were cats. "I have seen enough," wrote Pleimes, "to convince me that animals do have a special psychic power to sense danger before it happens. We are fools to ignore them."

Dogs also exhibit the homing instinct: Bobbie, part Scotch sheepdog and collie, was taken on a long automobile trip. The family drove east from their home in Oregon, and when they stopped in Indiana, a distance of more than 2,000 miles, Bobbie jumped out of the car and disappeared.

His owners spent a long time searching for him but eventually gave up and continued their journey. Three months later an exhausted Bobbie appeared on their Oregon doorstep. Research revealed that the animal had to cross the Rocky Mountains in midwinter and swim several icy rivers.

(Our most challenging and satisfying experience in communicating with another creature came when we brought up a baby robin that had fallen from its nest. The bird was fed ground beef on a matchstick, given a daily dose of Vitamin E, granted time for worm pulling, and we trained it to perch on our shoulders. There was no need to warn the little thing that the salivating observer with claws was "Moonshine" our house cat—that apprehension was instinctive. We, the foster parents, knew when it was time to say good-bye. We placed the robin on the limb of a tree and stood back. The bird looked at us and at the sky—it was a moment of sadness and exhilaration when the robin flew above a stand of trees and disappeared.)

The following is a 1980 tale of animal communication published in several New England newspapers. Miss Rachel Flynn, an eighty-two-year-old resident of Cape Cod, enjoyed her daily walks along a bluff near her seaside home. One day, on a solitary outing, she fell from a thirty-foot cliff and landed on a deserted strip of beach at a time of rising tide. When she regained consciousness, the woman found herself too badly hurt to move. Nearby, a seagull stood looking at her. Miss Flynn wasn't sure—since gulls look much alike to humans—but she hoped that this bird *might* be Nancy, the one she and her sister had befriended and fed regularly at home. "For God's sake, Nancy," the woman called, "get help!"

The gull flew away, and minutes later Miss Flynn's sister, June, heard Nancy tapping at the kitchen window. "Shoo off," she insisted as the bird continued its drumming with an occasional flapping of wings, "you're making more noise than a wild turkey!" But the seagull kept it up, and after fifteen minutes of this unusual behavior, the sister realized that Nancy was trying to tell her something.

The gull led the way with stops to make sure that the woman was fol-lowing. At the cliff's edge, June saw her sister below. A rescue squad was called and Rachel was taken to a hospital with severe bruises and a badly twisted knee. "It was simply incredible," June told reporters, "the way that gull came to the window and caused all that racket and saved my sister's life!"

George Washington Carver had an amazing rapport with all types of vegetation and was renowned for his ability of bringing ailing plants back to life. "All flowers talk to me and so do hundreds of little things in the woods," he replied when asked how he brought about these miracles. "I learn what I know by watching and loving everything." The botanist would get up at 4:00 a.m. to prowl the woods near his home. He listened to plants because he felt the "still dark hours before sunrise" to be the best time for such dialogues. "The secrets are in the plants," he observed. "To elicit them you have to love them enough."

Parapsychologist Sylvia Fisher brought home six philodendrons. She named two of them Leda and Venus, after two dogs she loved; two plants were called Kenny and Tippy, named after two dogs Mrs. Fisher disliked; and the two remaining philodendrons were called Dusty and Okie—for no particular reason, just names to color her experiment. The six plants were placed on a windowsill and watered daily. Leda and Venus, the recipients of loving thoughts, grew fast and thickened with leaves; Kenny and Tippy, the two insulted with bad thoughts, were soon scraggly and in need of pruning; Dusty and Okie, the ignored plants, were healthier than poor Kenny and Tippy but noticeably inferior to Leda and Venus. "I see all of earth's life-forms," wrote Penelope Smith in *Animal Talk*, "including plants, rocks, water, air, and all we experience around us, as a symbiotic whole."

APPENDICES

ACKNOWLEDGMENTS

Books by the following authors and editors proved immensely helpful in researching material:

Ater, Bob, *Dowsing With a Pencil*, American Society of Dowsers, Danville, Vermont, 1970.

Atwater, P.N.H. with Morgan, David H., *Near-Death Experiences*, Alpha Books, Indianapolis, Indiana, 2000.

Bardens, Dennis, *Psychic Animals*, Barnes & Noble Books, New York, 1987.

Beckley, Timothy Green, *Mysteries of the Men In Black: The UFO Silencers*, New Brunswick, New Jersey, 1990.

Bender, Albert K., *Flying Saucers and the Three Men In Black*, Saucerian Press, Clarksburg, West Virginia, 1962.

Biley, Ria, *Angel Country*, Angelis Press, Rockland, Maine, 1996.

Bord, Janet and Colin, *Unexplained Mysteries of the 20th Century*, Contemporary Books, Chicago, 1989.

Brookesmith, Peter, *UFO: The Complete Sightings*, Barnes & Noble Books, New York, 1995.

Browning, Norma Lee, *The Psychic World of Peter Hurkos*, Doubleday & Company, Inc., New York, 1970.

Cabot, Laurie with Cowan, Tom, *Power of the Witch*, A Delta Book, New York, 1989.

Clifton, Chas S., Editor, *Witchcraft Today: The Modern Craft Movement,* Book One, Llewellyn Publications, St. Paul, Minnesota, 1997.

Cone, William P. and Estes, Russ and Randle, Kevin D., *The Abduction Enigma*, Tom Doherty Associates, New York, 1999.

Cousineau, Phil, *UFO: A Manual for the Millennium*, Harper Collins West, New York, 1995.

Curtis, Anita, *Animal Wisdom: Communications With Animals*, Gilbertsville, Pennsylvania, 1998.

——*How To Hear The Animals*, Gilbertsville, Pennsylvania, 1998.

De Givry, Grillot, *Witchcraft, Magic & Alchemy*, Bonanza Books, New York, No date given.

Doore, Gary, Editor, *What Survives? Contemporary Explorations of Life After Death*, Jeremy P. Tarcher, Inc., Los Angeles, 1990.

Fowler, Raymond E., *The Allagash Abductions*, Wild Flower Press, Tigard, Oregon, 1993.

Gerwick-Brodeur, Madeline and Lenard, Lisa, *Astrology*, Alpha Books, Indianapolis, Indiana, 2000.

Gile, Robin and Lenard, Lisa, *Palmistry*, Alpha Books, New York, 1999.

Goldberg, Bruce, *Past Lives, Future Lives*, Ballantine Books, New York, 1982.

Guiley, Rosemary Ellen, *The Encyclopedia of Ghosts and Spirits*, Checkmark Books, New York, 2000.

Hammerman, David and Lenard, Lisa, *Reincarnation*, Alpha Books, Indianapolis, Indiana, 2000.

Jaegers, Beverly, *The Psychic Paradigm*, Berkley Books, New York, 1998.

Knight, David C., Editor, *The ESP Reader*, Grosset and Dunlap, New York, 1969.

Lagerquist, Kay and Lenard, Lisa, *Numerology*, Alpha Books, Indianapolis, Indiana, 1999.

Loring, Rev. Amasa, *A History of Shapleigh, Maine, 1854. (The Ghost of Shapleigh Plains* as told by Julia Anna Clark), Sanford, Maine, 1983.

The Mind and Beyond (Mysteries of the Unknown), Edited by Time-Life Books, New York, 1991.

Monroe, Robert A., *Far Journeys*, Doubleday, New York, 1985.
——*Journeys Out of the Body*, Doubleday, New York, 1977.

Moody, Raymond A. with Perry, Paul, *The Light Beyond*, Bantam Books, New York, 1989.

Muldoon, Sylvan and Carrington, Hereward, *The Projection of the Astral Body*, Samuel Weiser, Inc., York Beach, Maine, 1987.

Ogden, Tom, *Ghosts and Hauntings*, Alpha Books, Indianapolis, Indiana, 1999.

Opie, Iona and Tatem, Moira, *A Dictionary of Superstitions*, Barnes & Noble Books, New York, 1989.

Peel, Robert, *Mary Baker Eddy: The Years of Discovery*, Holt, Rinehart and Winston, New York, 1966.

Psychic Powers (Mysteries of the Unknown), Edited by Time-Life Books, New York, 1987.

Roberts, Jane, *The Coming of Seth*, Pocket Books, New York, 1976.
——*The Seth Material*, Bantam Books, New York, 1970.
——*The Unknown Reality* (Volume Two, Parts One and Two), Bantam Books, New York, 1989.

Roberts, Kenneth, *Henry Gross and His Dowsing Rod*, Doubleday and

Company, New York, 1951.

——*The Seventh Sense*, Doubleday and Company, New York, 1953.

——*Water Unlimited*, Doubleday and Company, New York, 1957.

Robinson, Lynn A. and Carlson-Finnerty, LaVonne, *Being Psychic*, Alpha Books, Indianapolis, Indiana, 1999.

Rogo, D. Scott, *The Poltergeist Experience*, Penguin Books, New York, 1979.

Schulte, Carol Olivieri, *Ghosts on the Coast of Maine*, Down East Books, Camden, Maine, 1989.

Sherman, Harold, *How To Make ESP Work For You*, Ballantine Books, New York, 1964.

——*You Can Communicate With the Unseen World*, Fawcett Publications, Inc., Greenwich, Connecticut, 1974.

Slate, Ann B. and Berry, Alan, *Bigfoot*, Bantam Books, New York, 1976.

Smith, Penelope, *Animal Talk: Interspecies Telepathic Communication*, Pegasus Publications, Point Reyes Station, California, 1998.

Stevenson, Jay, *Vampires,* Alpha Books, Indianapolis, Indiana, 2002.

Superstitions: The Little Giant Encyclopedia, Sterling Publishing Co., Inc., New York, 1999.

Tanous, Alex with Ardman, Harvey, *Beyond Coincidence*, Doubleday & Company, Inc., New York, 1976.

TenDam, Hans, *Exploring Reincarnation*, Viking Penguin Inc., New York, 1987.

Tognetti, Arlene and Lenard, Lisa, *Tarot and Fortune-Telling*, Alpha Books, New York, 1999.

Verde, Thomas A., *Maine Ghosts and Legends*, Down East Books, Camden, Maine, 1989.

Wambach, Helen, *Life Before Life*, Bantam Books, New York, 1979.

Watkins, Susan M., *Conversations With Seth*, Volume One, Prentice Hall Press, New York, 1980.

Wilson, Colin, *Afterlife*, Doubleday & Company, Inc., New York, 1987.

——*Beyond the Occult*, Corgi Books, London, 1989.

——*Beyond the Outsider*, Carroll & Graf Publishers, Inc., New York, 1991.

——*Mysteries*, G. P. Putnam's Sons, New York, 1980.

Wilson, Colin and Damon, *The Mammoth Encyclopedia of the Unsolved*, Carroll & Graf Publishers, Inc., New York, 2000.

Zimmermann, Denise and Gleason, Katherine A., *Wicca and Witch-*

craft, Alpha Books, Indianapolis, Indiana, 2000.

Acknowledgments are made to the following individuals and producers for video presentations:
Ater, Bob, *Dowsing for Water and Treasure*, (2 hours), Bath, Maine.
——*Some of My Spiritual Experiences*, (65 minutes), Bath, Maine.
——*The Tactual Detection of Subtle Energy*, (about 90 minutes), Bath, Maine.
Questar Video, Inc., *UFOs: Above Top Secret,* (60 minutes), Chicago.
——*UFOs: From Legends To Reality*, (60 minutes), Chicago.
Tanous, Alex and Osis, Karlis, *Is There a Ghost In the House?*, Alex Tanous Foundation for Scientific Research, Portland, Maine.
TBS, *Unsolved Mysteries*, Atlanta, Georgia, 1996.
Thomson, William O., *New England's Haunted Lighthouses*, Thomson, Kennebunk, Maine
WCSH Television, *Maine Mysteries*, Channel 6, Portland, Maine, 1998.

These publications, archives, websites, and research organizations are cited for providing helpful information and material: *Belfast Republican Journal*, Bigfoot Field Researchers Organization, Bigfoot/Sasquatch Database, *Discover Maine: Maine's History & Nostalgia Magazine,* Gulf Coast Bigfoot Research Organization, Lewiston *Sun Journal*, *Lighthouse Digest*, *The Maine Eagle Magazine*, Maine State Library, Mutual UFO Network, Association for Past-Life Research and Therapies, Inc., *Portland Press Herald, Space Review*, and UFO Roundup: American UFO News.

The following individuals have been generous in sharing information: Gary Baril, Elaine and Hyland Barrows, Georgina and Leland Bechtel, Richard Brown, Harold W. Castner, Susan Cormier, Pamela Coupe, Dennis Creaser, Anita Curtis, Jane Curtis, Juanita DeMello, Scott Desjardins, Bonnie and Delbert Gardner, Laurie Goodie, David Hall, Gary and Lorna Howard, Stephany Hurkos, Sam Kubic, Rita Lachance, Diane and Maurice LaForce, Hedy Langdon, Loy Lawhon, Monique Levesque, Sheila Lizotte, Madelon Rose Logue, Jennifer Maguire, David Masse, Paul and Verla Ouellette, Harvey Packard, Lois Palches, Frank Perham, John Perry, Alex Pratt, Marjorie Richard, Tamaranda (Jean Laier), Gladys Taylor, and Leigh Walton.

INDEX

ABOUT THE AUTHOR

C. J. Stevens is a native of Maine. His poems, stories, articles, Dutch and Flemish translations, and interviews have appeared in approximately five hundred publications worldwide and more than sixty anthologies and textbooks. He has taught at writers' conferences and seminars and has lectured widely. Stevens has lived in England, Ireland, Holland, Malta, and Portugal.